Finding the G[...]

Daily Meditations
for *Mindfulness*

To your gifts !!

Angela Howell

ANGELA HOWELL

Praise for Finding the Gift

"Angela Howell's *Finding the Gift* offers powerful perspective, hope, and encouragement for daily life. Engaging, spirit-driven—it's a collection to keep nearby and refer to again and again."
Dr. Tami West, Author of *A Woman's Guide to Personal Achievement & Professional Success*

"Angela Howell gently guides you to face what's true and then brings you full circle to remembering that 'now' is all that exists. Brilliant!"
Denise Simone, Empowerment Coach and Intuitive Counselor

"Angela Howell generously opens the door to her life to help others solve their own puzzles and find their way back to themselves, through the maze of life."
Todd Cecil, Artist, Musician

"Authentic, captivating, thought-provoking! Angela Howell's insights remind the reader that in every life experience there is a gift waiting to be found ... if we only dare to look deeper."
Rachel Martinez, Certified Addiction Counselor

"Angela Howell brings fresh hope to light your daily path of life. You will find encouragement and insight as you read these daily meditations."
Sue Detweiler, Author, Speaker, Pastor, and Radio Host

"Angela Howell is an author who takes the 'ordinary, everyday stuff' and causes us to look at it once again through her grace-filled eyes. Her deep sense of commitment to her Creator has infused her writings with much joy and self-awareness. While reading an excerpt each day, it causes one to truly reflect and 'take time to smell the roses.'"
Paul S. Frank, Retired Minister

"*Finding the Gift* can inspire and change your life!!!"
Susan Underwood, PT, Founder and Owner of Susan Underwood Physical Therapy

"*Finding the Gift* is GREAT! The daily thoughts are inspiring and challenging. Without a doubt, Angela Howell is going to help a lot of people."
Dan Smith, Pastor

"*Finding the Gift* redirects the mind, refreshes the soul and motivates the heart. Fantastic! Amazing daily read and a thoughtful gift for family and friends."
Kathleen Moore

"Finding The Gift isn't about pursuing talent, but rather, discovering ourselves through the hidden treasures of life. We find our gifting in the small things in life that refine our purpose. We all have value and it isn't measured by our bank account or the size of our house. This will be a game changer!"
Brad Lukacic

"Helping people connect to themselves and to their higher purpose through everyday encounters is a gift and a blessing. I too want to let my wings continue to grow knowing, 'One day soon I will soar with ease.'"
Deborah Ezell Denson, Conflict Management Coach

"Angela Howell has a wonderfully positive and spiritual way of looking at life and its everyday-ness. It's so helpful to stop and see all the great blessings around us every moment."
Miriam Frank

"Angela Howell's idea of *Finding the Gift* is a great way to use Consciousness, moment by moment, to see beyond the physical eyes. Angela demonstrates this spiritual acuity in relating her mindful meditation experiences. She encourages others to also Find the Gift in seemingly everyday occurrences. There is a Greater Reality to be experienced and appreciated when we are looking for it."
Mahria Thompson, M.A., Author of *The Consciousness Code, 7 Keys to Awakening*

"Angela Howell is now God's person who has received mercy that she may proclaim the excellencies of Him who called her out of darkness into His marvelous light!'"
Reggie Tryon

"What a remarkable, insightful book. *Finding the Gift* touched my soul, and your daily practical suggestions make me want to share this with all my friends."
Priscilla Craig

For information contact: www.FindingTheGift.com

Cover Illustration by Thalia Nguyen
Author Photographs by Tim West Photography
Cover design by Kathleen Johnson, Moore Creative
Book interior design by Melissa Craven, The Writer Lab

ISBN 13: 978-1517163723
ISBN 10: 1517163722

First Edition for print: September 30, 2015

Dedication

I dedicate this book to myself and all the souls who join me in seeking to create their best life; all those who won't let their past keep them from *Finding the Gift*.

And to my son, Canaan, my man of promise! I pray you will always seek and find the gifts along the way.
¡Te amo mi hijo¡

Contents

Acknowledgments

Most importantly, I have to thank and give this book back to God, with gratitude for His constant protection and guidance. He opened my eyes to see insights for this book and my life, and He continues to illuminate my world, using everything for my good! I still don't have all the answers, but I wouldn't trade a moment in His presence for anything. I am thankful for this incredible journey, which is far greater than anything I could have ever imagined.

I am grateful to my husband Patrick, the love of my life, for always believing in me and encouraging me to finish this book. You will always be one of my greatest gifts! Thank you, Canaan, for patiently listening to my every day epiphanies and cheering me on!

I thank my mom for sharing her love of beauty, and my dad for showing me how to persevere. I'm grateful for my siblings: Kurt, Jubal, Samuel and Rachel—my comrades on this journey who understand me better than anyone.

I'm grateful for the teachers and coaches who showed me love, and gave me a place to belong. Thank you, Jeff, for showing me that my pain is average. Thank you, Ginger, for taking me into the darkness and bringing me out on the other side. Thank you, Priscilla, for always bringing it back to gratitude. To Paul and Miriam, I could never express what your unconditional love, friendship and support have meant to me and my family—thank you so much. I'm grateful to you beyond words, Susan, my angel, for being a steady light in a dark time, and my joy partner here on the other side. To my "oldest" friend Jennifer, I love you always. To Todd, thanks for showing me how to live sunny. Thank you

Denise, my *Finding the Gift* friend and co-coach. Your support and accountability greatly helped me cross this finish line! Thank you Dan, Connie, Tim and Tami for giving me a safe place to grow. Extra thanks to Tami, for having the great hair that launched our friendship! I'm thankful for the mentors who guided me, and the reverse role models who challenged me to find a better way. And to all the authors and speakers who provided light for my path—many thanks!

Special thanks to my "gifted" designer and awesome friend, Kathleen Johnson, for creating the perfect book cover. Besides that, you are one of my greatest cheerleaders, and valuable beyond measure. Many, many thanks to my incredible, patient and dedicated editor, Melissa Craven, who challenged me to make this book even better. You are a true find, a treasure, and I could not have done this without you. Cheers to both of us finding the sleep now!

*Plunge boldly into the thick of life, and
seize it where you will, it is always interesting.*
~ Johann Wolfgang von Goethe ~

My husband and I finished a convention in Houston, with an afternoon and evening to burn before flying back home. My lack of geographical awareness is a running joke in my family, but when I found out how close we were to the ocean, I told him we had to jump in the car, drive to Galveston Island just so I could feel the sand on my feet and dip my toes in the water for a half hour. My husband lovingly obliged.

I tried so hard to be careful not to get wet or dirty! And then I couldn't take it any longer and was overcome by the moment. I love the ocean! I didn't care that my pants were going to get wet and sandy, and that we were going to dinner right after I finished splashing in the water. I was not about to be that close to the ocean and go quietly. I had to indulge the moment! Life is short. Make memories and grab every gift you can! They are all around us!

Introduction

A therapist once told me, "Suffering is ordinary." That *really* ticked me off! After all I'd been through as a child, adolescent, and adult—that's what he had to say to me? Chaos and violence. Religious extremes and kidnapping. Held hostage at gunpoint. I could go on. Life put me on an early path to personal discovery and emotional healing, as I began pursuing recovery from anorexia and bulimia in my late teens. Over the years, I gradually adopted my therapist's philosophy. (I paid for it, I might as well use it.) I survived much. Still, I am … *ordinary.* Because many of you have been hurt significantly too. In the first century, a Greek-born slave of Rome named Epictetus said, "It's not what happens to you, but how you react to it that matters." One thing my mother instilled in me as a child is the solid belief that everything works for my good. That belief has carried me and taught me patience and trust, even in the most trying situations. I guess in a way, I've been looking for the "gift" my whole life!

My journey with metaphors in nature and everyday life lessons started in November, 2003. I was hiking through Radnor Lake in Nashville—somewhere I went frequently—when I saw the most unusual tree I had ever seen. I saw it at eye-level first, and really thought it was dead. It had a big hole right through the trunk! I have gone back many times to take pictures of it, but I've never been able to find it again. That encounter inspired *A Lesson From Trees*, the poem I share at the beginning of my book. Looking back, it makes sense to me the metaphor I saw in that tree was the first one, because it was a clue about the journey I was to embark on. The one I'm on now, with you!

That one tree opened up a whole new world of metaphors for me. I GOT the lesson and my eyes were open! A year and a half went by and I didn't see anything else particularly profound. Then one day in 2005, I began seeing metaphors all around me, practically on a daily basis. That's when it really took off: ordinary life … *extraordinary* perspective! Each time it happened, I felt like my awareness expanded on the spot, as my mind absorbed what was being revealed to me in such an obvious, but never-before-seen way. And of all places, I saw these in everyday life, in things I'd seen or done a thousand times before. I savored each insight as a spiritual gift to capture and record for my own personal growth, as well as to share with others.

One time I was chasing a runaway feather while cleaning my house. The harder I pursued, the more it danced through the air, evading me. I grew frustrated and became more determined than ever to catch that silly feather! I even tripped over a cat trying to grab it, when suddenly, I saw the lesson! I could see uncanny similarities with how I approached my life. Too often, I have attempted to control every aspect of my world using relentless persistence, clenched teeth and a white-knuckled grip. All I had to do was back off and let the feather land on its own—effortlessly! I've made circumstances and relationships more challenging than necessary when I could have patiently surrendered, allowing a more natural flow to land easily in my hands at the right time (not in my time).

I'm excited to share these lessons, but I'm equally excited to reveal all the procrastination, doubt and resistance I've constantly had to overcome during the ten-year process of writing and bringing *Finding the Gift* to print. You may fight the same battles too, and I want to encourage you to never give up, because every little step will get you closer to your goal, if you just keep going.

When these lessons first started showing up, my life was both the best and the worst of times, all at once. I had just remarried my first husband at the end of 2004, and life was freshly filled with the hope and promise of restoration. Our first marriage had completely unraveled in the chaos of his demanding career as an undercover agent, and my own workaholic habits in corporate sales.

We gave it our all for seven years, but our marriage ended after a devastating separation in 1999, which left me a divorced, single mom of a three year old. Realizing the love of my life was gone, I married the first nice guy who showed up and liked my son. My ex-husband remarried too, and ironically, both of our brief marriages ended due to unrelated issues, two years later. In the same week, we both were newly separated. Reconciling six months later with my first husband was totally unexpected, and I felt like I was getting a do-over. It never crossed my mind that God could, or would, put us back together, despite all we had done and said to each other. I had never felt more thankful, nor more fully aware of the inability to make a mistake that God couldn't fix and use for my good. Gratitude and taking risks, despite what other people might think, is a recurring theme in my meditations, and I do have much to be grateful for.

On the downside, my successful, twelve-year career in corporate sales ended abruptly in May, 2005. I had suffered for almost a year in inexplicable pain that left me struggling to brush my teeth, let alone do my job. Within months of changing to a different company the previous

January, I began to experience significant pain and neurological problems, which ultimately resulted in a decade of surgeries, a worker's comp lawsuit, disability and ongoing physical therapy. When I was taken off work permanently that May, a significant part of my life ended, leaving me with lots of looming questions about my life's direction.

However, right in the midst of that terrible time, my family life was beginning anew and life handed me another gift! I discovered a love and talent for photography, which brought a bright light into a very dark time. It also served as an opening to use my creativity in a professional capacity. Over and over, I have learned that gifts are often gift-wrapped in obstacles. Not coincidentally, in that same year, I began writing this book!

Looking back, I would go through all the surgeries and rehab again to become the person I am today. Despite the physical limitations that persist, I don't know if I would have left my comfort zone any other way. For so many years, I gave in to what was familiar, and kept chasing money and status. I was playing it safe, instead of finding the courage to pursue my authentic, yet unknown calling. My heart aches for anyone who feels trapped in their present circumstances—certain there must be more to life, but afraid to make a change. I write a lot about pushing past mediocrity and staying comfortable, challenging all of us to embrace fear and summon the courage to pursue dreams. I might still be stuck, if I hadn't been lovingly shoved out of my nest!

Amidst the devastating pain and the joyful restoration of my family, I saw random life lessons as I traveled through each day. Suddenly, I could see situations more clearly and relate them to various aspects of life and the common things we all struggle with. At first I dismissed these as just strange occurrences, or assumed everyone else could probably see what I was seeing. I pointed out an insight once to my son, as we walked through downtown Nashville. I said, "Look at that guy right there. Don't you see it? Can't you see his world is just as important to him as ours is to us? He is special! He's a son, a friend, maybe someone's dad. He's a stranger to us, but he is just like us, living a life as big and relevant as ours! He means the world to someone! My son said, "Mom, no one thinks like that. No one looks at him and sees that, but you." I felt sad. I thought, *Why can't we all see that? Why can't I see it all the time?* I get so wrapped up in my own life, and I forget other people's lives are just as valuable as mine. Whether it's full of joy or crisis, their lives are exactly like mine is to me—important!

After receiving several of these unexpected lessons, I felt an obligation to start writing them down, if for no other reason than because I wanted to remember these nuggets, these keys to life. If I put enough of them together, I could create a great road map for how to live my life. I'm a very visual person and I can grasp something much easier if I can actually see it. So I captured these for me, but I also had a sense that other people could benefit from helpful insights too, and I wanted to share them.

Throughout the last ten years of receiving these insights, I noticed a pattern about myself (which of course, became another day's entry to write about). When I was expectant, when I was *intentionally* looking to be shown something to write about, I was given "the gift" a lot more often than when I was going through the day with my receiver off—with my mind less open to spiritual input. Put another way, when I wasn't looking, I wasn't finding. How can we find something we aren't looking for? I can relate this to all the ways I used to avoid naming the desires of my heart. Maybe because I doubted they could happen, or because I didn't want to be responsible for actually doing something about them. If I keep my head buried in busyness and day-to-day monotony, never seeking a way to grow or change my circumstances, I'm not going to find anything new, and I get to keep my "present." (Like it or not.)

Despite my best intentions, life happened and for several years, I stopped writing insights consistently. Another lesson demonstrated: without action, a dream remains a wish. And yet another: I can't do it all in one day—a big goal is accomplished by taking small actions repeatedly over time. I resolved to make myself available to receive insight ... daily. However, I learned to celebrate progress instead of perfection. The insights came regularly by either sitting outside journaling until something came to me, or by looking out into nature until I saw it. I couldn't believe how they just kept coming out of nowhere! Some days I went for a walk and was shown something, and other days I just kept my eyes open as I traveled throughout my everyday activities. I saw lessons in birds, trees, water, feathers, my own pets—even the neighbor's trash on the curb! Day in and day out, my creator had something to share with me, because I was open.

Finding the Gift is not simply one year of my life recorded through these daily lessons, but many years. You will notice the passage of time during my process of writing this book. I discuss multiple vacations that happened over several years, and several beloved pets that have come and gone. We've also moved throughout beautiful, middle Tennessee three times during the course of this book, and I frequently found inspiration in my own backyard, which varied depending on the home I lived in. My goal has always been to deliver a daily meditation with a seasonal flow, where each entry is relevant to that specific time of year, instead of a chronological passing of my life. Additionally, I knew I wanted to find encouragement by topic as well. I've created an extensive index based on topics and keywords where readers can search for just the right entry for their mood or circumstance. I am excited to read this book with you, and be inspired all over again by the insights I've collected over the last ten years. Life can throw curve balls and cause me to forget what I already know, so I need constant reminders to encourage me and keep me on track!

Thank you for joining me on this wonderful journey of *Finding the Gift*. I applaud your open eyes, your open heart, and your mindfulness. When you look, you will find. And when you're willing to be present, more gifts will appear. Please visit me at www.findingthegift.com to share your comments and insights with me and my other readers. I will have a free gift waiting for you, just to thank you for dropping by and joining my community. Cheers to you and me both for *Finding the Gift* today!

A Lesson From Trees

All kinds of trees.
Living ones. Dead ones.
New ones. Old ones.
On the rise. Old and wise.
New and eager. Barely breathing.
Fragile. Strong. Healthy.
Wasted. Flourishing. Fallen.
How is their fate determined?
What chances did they take?
What lessons could they tell?
What mistakes did they make?

Easy to predict the future of some trees.
Strong foundation. Steady nourishment.
Support from balanced roots.
Thankful for their beginning
Yet instinctively they knew;
Roots must continue to grow
If they are to stand strong on their own.
With arms lifted high, and roots running deep,
In gratitude, more gratitude,
Ever growing right on through.

Two other trees more complex than these.
One with a strong foundation;
Broad trunk grew tall and bold.
Why then when nature called
Did this one topple and fold?
Self-will. Self-reliance.

Rotted roots never intertwined with others.
Pride alone left nothing to hold
In times of trials and troubles.
Now on his belly, all that remains is ... firewood.

And yet another tree.
Different, but not unlike many.
Foundation fatally flawed.
How could she possibly evolve?
Gaping hole, clean through the base of her trunk.
Nothing there but air, full of emptiness and stares.
One more good blow and she would surely fall.
Not at all.

How then did this tree grow beautiful and tall?
She wanted to. She decided to. She was born to.
She acknowledged the hole and then looked skyward.
Slowly. Steadily. She used what she had
And joined her roots with others.
She stretched and grew tall,
And encouraged all to follow.

You will never know about the hole
Unless you look up close.
From the sky she looks the same.
Her Maker knows her name.
Those who can see all of her
Delight in growing strong with her.
Gratitude. Peace. Endurance.
Truth. Hope. Care.
With healing and self love,
She now has fruit to share.

Angela Howell
November, 2003

January

All glory comes from daring to begin.
~ Eugene F. Ware

In the gray stillness lies the spirit of incubation birthing the hopes and dreams of the New Year ahead. Some might say it's a cold and dreary season, but not me. This is a time for reflection, planning, and repurposing. Maybe it's also time for redirection? Maybe we accomplished what we hoped to in the previous year? Perhaps we took a detour? Every choice teaches us and propels us forward. There is no right or wrong, only clarity if we are willing to spend time in reflection and be honest with ourselves.

What are you grateful for? What do you want more of this year? Where do you want to spend more time? Less time? Who do you want to spend time with? If you and I were to meet for coffee one to three years from today, what needs to happen in that time for you to be happy with your progress, both personally and professionally? Sometimes I find it easier to look at a big goal and then work backwards, breaking it down into smaller pieces. I'll ask myself, *Well, if that goal was true one year from now, what else will be true?* For instance, if I had aspirations to become more fluent in a foreign language one year from now, I could start by finding other people to regularly converse with. Boom. I just created a tangible action step I can do today, which will help me get where I want to be a year from now. This sounds so obvious, but too often we get overwhelmed and intimidated by the idea of attaining huge goals. We can't think of how to get started and we stay frozen.

As the New Year begins, bask in the stillness of January and start to get clear about what you want and where you want to go. Chart your course for the next three years, one year, six months and even this week. Align yourself with nature—new growth may be dormant now, but it's stirring underground. Bring to the surface the desires of your heart, and the desires of your heart will surface in your life. Refine your life, starting now!

January 2   Wide Open Spaces

"What you can do or think you can do, begin it. For boldness has Magic, Power, and Genius in it."
~ Johanne Wolfgang von Goethe ~

It's sunny but well-below freezing and bitterly cold, so I will NOT be venturing outside this morning! I opened the blinds for inspiration, looking expectantly for something to write about. I started first with one set of blinds on the French doors. I sat back down and looked and waited. Nothing. I opened the blinds on the side window and sat down. Ahh … there it is! A beautiful view of the acreage running across our backyard and several of our neighbors' yards—about three or four acres of frosted grass leading off to trees in the distance. The window is a bit dirty, making it look like there's a light dreamy fog across the icy field.

Open land steals my breath away, it's so beautiful. I see freedom, opportunity, stillness, serenity, and acceptance. I feel captivated and present. I see untouched land and feel like anything is possible. I feel called and inspired to do and be something great. I feel a direct connection to my higher guidance and inner knowing, and I'm quieted so I can listen. Find a view of open land, preferably real but a picture can work also. Let it speak to you, touch you, give birth to new dreams, bathe old dreams with new life. You really can do and be anything you want. We are only limited by our beliefs and those we borrow from well-meaning friends and loved ones. The open land tells the truth. Tune your spirit to it and be grateful for the guidance it offers.

Setting goals is great. *Achieving* goals is much better! We can spend a lot of time writing out detailed goals and elaborate action plans, but unless we begin to change some of the things we do every day, we can't hope to see any real movement toward attaining our hopes and dreams. Without action, our best goals will remain wishes.

We can plan our lives, but we can't just decide what our futures will look like and then sit back, waiting for it to happen. We *can* decide what habits and disciplines we will do daily, and those daily practices are what ultimately decide our future. As we evaluate where we would like to be in six months, one year, three years, or even ten years, let's also evaluate what needs to happen daily to bring about the progress we seek. For instance, a new daily discipline to consider could be waking up twenty minutes early every day to read or listen to ten pages of a book that inspires, challenges and makes you think. An inspired mind fed daily will help you accomplish anything you set out to do. Maybe you need to commit to ten minutes daily of making phone calls to expand your business, instead of just putting out fires, or handling existing issues? I don't know what you need to do, *but you do*. However, don't overwhelm yourself with a commitment you dread and won't keep. Keep it bite-sized and pick something you will actually do. It's the small change that leads to the big change. Allow twenty-one days of repetition for a new habit to form. One day won't make a difference, but consistency over time will change our lives and we will achieve more of the goals we set!

When it comes to reaching goals, the slow, consistent turtle usually beats the rabbit. Try taking a few small steps today—even if it's just ten minutes worth of action or one phone call. Then join my community at www.findingthegift.com (a free gift awaits!) and message me to let me know you're one step closer toward changing your wishes and goals into reality.

January 4   Blessings in Unexpected Packages

Today is an unusually mild, January morning—perfect pajama weather for the deck. I heard the wind howling and screaming all night and now I know why! It was blowing in this incredible warm front!

Sometimes, to get us to the good stuff, we must endure some rough weather. We might get whipped around a little, tossed here or there, and begin questioning why things suddenly got so tough. Trust. Hold on. Weather the storm, because sometimes blessings come in unexpected packages. A warm sunny day may be right around the corner, and you just don't see it yet. Welcome the winds of change—they bring tomorrow's gifts!

January 5   Savor the Moment

Today is sunny and COLD! Whoa! What happened to the exceptionally nice weather that blew in yesterday? Today it's barely above freezing again, quite a shock from our balmy winter break, which unfortunately only lasted one day. I guess the lesson is to enjoy a warm, sunny day while it's here!

Soak up every minute of the good stuff. Take nothing for granted. We're not guaranteed a tomorrow, and we're certainly not guaranteed tomorrow won't bring unexpected change. If I can take what comes and find the blessings in it, I can remain content and stable no matter what's happening around me. If I constantly put expectations on everything and everyone else, (which naturally can't always be met), I'm setting myself up for disappointment. I'm also dancing with yesterday and tomorrow, and missing the good stuff available today. Enjoy the moment. Stay present. Find the gift!

*I find the great thing in this world is not so much where
we stand as in what direction we are moving.*
~ Oliver Wendell Holmes ~

What a beautiful, chilly morning! I feel as sunny on
the inside, as it is outside, after attending a goal-setting
workshop yesterday that really ignited my passions. I
found clarity about what's important to me this year and
in the next five, ten and twenty years.

Take a moment. Stare out a window. Let yourself
dream of a life that is to come. If you could do or be
anything—no limits based on finances, present
circumstances or past experiences—what would you do?
Where would you go? What would you invent? What
new hobby or interest might you explore? Who would be
in your life? (Who would you let go of?) Who would you
help? How much money would you see in your account?
Where would you live? What would your body look like,
and how strong and flexible would you be? What charity
would you support or create? What would your doctor
say at your annual checkup?

This is YOUR dream. STOP the limiting chatter! Find
a great tree, creek, ocean, mountain or expanse of sky to
stare at. They will help you dream. Dreaming without
limits is a challenge for many people. Read *The Dream
Giver*, by Bruce Wilkinson to explore your resistance. I
don't know how it works, but dreaming, writing dreams
down, and attaching your vision, energy and passions to
them starts a chain of events (sometimes quickly,
sometimes slowly) that move you in the direction of your
dreams.

Give it a shot! Remember, you don't dream the *how*,
just the *what*. The *how* will appear on its own if you open
the door to your imagination. No limits!

A friend of mine recently shared with me she had discovered squirrels in her attic. It seemed like everything she tried could not keep the squirrels from getting back in. Christy told me she even put moth balls all throughout the attic, only to find a fair amount of them had been tossed out into their backyard the next day! Scratching around and running incessantly, it seemed they were taunting her. Finally, my friend and her husband found something that worked and they successfully blocked off all avenues into their attic. The squirrels responded by screeching from the trees, loudly protesting their eviction.

Christy likened the squirrels to all the mental pests that chatter away, disrupting our peace of mind. So true! We can spend countless hours chasing those thoughts, and running scenarios round and round in our heads until we are absolutely at our wits end, distracted and exhausted. When we do find a way to finally surrender those thoughts that have held us captive, they don't go quietly. They will wait patiently, reminding us they are still there, ready to resume mental havoc the second we drop our guard. How many times have we re-played conversations in our minds, saying what we *really* wanted to say? Or worse—we are having conversations in our heads about assumptions we're making for things that haven't even happened yet! If I'm engaged in mental warfare, I am definitely not able to be present in the real world. This is a perfect time to write those thoughts down, place them in your God box and let them go! (Jump ahead to October 24 to discover what a God box is and how it works.) When they resurface (and they will), remind yourself you have surrendered that situation and you're off duty right now. With repetition, those same thoughts will show up less and less. And when new "squirrelly" thoughts show up (worries, doubts, fears, concerns, indecision, resentments and imaginary conversations), repeat the process with them as well. We get to decide who is running our lives today—us or the squirrels. When we master our minds, we master our worlds.

January 8   **Tuning Into Your Spirit**

Every spirit builds a house, and beyond its
house a world, and beyond its world a
heaven. Know then that world exists for you.
~ Ralph Waldo Emerson ~

Throughout this book, I will frequently use the word spirit, spiritual connection or spirituality. In many cases, I'm not speaking of religion or my relationship with a higher being beyond me (although I do believe in God). When I talk about my spiritual connection, I'm often referring to my spirit and the essence of me—the spark of life inside me that makes me who I am and determines what I care about, what I desire. My spirit is what lies at the core of my soul, my innermost being. My spirit holds my creativity, my passion, my fears, my love, my hopes, my dreams, my curiosity, my trust and so on.

How is your spiritual connection? Are you tuned in? Is the signal coming in loud and clear, or do you hear a lot of white noise and have to strain to discern anything that makes sense? When someone asks you how you are, do you ever really think about that? Maybe today your answer would be, "(Spiritually), I am grateful, excited, curious, and trusting, with just a hint of loneliness." I know, that would surprise most people, so we usually just say, "I'm fine." That's okay, but I encourage you to be in tune with the real answer to that question.

Our spiritual health has to be nurtured intentionally and pursued the same way we seek to maintain and improve our physical health. We can't just buy a gym membership and expect to get fit if we never go. We can't benefit from a journal that remains empty, or books that go unread. We can't run ninety miles per hour all day, every day, with no quiet time and wonder why we feel so frazzled and out of touch with ourselves, and as a result, with our other close relationships also. Some of us may have neglected our spiritual selves for so long, we're not really sure how to access that part of us.

What follows are some of my favorite paths to meeting up with my spiritual self and inviting God to show up too: taking a moment to be still and look out the window, going for a walk in nature, taking a hot bath, journaling, praying, putting dreams on paper, indulging a long country drive, looking at meaningful pictures, listening to music, and letting my brain go soft and unfocused.

Regardless of your religious beliefs, every one of us has a spirit, and is thus, spiritual, at least as I defined it earlier. If your cup is full, if you're cramming so much activity and stuff into your life that there isn't time for getting in touch with your spirit, something's got to give! No more can go in until something else comes out, or you push the pause button! Radios and instruments must stay in tune to produce a desired sound, and you are the finest instrument of all! Stay tuned! Cherish and regularly pursue your spiritual fitness and remember, just like your physical health, it's easier to maintain, than re-gain, so keep your maintenance plan in action.

January 9   Schedule Regular Time-Out

I'm parked at the gym to write before my workout. Kids are back in school after the holidays. My routine of taking my son to school and then coming to the gym has resumed. I am happy for the return of daily rhythm, which includes writing in my car during the time I have before my class begins.

Today, however, it's a struggle to write amidst some unusual distractions. A dog is barking. A child is crying.

The lady who just pulled up next to me has her talk radio show turned up really loud. Birds are singing, but they are drowned out by cars coming and going, doors slamming and that barking dog! How critical it is to find time to bask in the silence of nature without the man-made confusion which surrounds us much of the time. I cannot possibly access my deeper wisdom and insight when constantly immersed in chaos.

Find the time to take a timeout. If that time stops working, or your usual place is too distracting, be flexible. Adjust your schedule and location to get those moments of quiet solitude so you can hear yourself, so you can breathe uninterrupted, so God can whisper words of comfort and guidance to you. With all you do for everyone else, do this for YOU! Everyone else, including you, will reap the rewards of your personal dedication to daily peace and divine impartation—the goods.

January 10   The Dreaded G Word: Gratitude

Every morning sets the tone for the next moment. We can change our day by changing this moment. If you like how you feel right now, don't do anything! If you want to feel different, let's get to it! Making myself available for spiritual connection is one approach I use. Writing a letter or talking to the part of me who is scared, sad or angry is another tool.

One of the most successful ways to transform my mood, however, is gratitude. That's the *G* word I will use a lot in this book. I had a friend at one time in my life who, no matter what I was struggling with, would always recommend I make a gratitude list. It really irritated me.

But did you hear what I just said? I wanted to yell. *THIS* (awful thing) *just happened to me!*

"Make a gratitude list anyway," she would tell me.

But what about what she did to me?

"Gratitude list," she repeated.

But I don't know what I'm going to do about XYZ!

"Gratitude list," she said rather smugly.

Ugh!

The funny thing is when I would sit down and poke a hole through my resistance, and just start making the stupid list, it worked. Especially, *especially* if I could find reasons to be grateful for the very thing or person that was troubling me.

Gratitude has a way of softening my heart and breaking down my walls so compassion, serenity and solutions can find me. If I am feeling pretty good, a gratitude list helps deepen my hold on peace and joy. Being grateful can't in itself solve every dilemma. However, it can alter how I feel in this moment, which can alter the next and the next, leading me to a state of being where I can approach my life from a much better place. Go ahead! Try it for five minutes. As a bonus, humility and compassion will find you too! Exercise your heart without ever breaking a sweat. You're welcome.

January 11   **Welcoming Change**

I'm sitting outside this morning, and it's a sunny, fifty degrees, which is pretty awesome for January, and warm enough for me to bundle up and write outdoors. I just love my covered deck, my view of rolling Tennessee hills, and hearing the cows moo across the way. Though we love it here, we've decided to put our house up for sale. We bought it as an investment and it's time to do something different.

I enjoy this house inside and out. It's difficult to even imagine finding something just as good. It's so easy and natural to want to stay where we are—the same house, city, job, relationship, or school. Even when it's not so great, it's often difficult to imagine making a change. Maybe there is something better? Maybe something different would open new doors we hadn't even thought about before?

Many times change, voluntary or not, has brought about unexpected blessings and rearranged my life in a way I never would've planned for myself. Maybe we'll sell and maybe we won't—we're going to put the house on the market and see what happens. That's called taking action and surrendering the results. Meanwhile, I'm going to savor every moment spent on my secluded, covered deck, overlooking my little piece of heaven. I will enjoy today and all that's exactly right in my life, right now. Join me in being grateful for today, and expectant of blessings to come.

January 12   Getting Comfortable with Calm

Somewhere close by, I can hear a very curious, or otherwise, incessantly noisy dog. (Not mine!) I can let him ruin this moment for me—or not. Certainly, it's a challenge to see and hear everything else around me. Actually, without the barking I wouldn't appreciate the absence of it. Though I do love my quiet, mornings outside, I appreciate the interruption, because it makes me cherish what I love even more. I find this is true in all things—the noise in our lives (the obstacles, the distractions) and then the silence and still moments (calm, serenity). I need one to appreciate the other.

Now conditioned to expect noise every few minutes this morning, I'm noticing my tendency to listen for the dog even in the peace and quiet. I can't even enjoy the silence, because I'm waiting for him to ruin it! How often have I done that in life, rather than relish a moment of serenity for however long it lasts? It takes faith and a conscious effort for me to allow myself to get comfortable in peaceful times, because that's just not as familiar to me.

I have experienced the "barking dog" in life many times, and admittedly, have trained myself to listen for it, expecting problems to return any second. I must have decided at some point it was safer to stay expectant of trouble (waiting for the other shoe to drop), than to relax and enjoy a stress-free outlook. When Fido barks again and the silence is broken, I see how that fosters my idea that it's just easier to just not embrace peace, knowing it will be interrupted. So why hope at all? Because like today, the disturbance is never permanent.

I can re-learn to be comfortable in a season of calm—allowing myself to experience the fullness each moment offers, without worrying about when it's going to end. Today, I will consciously choose to trust I am safe to be, to dream, and to hope. Interruptions are temporary. I will keep my focus where life is, not where chaos is, or might be. Faith can set me free, despite nothing and no one else changing.

January 13   Aligning Intention and Focus

This morning, I went for a walk and experienced a couple of insights about the different ways I tend to approach my suburban adventures. Do I walk with my head down, constantly looking to see what might trip me up? Or do I keep a casual eye on where I'm placing my next step, but spend most of my focus on the sights and sounds of the walk?

I can appreciate the trees, the sky, birds, landscape, squirrels, architecture, neighbors, flowers and creeks and whatever else I might encounter if I'm not staring at the ground. Sometimes I even get extra surprises, like the occasional deer or rabbit! I love to walk because it brings me back to the present and keeps me there, as long as I set my intentions to ignore the nagging thoughts that can easily distract me from the moment, and steal my joy along the way.

Sometimes I've been guilty of walking through my life more focused on the people and circumstances (obstacles) that might potentially trip me up, to the point I have missed other wonderful blessings. The key is my intention. My feet will go wherever I intend them to go. My mind will go wherever I let it wander. Today I will focus on what is—the good that is all around me—with just an occasional glance at the road ahead to keep me safe and determine my next steps.

January 14   Listening to Your Inner Requests

Whew! It's near freezing and drizzly. I went outside on the deck to see if I could bear the chilly temperature to do my writing. I decided my best chance of enjoying nature today was to sit close to the house and the cozy warmth on the other side of the wall. Even with the most thought-out, ideal circumstances, I was not comfortable. I was not relaxed. I was too cold to allow myself to sink into the moment and relish my morning time.

News flash! I can change my mind! Sometimes I just don't know how something is going to feel until I try it. Yesterday I had some time to kill waiting for a store to open so I decided to park my car and read. Without thinking, I pulled into the closest space possible. People were coming and going by my car into a neighboring office building, and my soul was pleading for me to move to a space further out so I could read undistracted. But I didn't want to look silly. Really? As if anyone is watching me, paying attention to whether or not I move my car and don't get out? Who cares!

More than ever, I'm ready to please the inner voice inside and forget the worry of what others are thinking about me. In most cases, they aren't thinking of me at all! So yesterday, I moved the car away from all the distractions, to read in peace. And today, I listened to myself say, *It's cold! Please take me back inside!* That sometimes-not-so-small voice is there for a reason. It's my inner compass. When I trust my inner guide, I'm more loving, not only to myself, but to everyone else around me. I feel heard and the inner battle subsides. Today I will listen for three inner requests and I hope you will do the same. For example:

- ❦ What I really want for lunch is_____.
- ❦ How I really want to exercise today is _____ instead of _____.
- ❦ I would like to take a break right now.

Listening and honoring my needs are the greatest gifts I can give myself today!

January 15   Rewards of Listening to Yourself

Yesterday I suggested a challenge of listening and honoring three inner preferences from that small voice inside. Here's how that worked out for me. First, I made a trip to the grocery store and initially took a parking place pretty far from the door. My intuition said she would prefer to move to another row to find a space closer to the door. I remembered my intention to look for three inner requests and here was the first one. I thought, *That's silly to move the car, but I'll do it for you anyway.* I drove over two rows and got a place about three spots closer to the door. As I was about to pull in to that one, I noticed the very first parking space was open. I shouted, *YES!* and then, *Ok, smart girl, so that's why you wanted to move? Thanks for telling me there was a place right up front!*

Secondly, while in the grocery store for milk and bananas (it's never just milk and bananas), I saw fresh sushi. My inner voice said she would really like to have sushi for lunch as a special treat. *Okay. Fine.* I bought sushi to go. She felt heard and delighted.

Third, back at home, I was getting ready to eat my special sushi lunch at the kitchen table when I received an inner request to eat outside on the deck to make it a real treat. Though chilly, the sun was shining, so I prepared a tray and ate outside. It WAS a nice treat! Wow, in each situation my spirit felt heard! I took just a few extra steps to honor her inner desires, and I felt not merely contented, but delighted! She really doesn't ask for much, so why do I refuse to indulge her little nudges so often? If someone I love asks me for a small kindness, wouldn't I do it? Especially if it's a little thing that can bring big joy?

It's like I have another voice that dismisses her "silly" wishes and likes to stick to a routine. Every time I ignore my spirit, I tell her she doesn't matter. I think she's heard and felt that rejection from me enough, and it's time to heed her voice. Imagine a week, a month, a year or a lifetime of listening to and honoring my inner requests? I believe my self-esteem might be completely restored, my daily contentment level would go from often nonexistent to never ending. Imagine what that level of well-being would do to my relationships? My ambitions? I think I'll try it again today!

January 16   **Mindfulness Makes Sense(s)**

I have a lot of animals and I'm a sucker for a stray! Throughout the course of writing this book, some have come and gone so you'll see different names from time to time. God bless all furry creatures and to the ones we've lost, may they rest in peace!

Today my senses feel like they're heightened, and I'm extra aware of everything, anything. I'm out on the deck and it's chilly and dreary. That same dog a few houses over is barking like crazy. Harvey is meowing. Goldie and Lucky are quiet. A truck passes down the distant road. Birds fly by; others are singing. The trees and clouds are still. Two more cars go by. Several cows are grazing in the field across the road (occasionally one speaks, or rather moos). A new dog starts barking and Goldie goes down the stairs to investigate. (Her collar jingles.) The neighbor's pool ripples just slightly, sounds peaceful. I hear another neighbor slam a car door. A plane emerges from the clouds. Smells like winter (cold, moist).

Take a moment ... or two! What do you notice? I just took ten minutes to see, smell, hear, notice and appreciate my environment. I feel calm, centered, grounded, peaceful, and grateful. I did not experience one second of fear, worry, hurry, anger, sadness or loneliness. I truly experienced those few moments—a unique sliver of time in my life. Patience, consistency, acceptance, peace, familiarity—it's all around me. Breathe it in. Take a moment, as often as necessary, to hit the restore button and come back to the here and now—the fabric of your days, the mosaic of your life.

January 17   Fear of Success

We've all heard the phrase, "We are never given more than we can handle." I've always applied that to difficult situations and tough times, but I recently heard the idea that it's also true for our talents, our potential, and thus, our destinies. Fear of success is just as real as fear of failure.

In Nelson Mandela's famous inaugural speech, he quoted Marianne Williamson by saying:

"Our deepest fear is not that we are inadequate. Our deepest fear is that we are powerful beyond measure. It is our light, not our darkness that most frightens us. We ask ourselves, Who am I to be brilliant, gorgeous, talented, and fabulous? Actually, who are you not to be? You are a child of God. Your playing small does not serve the world. There is nothing enlightened about shrinking so that other people will not feel insecure around you. We are all meant to shine, as children do. We were born to

make manifest the glory of God that is within us. It is not just in some of us; it is in everyone and as we let our own light shine, we unconsciously give others permission to do the same. As we are liberated from our own fear, our presence automatically liberates others."

The biggest role we will ever play on the stage of life is ourselves! We must not be afraid to trust and follow the mysterious greatness inside us, no matter how unknown, unpredictable, or scary it may seem. Change will happen at a speed we can handle. Me being all of ME, you being all of YOU, inherently came with the equipping we would each need to be that person in full. Being all that we are meant to become, letting all of ourselves float to the surface for the world to see is never a mistake. It's who we were born to be and it's our role in the symphony of life. No one else can do it for us.

Let's each play our part loud and proud so we can all be blessed by every individual's contribution to the music we were born to create together. As we contribute to the whole, the essence of each one of us is also fully realized and fulfilled. While this doesn't happen overnight, we can all take a step in the right direction today by being honest, and asking ourselves if we are thriving or merely hiding out in the roles we've taken on. I know I've hidden a lot in my life, but I'm taking small steps to correct that, and I hope you will join me.

January 18   **Replay or Try a Different Way?**

On my walk today, a car approached and was forced to move over to the oncoming lane to avoid me, before moving back to the right side of the road. I started to think about the various obstacles I often encounter on my walk: a rock that wasn't there before, a new pothole, a recent gift from man's best friend (definitely like to avoid stepping in *that*). Even if I'm really enjoying my walk and taking it all in, occasionally I might have to alter my steps to avoid a mishap. It could be something new, or maybe it's something that's always been there, but I get distracted and forget about it, and it trips me up again.

There's a particular concrete spill along a stretch of road I frequent. I've tripped over that same spot more times than I care to admit! It keeps happening because I'm looking all around and forget to avoid it. How many times have I encountered obstacles in my life—the same ones over and over? I let the same people or circumstance trip me up, hoping maybe this time things will be different. Maybe *they* (parent, boss, lover, spouse, or child) changed and have miraculously become the person I always hoped they would be? A spilled, hardened lump of concrete isn't going anywhere and often the people or other obstacles in our life are not going to change either.

Instead of stubbornly clinging to old hopes, dreams and behavior patterns, waiting for them to change, *we* can change! We can put the focus on our safety, happiness and well-being and go over, around or through the obstacles with our peace intact.

I love the phrase, "Obstacles or opportunities?" We get to choose. Get the lesson. Get the gift. Adjust your steps and move forward.

January 19   Expect the Unexpected

The wind has been howling all night, bringing a dreary, overcast morning. It's dark enough to turn on a lamp, thanks to the thick clouds rolling across the sky. All of a sudden—literally out of the blue—the sun burst through. It really startled me! A huge stream of light came through my window, lasted for about six seconds, and was gone. I thought to myself, *It's impossible to see the sun on a day like today, with the clouds so dense.* I totally wasn't expecting it, and in a way, I missed it. I was so startled when it happened, I didn't soak it in. I doubted myself the second it was gone and wanted to hit replay!

I feel humbled and reminded that anything is possible. I can't look around at my circumstances and decide they can't possibly change, because I'm not in charge! I do believe there is a power greater than me. There is a God and I'm not it! The impossible *can* happen. Unexpected gifts *can* fall into our life. They may last. They may be fleeting. Enjoy them for what they are for as long as you can. Don't be so full of disbelief that you miss the gift while it's here.

The wind is screaming again and yet I just got another two seconds of sunshine as it parted the clouds for an instant. Another ten seconds. Now it's blinding me! Now it's gone. This time I didn't miss out. Each time, like a kid about to burst with anticipation, I waited expectantly for it to return. I enjoyed how it felt and the way the light sprayed across the room in a stark ray. It could come back again any second, even though at this moment, I don't see a break in the clouds. But I didn't see the last break coming either—it just happened.

I will expect the unexpected today. I will open my heart, my mind, my ears and arms to receive. I am full of gratitude for what I've already received. I feel smiled upon. What's next? I'm ready and up for anything.

January 20   **Everyone Needs a Little Color**

Sunset is still my favorite color, and rainbow is second. ~
Mattie Stepanek ~

Winter has brought another overcast day and it's very, very cold! It seems like the sky has been gray and bleak for several days in a row. This morning, I happened to be glancing out my bathroom window at just the right time to suddenly see a piece of blue sky! It changed the color of everything outside, adding warmth and brightness. I felt like my world literally went from black and white to color!

I thought about how big of a difference that small amount of color had on my attitude. Sometimes life can get so monotonous it's like living in black and white, and we need some "color" to stir things up! A new hairstyle or lunch from somewhere we've never been before, a visit to a toy store, a different route to work or home. Mix it up! Ask yourself for ideas and listen for the answers. You'll find them if you look. A little variation can make a world of difference if we are willing to experiment and invite some change. Play! Live! Have some fun with it! You'll renew the bounce in your step in no time!

January 21   **Nature Soothes**

*In all things of nature there is
something of the marvelous.*
~ **Aristotle** ~

Take yourself to the park! Watch the birds, pigeons, and ducks just hanging out, living life. I can't think of anything else when I'm watching, fascinated by God's creatures.

I am sitting in a parking lot killing time right now, and just tossed my apple core into the grassy field beside my car. Busy writing, I didn't notice the influx of birds nearby, taking turns feeding on the apple. Off in a distant tree, a blue jay appeared to watch.

Wherever you are, whenever you can, take a five-minute break and let nature and her creatures draw you away from the noise and chatter of life. Instantly my gauges are reset. I am balanced, grateful, calmed and ready to carry on with my day taking my renewed appreciation for life with me. Even the people I encounter the rest of today will benefit from the smile I'm feeling on the inside.

January 22   Breaking the Rules is Good

I woke up extra early this morning and the sun was just breaking through on the horizon with a warm yellow, orange, pink and purple glow. Big, fluffy clouds are making the view even more spectacular. It truly fits the description of majestic. When I sat in my usual chair, I couldn't see it. I tried my husband's chair, but the view was even worse.

I got the idea to move my regular chair sideways so I could see the sunrise better, but I've never moved that chair before and I didn't want to bother with it. I sat back down, still not satisfied with my view. I got back up, and decided to throw out my chair-moving rules and slightly turned the chair. What a simple, thirty-second solution! I will move it back when I'm done.

Where do we get all these crazy rules in our heads anyway? It's my life! I want and deserve a front row seat with the best view! Get rid of the self-imposed limitations! Embrace the solutions we're given, even if they are outside the box and something we've never tried before. Trust that inner guidance when it speaks and we just might discover we like what appears.

January 23   Where to Find Stillness

Today is very still and quiet, but it's not too cold, so I'm outside on my patio swing. I remember the day we picked it out, brought it home and hung it up—I felt like I had really *arrived*! It's amazing what a relatively small purchase can do for our well-being, but that's another topic for another day.

I'm discovering I have some built in patio-swing philosophies to go with the inside-chair-moving rules I discussed yesterday. A patio swing was created specifically for pleasure outside. It's not just a piece of furniture—we have other outdoor chairs for simply sitting. No, a patio swing is for fun, companionship, solitary reflection, or a cozy place to curl up and read.

I use my swing very intentionally, when the mood or circumstance calls for it. Today I'm using it to slowly swing and enjoy the quiet stillness of the morning. I hear very little traffic on the nearby road behind my home. Just a few birds tweeting to each other. The sky is a blanket of grey clouds, illuminated by the light behind them. At this very moment, everything in my world is calm and peaceful. I am content. Stillness in nature is like ointment for my soul. It soothes whatever is ailing me. Today I just needed a big dose of calm. I'm grateful and giving thanks!

January 24   When Grief Settles in Like Fog

Today is cold and foggy, and that pretty much describes how I feel. I woke up early, right after a bad dream left me with a lingering feeling of sadness and grief. As I stare outside at the fog settling over the houses and fields, I realize that's how my grief and sadness would look if I could see them. It feels like I have a hovering layer of heavy emotion around my heart today.

Some days, there are no magic words to move or uplift me. Grief is a part of life and when it comes, I feel it serves my best interest to feel and experience it. I will journal and explore the nature of it to see if I can learn more about it or possibly help the feelings move through me more easily. Sometimes I know what it's about, but other times I never really understand what brought it up on a particular day. If I feel like crying, I do. I honor my grief. It's real, even when I don't understand the nature of it. No more than if I could sweep away the fog outside. I just let it be.

I sit in feelings of grief for as long as it seems necessary and then ask myself what I need. Do I want to move my body, rest, take a walk or a nap, stretch, make something, paint something, watch a movie, feed the ducks or the birds, call a friend, listen to music, or just be silent? Whatever it is, I listen and give myself what I need and when it's time, the fog will lift and life goes on. It always does. I am grateful for the contrast.

January 25   Finding the Gift in the Storms of Life

We had really intense storms and wind last night. The clouds are still moving swiftly outside, sporadically allowing bright sun to shine through and dry everything up. As I drove my son to school, I noticed how the sun reflected brightly off the wet parts of the street, as opposed to the dry parts. I see the wet areas as residual evidence of the storm bouncing light more easily, and the dry areas as being back to normal.

After a storm in our lives where we might have been knocked around a bit, a dose of humility is likely to give us a reset, making us more open for help and guidance, and better able to shine brightly again. We can reflect the love and light that comes our way, provided we've been able to use the circumstances of the storm to gain a higher perspective. Our egos may have disappeared a little, allowing us to more effectively mirror God's light, as it comes back into our lives.

When the sun shines all the time (when life is going well), it's easy to take things for granted and let self-reliance take over, never asking for, or being open to receive help. Today, sunshine or not, I will reflect the love and light around me to myself and to others, grateful to receive with an open heart and mind.

January 26   Choosing My Reflection

There is something beautiful about a life that's transparent. Someone you can see goodness through. Someone who just feels good to be around. We can all be that person. When my heart and mind are open to be a channel for love and light, and when I'm living an authentic life full of action and purpose, I become that person.

I believe each of us has a mirror inside, reflecting to others how we're really feeling about life and about ourselves. If I let my internal mirror become coated with the haze of complacency, negativity, and poor self-care, what I project to those around me isn't too desirable to look at or be around. I can polish my internal mirror with self-love, nurturing, and being helpful to others. I can shine brighter when I'm doing things to seek guidance and cultivate curiosity and inspiration—like reading, journaling, praying, meditating, creating something, taking walks, sitting on a park bench, listening to music, viewing art or going to the beach (or the mountains).

When I make self-care a priority, I can be a clear reflection of goodness, passion, compassion and love. I enjoy being around me and so does everyone else! I will choose an activity today that will move me in the direction of openness and love.

January 27   Most of Our Life is Spent on the Way

It is good to have an errand to journey towards;
but it is the journey that matters in the end.
~ Ursula LeGuin ~

I welcome winter days to go inward, to sit in good company—my own!—and ponder my journey, with divine guidance. I can always look back and appreciate how far I've come, which is especially helpful on days when I feel lost or doubt I'm making any progress. Today, all I need to know about my future is the direction I want to go, and what the next step looks like. I become willing to take that step, then another, then another. I stop to rest and ask for directions, and to check my course regularly.

Let me never forget, life is the journey. Life is what happens along the way. We only spend a fractional proportion of time at any given destination, any anticipated place of arrival. We arrive, we look around, and when appropriate, maybe we even celebrate for a period of time. It's not long, however, before we begin looking toward what's next. In my experience, a soul that is idle and aimless is as good as dead—we just haven't had the funeral yet!

We all need a journey. We crave adventure and growth! It's in our nature to aspire to be more, to know more, to do more or to have more than we have today. Hope is the fuel for the future. Gratitude is the rest stop along the way. Is there a secret to life? Maybe it's to be grateful for where we are and what we have, while remaining hopeful for all that is yet to come. An object in motion remains in motion. An object at rest remains at rest. Take breaks when needed, but keep on moving! Moving is living! Movement is life!

January 28   Face Truth Then Play Make-Believe

You cannot change your destination
overnight. You can change your direction.
~ **Jim Rohn** ~

Seems like yesterday we were celebrating New Year's Eve and now January is practically over! Time flies when you're having fun, but the real truth is—time flies. Before you know it, half the year will be gone, then half a decade and so on.

Think back to five years ago, the goals you had and the challenges you faced. Are you happy with the growth you've made since then? Most of us have probably made some progress and maybe even hit a milestone of some sort. Many of us, however, may still be battling with some of the same issues today that we were wrestling with back then. Maybe the things we hoped would be resolved or much better by now haven't changed as much as we would have liked? Maybe we're still stuck in a job we hate, our relationships are still troubled, or we still have the same financial difficulty, health issues, or bad habits that we struggled with five years ago?

We have to be willing to do something different today in order to have something different tomorrow. Change requires two things—decision and action. Pick one thing you want to change over the next one to three years. What will be different after you make this change? How will your life improve?

Be that person today, the one you'll be when the change is in place. Get up tomorrow morning when your future, changed person would get up. Go to the gym *now*, as often as your future, changed person would go. Treat your current spouse or significant other in the same way the changed you would treat them. Walk into work today with the posture and confidence that you envision yourself having one to three years from now. Be as grateful today as you will be in your changed life, and watch your life begin to shift. Remember the game of make-believe? Let's play! Just for today, act as if you've already made the progress you seek. It may feel so good, you want to play again tomorrow!

January 29   Take Action and Trust in the Process

My neighbors and I share a long row of tall evergreens that run across the far end of our backyards. A few of the trees died, leaving some gaps, which wasn't a big deal until the neighbor behind the tree line constructed a big green shed. The view from our house wasn't greatly affected thanks to the evergreens that remained, but several neighbors were very unhappy about the unsightly shed.

Our next-door neighbors took action and planted two eight-foot evergreens in the gaps which will solve their problem in time. The existing trees are at least twenty-four-feet tall. It's hard to believe they'll ever be as tall as the others, but we don't have to understand how a tree can triple in size over time. It doesn't even matter if we believe it's possible. All my neighbors had to do was plant them and trust in the process. They've surrendered the outcome to nature and time.

If we want a desired outcome, we just need to do the next right thing and take some action, whether or not we possess complete confidence it's going to work, and regardless if we feel like doing it or not. If other people have what you want, do what they did to get it. Chances are good it will work for you too. Faith and footwork can change almost everything.

January 30   What Feels Like Forever, Never Is

Here we are in January, in the thick of winter. It's well-below freezing and overcast—again! My soul longs for sunlight and warmth. Even though my steady goal is to be present in the moment, I can't help sometimes just wanting to fast-forward to spring. A few days ago, I did just that!

I've been writing this book on and off for nearly eight years, and only a year ago did I decide to be diligent and write regularly, with a completion date defined. All my thoughts have been hand-written in journals, so on top of continuing to write, I'm also in the process of dictating the content into digital form.

A few days ago, I was converting some April entries, when I ran across one that was exactly what I needed to read at that very moment. In that entry, I talked about how it was so beautiful, and warm enough for me to be able to write outside again. Flowers were already blooming. Ironically, I also wrote about how, not too long ago, I had been in the dead of winter, wondering if it would ever end.

When I read that, I felt like I had time-traveled! I was encouraged to remember, *This too shall pass.* I got to read encouragement from my spring-self, talking to my winter-self, saying, *Yes, a new season is coming, hold on!* This book has no rules, nothing that says you can't read an April meditation in January. If I need a taste of spring and winter, I can fast-forward for a moment. If the long, hot days of summer create a craving for a chilly winter day, I can turn the page and read a December entry. I can go there in my mind for a quick temporary reprieve.

Life really is short. Each season of nature is roughly only three months. Seasons of change, struggle, joy, grief, etc. can vary, but in the big scheme of things, most seasons of life are brief. Today, I will ask what I can learn from the season of life I am currently experiencing. It will be gone before I know it, so I will not wish it away. I will make it count and I will grow!

January 31   **Setting Life's Thermostat**

Sometimes just moving the dial a little can create a life that feels a lot more comfortable. Winter is upon us! It may be thirty degrees outside and raining, but here on the other side of windows and walls, I am toasty and warm inside. Isn't central heat and air amazing? I set the dial to create the environment of my choice.

Is life really that different? We've all made the choices that created our present environment. If we get uncomfortable, we can turn the dial, or in other words tweak our choices. We can seek knowledge, personal growth and development. We can change our habits. We can change jobs, geography and relationships. Perhaps the most powerful change of all also lies within our reach—we can change how we perceive our situation. Even when nothing else is different, we can have a whole new reality based on how we choose to approach and interact with the circumstances and people in our lives,

AND where we decide to focus our energy, love and thought.

Norman Vincent Peale said, "Change your thoughts and you change your world." If your environment needs to change, pray for the willingness and courage to make some new choices and take action. If your perception needs to change, make a gratitude list of what's working well right now and pray for an open mind, acceptance, and a new way to look at the situation. Be encouraged! A one or two degree shift can make a world of difference!

February

Half an hour's meditation is essential except when you are very busy. Then a full hour is needed.
~ Francis de Sales

Yikes, we had frightening wind last night, howling so fierce, I just couldn't go to sleep. I felt sure something bad was about to happen, or something was going to break or shatter. I finally got up at 3 a.m. to look around outside, checking the view from several different windows. Other than our outdoor furniture being a little scattered, everything looked okay. It sounded awful though—it was the worst wind I can ever remember.

I went back to bed, and not twenty minutes later, our son bolted into our bedroom and said we were under a tornado warning! The wind got louder than ever and then everything grew very quiet. We ran down to the basement right away, but I believe the tornado had already passed.

Sometimes we get a feeling in our gut so strong, but ignore it when we don't know what it's trying to tell us. Over and over, I've been able to look back at inner warnings and realize my intuition was trying to tell me something. If we're tuned into ourselves and listening to our source, we will hear the sirens go off in times of danger or when we need to be concerned. I don't just mean natural storms, but also storms brewing in life: a new relationship that just feels off, a job interview that looks great on paper but doesn't feel right, or an offer for help that seems too good to be true. Whatever it is, listen and proceed with caution. Talk things out with a trusted friend. Hindsight is 20/20 and we won't always avoid trouble, so give yourself grace if you miss the warning signs. It seems obvious now, but it didn't occur to me at 3 a.m. to watch a weather report.

For today, practice listening to yourself. Trust your gut, even if you can't prove it or make sense of it, yet. Intuition is a gift we've been given, but it's up to us to use and develop it. The more we practice trusting ourselves and the nudges in our spirit, the better we'll be able to dodge unnecessary storms in life.

February 2 Rainy Days are Good for Going Inside

The best thing one can do when
it's raining is to let it rain.
~ **Henry Wadsworth Longfellow** ~

Rain has a way of driving me inside, not just under a roof surrounded by four walls, but all the way into my soul. Thoughts of goals, longings and aspirations still linger in my mind over the coming year. What do I really want? Where do I want to change? I ask God, *Where is the bridge to get me from where I am now, to where I want to go?* I silence all chatter and wait for a reply.

Meanwhile the rain keeps falling constant and steady—nurturing the earth and preparing for the miracle of spring. My changes are in motion, too. The answer I get is to just keep doing what I'm doing: dreaming, seeking, stretching, exploring, facing fears and taking action. My success isn't determined by individual outcomes, but by the fact that I'm persistent and keep taking steps in the right direction. I'm open to whatever I may find, and I trust I'm on the path toward my highest good.

February 3   Get Busy Living!

Death. The very word brings darkness and weight. I believe the secret to really living out loud is to accept we're not getting out alive, and we're not promised tomorrow. Intellectually, we know this is true, but are we living it on a daily basis? On this day in 2013, a beautiful young soul left this life too early at twenty-one years of age. Though we will never understand why a life is ended too soon, let it serve as a reminder to the rest of us to get busy living!

As they say, "The only difference between a rut and a grave is the depth of the hole." If you're in a rut, get out while you still can! Live and love like there's no tomorrow! Make each day count by doing or saying something memorable. Forgive and forget. Life's too short to carry resentments around. Be grateful for every second—it's a gift not to be taken for granted. Make peace with others and even more importantly, with yourself. Stop living for everyone else and start living for you. If there's something you really want to do—DO IT! Make plans to make it happen this year, or in the very near future. A life full of dreams and hopes and plans, and even disappointment, is a life full of LIFE. Failure to try may be the worst regret of all. Today is a new day, which can mark the beginning of your decision to really live. Get honest and then GET BUSY!

February 4   **Illusions Aren't Real**

I'm sitting by the lake at Foggy Cove, which is anything but foggy today. Though it's bitter cold, bright sunshine spills everywhere, without a cloud in sight. The water has a gentle movement and the reflections are mostly soft and muted. However, the closer the reflection, the sharper the image. The reflections of the trees on the far side of the lake are much more exaggerated and abstract, but it's an illusion, not an accurate reflection of what's real. Reflections are distorted when viewed from a distance.

When I evaluate my own life—my feelings, my relationships, financial success, and behaviors—my reflection is a fairly accurate perception. It's my world. I'm close to it and I know what it is, and what it isn't. When I look out and try to judge or compare my insides with other people's outsides, it's natural for them to appear happier, have more success, and have better relationships. But it's an illusion—distorted thinking. I can't possibly know what it looks like or feels like to be them. I can only see the reflections of their lives, what they allow me to see. What they are projecting may or may not be accurate.

We see a man with a beautiful woman, a nice car and we automatically assume he has money and a great life. We see a single mom in a rundown home and we feel sorry for her. We assume she is unhappy, poor, and maybe we even judge her worth by her possessions. We could be wrong in either case. My best bet is to keep the focus on myself and what I'm reflecting to the world. Look for the good in others and know that everyone gets their share of ups and downs, wins and losses. Let go of mind-reading and be your best—whatever that is on any given day. Today, be grateful for this very moment. It's yours. It's real.

February 5   Embrace the Void

Today is cold and damp, solemnly overcast by thick clouds. Quiet. Still. The trees are empty of leaves. The only sound is the faint song of birds echoing off in the distance. I can't often say this but today, things look and feel quite lifeless outside. A void. Avoid. I've never thought about the word play or irony in that. I have always wanted to completely avoid, or rush through the voids in my life, but they show up for a reason.

We are to embrace the voids in life as a much-needed rest and a season of reinvention or re-creation. A void can serve as a period of restoration, regrouping, reflection, renewing, and redirecting. This is when we store up energy, inspiration and focus for our next chapter. Today I will appreciate the void and allow myself to be fully in it, knowing it won't last forever, and trusting it bears the gifts tomorrow will bring.

February 6   Spring Always Follows Winter

It has been so cold, wet and gloomy the last several days. Today the temperature has risen to just below freezing, and it's spitting snow. Thankfully, the sun has made an appearance now and then. I feel a bit down today, winter blues I guess. As I look out at the barren trees, I know without a doubt that in just a short while, they will be covered with full, green leaves once again.

It helps to be reminded that even when, on the surface, life feels a little dull or maybe everything isn't going exactly as I hoped, major transformations are happening behind the scenes. This may be a winter season in my life, but spring always follows winter—always! Be encouraged! Even if I cannot see things are changing or growing, they are, and I can trust I will soon see evidence of the changes that are taking place right at this very moment. Today I thank the trees for their faithful reminder that, *this too shall pass*.

February 7   Winter Offers a Blank Canvas

We cannot stop the winter or the summer from coming. We cannot stop the spring or the fall or make them other than they are. They are gifts from the universe that we cannot refuse. But we can choose what we will contribute to life when each arrives.
~ Gary Zukav ~

Winter brings much stillness, and with it, a time to regroup, reorder and restore. What is working? Where do I feel lacking? What do I need more of? Less of? The winter landscape is bare like a fresh canvas. I am the artist. I hold the brush. I choose the color and the brushstrokes. I can paint whatever I choose.

I will use this time to reflect. What do I want the picture of my life to look like? Ask the questions. Be still and you can hear the answers. Then grab your brush and dip it into the paint. Every masterpiece began with the first brushstrokes and evolved from there. I don't have to know exactly what the finished piece will look like, but I do have to get started and trust that my next stroke will be guided. It will be, as long as I keep asking questions and keep listening for the answers.

February 8　　　　　　　**Gratitude Feels Better**

Today is cold and bleak. When it's dark outside, we have all the more reason to turn inward to find the sunshine. I can choose to reflect my outer circumstances by brooding and dragging myself through the day. Whether it's literally the gray winter season that has me down, or it's my work, relationships or other circumstances, there's always a good enough reason to be down in the dumps. Guess what? That still leaves me down in the dumps!

I heard a quote once that I'm going to modify here: "What's bigger—your ego or your smile?" Even if we have a great excuse to sing the blues, and though sometimes it's a battle with our pride to walk away from misery that is justified, choose happiness and gratitude anyway. It sure feels a lot better to make the decision to let something go and *choose* to be happy.

A gratitude list is always a powerful tool to transform my mood. Doing something nice for someone else, or making a phone call to just say hi, is a great way to get out of a funk and be of service to others. I have never been able to stay in my own pity party while reaching out to be a light to a friend or family member. However you do it, I hope you find some sunshine today!

February 9　　　　**Using My Senses to Find the Gifts**

It has been so cold that I haven't gone outside to write in weeks. Each morning, I sit in my chair and gaze out at the same gray, winter scene and wonder how I will find something new and inspiring to write about. Before creating an entry for this book, I usually journal a few pages, pray, and read several of my favorite daily meditation books to get my mind and spirit flowing. After spending at least thirty minutes going through my routine, I got out my book to write today's entry, looked outside once more at the bland landscape, and still felt uninspired. Something made me close my eyes and immediately I heard birds singing. It was like someone just un-muted them! I am sure they were there all along, but I was so focused on trying to get inspired by what I could see that I forgot to turn my ears on.

In the hustle and bustle of our daily routines, how much are we missing in the world around us? Stop. Look. Listen. Smell. Touch. Now as I write using all of my senses, I can hear the birds just chirping away. How did I not hear them for a full thirty minutes before? What changed? Me. My intuition (aka God) nudged me to open myself to what was here all along. How exciting to know my world can instantly offer more if I intentionally look and listen for the gifts! They are already here and waiting to be discovered. Enjoy!

February 10   A Little Sunlight Goes a Long Way

Today is another cold winter day, but just now, the slightest break in the clouds is illuminating our backyard and the neighboring farm with the most beautiful, golden sunlight! It's amazing how just a little bit of light can turn a cold, gray landscape into a rich, warm scene of beauty. The grass is a shimmering green. The colors on the houses have so much more life and intensity—the reds are redder and the browns are richer. Just gorgeous!

I am reminded that one small action or choice can have a large impact on my day and on the people in my life. Sometimes the smallest effort can color my world with a whole new perspective. I can choose to pass that along by sharing a smile with everyone I see today. I can read something inspiring for five minutes. I can turn my radio up and sing really loud. I can think of five reasons I am grateful. I can call someone and tell them they're pretty awesome. I can take a second to stare at the stars and wonder at their beauty. Let in the light, and see how you can pass that light along to touch others.

February 11   Contrast Makes Everything Better

There are dark shadows on the earth,
but its lights are stronger in the contrast.
~ Charles Dickens ~

Yes! Sunshine and blue skies! Oh joy! Even if it is still cold and wintery, what a gorgeous day! Contrast is so key to appreciation. We've had so many rainy days in a row that I'm more than excited to see my world lit up with sunshine today. But when sunny days run together, it's wonderful to have a rainy day to bring perspective. Neither is good or bad. I love both because each brings variety and its own unique gifts. The only thing about weather that is constant is change! So true, are the seasons of life. We can find gifts, and challenges can give way to sweet rewards. Unwrap your day and enjoy!

February 12   Fresh Air, Fresh Perspective

This cold, wet winter has kept me writing indoors for far too long! This morning I sat in my chair and waited for inspiration. Hearing the birds outside and seeing the sun shining made me long to go outside and join them— so I did! Bundled up in my coat, hat and scarf, I am now out on our sundeck. Yes, my hands and face are a bit cold, but there's just no substitution for fresh air and the sounds of nature. The birds are in full song, a live performance no longer muffled from listening indoors. The air is crisp and clean, and I'm breathing in as much as I can hold. Hope emerges with the impending new day, as the world wakes up around me.

Life really is what you make it. I can stay inside and let life pass me by, or I can jump in and make a big splash! Get your feet wet today. Get some fresh air and a new perspective while you're at it. How can I not feel serene out here where everything is in perfect order, and perfect harmony? My soul is soothed and quieted, yet stimulated at the same time. It's going to be a wonderful day. It already is.

February 13   Enjoy the Mysterious Gifts

I woke today to the sound of a gentle rain. I love sleeping in on a rainy day and fortunately, today that was possible. As I made breakfast, the rain turned into snow. It started slowly, but soon big giant snowflakes were falling thick and fast. My son said, "But Mom, that's impossible! It's almost forty degrees outside!" I didn't know what to tell him. Many times it has rained with the temperature barely above freezing, and my son has hoped and prayed it would fall just a few more degrees so the rain might turn to snow. How did it snow today at a higher temperature, and yet on other, colder days we saw rain but no snow? Who knows? We can't always explain everything.

We can follow all the rules, do all the right things, and yet sometimes things just don't work out like we hoped or think they should. Other times, to no credit of our own, the impossible happens and we are blessed with an unexpected gift. I believe in either case, I'm being given a gift, however in some instances, the gift may not be evident right away. Trust in the process. We don't always get what we want, but we do always get what we need. Nothing is impossible and when life smiles on you unexpectedly, say *Thanks!*

February 14   Be Your Own Valentine

Today is Valentine's Day. Be the love you wish to receive! Take yourself on a walk and soak in the beauty all around you. My tulips are peeking out of the ground, with the promise of spring right around the corner. Know too that your *tulips*—that is your new projects, new relationships, improvements in existing relationships, artistic endeavors—in other words, your future is pushing through to the surface right now!

If you don't have all the love you want in your life, quit waiting for it to show up in other people. Love *you*! Love your life exactly as it is right now. Happiness is an inside job! When I can maintain a spirit of love and gratitude for what I have today, my energy gives birth to a whole field of tulips and my future blooms forth with a variety of color and beauty. Happy Valentine's Day to someone special: YOU!

February 15   **Circle of Life**

This morning my cat, Lucky, went outside and returned thirty minutes later with a present for me—a live mouse he kindly left on the doormat. I thought maybe it was injured, but upon my investigation, Lucky went after it again and played with the poor mouse for another twenty minutes or so until it died. My family loves animals and we love to watch animal shows. In almost every case regarding the circle of life, I always feel sorry for the prey! I have to remind myself that even the prey are predators too.

In the human circle of life, we joyfully celebrate births and welcome new life. When it comes time to lose a loved one, it just doesn't seem right. We don't ever want to let go, and there's really never a good time for death. I read in *The Four Agreements,* by Don Miguel Ruiz that "What the angel of death can teach us is how to truly be alive... To live every day as if it is the last day of our life." This life is not a dress rehearsal! This moment, right now, will never come our way again. Make today count! Do something you have been putting off. Say "I love you" as much as you can. Forgive and forget. Make today memorable. Live.

February 16   **Focus on What *IS* Going Well**

This morning the rolling hills are covered with a beautiful frost. The sun is shining, adding an extra magical quality. I have to say a prayer for my tulips. We've had a fairly mild winter with some unseasonably warm days, prompting my tulips to prematurely push up through the ground about four inches. I trust they'll have what they need to survive and grow strong and beautiful. Why doesn't Mother Nature make sure everything is in sync, and not allow frost to kill early bloomers? That's a good question we will never know the answer to. While some years we may see damage by early bloomers or late frost, that is the exception not the rule. Most years, we will enjoy an abundance of gorgeous spring blooms. It's often no one's fault when things don't line up the way we expect. It can be frustrating, but sometimes, life just happens. If I have done all I can do, it's time to accept *what is* and trust that in the big picture of life, I am being cared for. Even if I'm going through some unusually adverse conditions right now, what can I focus on today that *is* going well?

February 17   **Keeping Calm in the Storm**

Remember, the storm is a good opportunity for the pine and the cypress to show their strength and their stability.
~ Ho Chi Minh ~

The wind was blowing fiercely just before dawn this morning and woke me up. I think it was hailing too. After a few hours passed, my alarm went off and I woke to an abundance of sunshine—not even a hint of adverse weather. Now, just an hour or so later, I am surrounded by fast-moving storm clouds, although occasionally I can see a small window of gorgeous blue sky.

Even when circumstances all around me are changing from one end of the spectrum to the other, even with an impending threat of storm, I can always find "blue sky" within. I no longer have to allow myself to be tossed about by the people and circumstances in my life. I can stay centered and grounded by taking care of me. There will often be chaos within arm's distance (and sometimes right up in my face!). It's my choice to determine how I react. Do I become a drama fan, seeking it out and staying immersed in it? Or do I seek to surround myself with calmer waters? I always have a choice. Today I choose peace and love.

February 18   **A Stolen Sunrise: Part One**

I woke up forty-five minutes before my alarm today, after a disturbing dream, and decided to get up and write to make use of the time, rather than attempt to go back to sleep. I am still almost speechless with what I just witnessed! Walking past the window, I immediately noticed the brilliant start of a sunrise bursting with pink and amber hues off to my left. I was drawn outside to my covered deck to watch the show, despite the cool temperature. In stark contrast to my right, I saw storm clouds brewing. Lightning flashed and thunder boomed! I whirled back around to my left to see the sunrise breaking through. It just happened again—lightning and thunder shot through the sky to my right—yet now on my left, I can see the sun rising above the trees, into a dense wall of clouds. More lightning. Now the sun is completely disappearing up into the storm clouds, as the lightning draws closer. At last, the sun is totally gone, with just a splash of pink glow remaining, and the lightning, thunder and rain are all around me now. The sun's glow has faded into the storm and the lightning is flashing bright in its place.

My alarm wake-up time is still thirty minutes away, and had I gone back to sleep, I wouldn't have seen this gorgeous sunrise decorate the sky before yielding to the storm. Had I ignored the early nudge to write, I would have missed all of this, and just risen to thunder, rain and lightning. Break out of your routine occasionally. Follow the inner promptings to deviate. A magical moment could be waiting for you just outside your box.

February 19   **A Stolen Sunrise: Part Two**

The sun's glow off to the left is completely gone, and it's raining now. As lightning illuminates the sky, all the clouds turn from stormy blue, to pink! The color of the sunrise flashes all around me just for a brief moment and then it's gone again. I've never seen anything like this before! In my mind, I say, *Again!* And within seconds, the lightning flickers again and stunning pink fills the sky. It happens so fast, I have to watch intently for it. If I gaze down to start writing again, and the lightning flashes, the sky is stormy blue again by the time I look up. No pink. The last time I watched for it, it didn't come. I can still hear thunder off in the distance, but the lightning has moved on. I could keep staring, hoping, but the magical moment has passed.

I feel so blessed and honored to have been awakened to see this spectacular light show—I could have slept right through it! I choose to believe I was deliberately given this gift, today especially. The dream that woke me up early had left me feeling disturbed and sad, so I had gotten up to use the extra time to journal about it, and I could feel the tears coming. And then I witnessed something I've never seen in nature before. I received the gift with humility, and my sadness turned to wonder and gratitude.

Open your eyes. Mix it up today. Take a different route to work or school. Look for the miracles that are happening all around you every day. Every minute. Let a moment of wonder replace your day-to-day worries or troubled thinking. Receive the gifts you are given with open eyes and an open heart. Say *Thanks*.

February 20   **Spring into Action**

Tap into the energy of the upcoming spring season. There is a universal force at work, ready to transform our world into brilliant color and beauty! Just think of all that is lining up to make that happen—sunshine, water, pollination—lots of effort happening behind the scenes in preparation for a glorious spring! Imagine that same universal force at work in you? For you. Can you trust that everything is working for your good? Can you feel the new life inside you, ready to burst into view?

Give yourself ideal conditions to manifest your destiny. Resolve today to eat better. Make your plate colorful and tasty! Drink lots of water, exercise, take yourself for a walk, dance, get plenty of rest, talk to mentors, meditate, be still, listen, look, and open your mind. Get ready. Get set. Go! Do your part, then surrender to the outcome and enjoy the ride.

February 21   Missed Opportunities and Turkeys

You must lose a fly to catch a trout.
~ George Herbert ~

I took a brisk, cool walk in the sunny afternoon today, walking my dog along our usual route. On our excursions, we frequently we pass a house where a lone beagle barks like crazy at my dog. On this particular day, the beagle barked up a storm as usual and suddenly I saw a flock of wild turkeys sneaking past, one by one, as if on tippy toes behind the back of the beagle's house. I tried to tell the little dog to turn around so he could chase much bigger things that were actually within the confines of his electric fence. My dog wasn't even accessible to him, but the beagle would not turn around and he missed an exciting opportunity that was well within his reach.

I laughed and laughed in amusement as maybe God might when He practically lays bigger opportunities right on our doorsteps and we still miss them because we are distracted by the small stuff. I was really encouraged by the idea that bigger dreams are right within my grasp. All I have to do is widen my perspective, open my eyes and look around. I have to be willing to lose sight of the familiar small stuff to bring the bigger opportunities into focus. I'm not sure if the beagle could have actually caught up with the turkeys had he chased them, but I do know he would have enjoyed the pursuit a whole lot more than barking at my dog. Dream bigger! Widen your perspective! Look under your nose and see what's right there waiting for you to notice. Pursue and enjoy!

February 22   Slowly but Surely

Sitting in my chair this morning, it's easy to look outside and see that everything is still—everything is the same. However, when I look up through the transom windows above my French doors, the view is continually changing as the clouds move across the sky. It's easy to stare at the bigger picture and feel like my life isn't moving forward as fast as I would like. Is there a smaller area I could focus on, where I can acknowledge some growth? Recognizing even the smallest changes can provide the assurance that even though I may not be where I want to be, I'm always exactly where I'm supposed to be, and I'm also moving in the right direction at whatever pace is right for me.

Change is happening. Slowly but surely I am becoming all that I am capable of being. This morning I give thanks and celebrate everything in my life exactly as it is today. I choose to focus on all that is, instead of all that isn't.

February 23   Recipe for Relationships

Frequently my mind is a music box that plays almost non-stop. Today, the song running through my head brings to mind the idea that some people are in your life for a reason, some for just a season, and some are here for a lifetime. Isn't it odd, in hindsight, to look at relationships that played a strong role in our lives, but for a relatively short period of time? Maybe one to five years? First we talk all the time, see each other frequently, share intimate parts of ourselves—and then life shifts. Things change and they're gone from our everyday experiences. Spouses, significant others, family members, bosses, teachers, coworkers, friends, neighbors. Were they just random connections? I don't think so.

I like to think we all have a jar of goodies and our role is to give and receive these gifts from one another to further each of us along our path. Many people inspire me and challenge me. Some teach me tolerance, acceptance and love. Others teach me boundaries and force me to get honest with myself. All are mirrors. I see in them what I dislike about myself, what I want to change, and who I aspire to be more like. Today, I give thanks for all who have crossed my path and everything they've taught me, shared with me, and blessed me with. I am grateful for the laughter, the love, the adventure, the envy, the anger, and the pain. Sugar and salt are frequently used together to make a recipe truly flavorful and awesome. I will continue to give and receive what I have to offer and be grateful for what I get in return.

February 24   **Warm, Sunny Reprieves**

I love the saying, "We are never given more than we can handle." It's true in life. It's true in nature. (Sometimes God's esteem of me is higher than mine though!) I am not a lover of cold weather. I am grateful for the seasons that give us variety and balance, but right about now, I've had my fill of winter, and I'm ready for warm temperatures. Maybe it's just grace, but I find it interesting that winter isn't consistently cold, at least not here in the Southeast. Today for instance, the high is supposed to jump into the sixties. Just an isolated day of sun and warmer weather, before it drops back down into the forties tomorrow with a forecast of rain.

If we look for them, I bet we can also find moments of warm, sunny reprieve injected into our tough circumstances and trying times. It might be just enough to lend a shot of encouragement, to give us a welcomed break and let us know this time—this season of our lives—won't last forever. "This too shall pass!" holds true even in good times, however, so whatever today has dealt you, embrace it. Learn the lessons and give thanks for everything. Tomorrow, a new season, will be here soon enough.

February 25   Grateful, Even For the Toothaches

Monday: no toothache.

Tuesday: suddenly a tooth begins to throb. It's slightly bothersome, but we carry on.

Wednesday: the toothache is unbearable. It's all we can think about. We say we would just be *so happy* if our toothache was gone.

Monday: we've been to the dentist and today our toothache is gone. We are … *so happy!*

Wednesday: our toothache is gone and so is the memory of the pain, and the gratitude about the pain relief. We are back to our pre-toothache state, as if it never happened.

We have all experienced pain and suffering. Remember when we longed for the situation to get better? Even if there is another "toothache" in your life today, the other ones are gone. Celebrate and give thanks today, for all the troubles and aches you no longer have to deal with. Can you think of five reasons to celebrate today? Abraham Lincoln said, "We are about as happy as we make up our minds to be." I will choose to be *so happy* … right now!

February 26   Setbacks Are Forward Progress

Two steps forward. One step back. It's all good—I'm right where I'm supposed to be. I had knee surgery recently. I've been doing so unbelievably well until yesterday, when I decided to get a jumpstart on physical therapy. All in all, I did too much and set myself back a little. I could beat myself up about it, but how else could I have known I wasn't ready without putting myself out there to see what I could handle?

We can stay in perpetual training for life, work, relationships, or creative endeavors. We can hone our skills, our growth, and our plans continually, but eventually we need to take action. At some point, we have to test our wings and leave the nest! If we fly, wonderful! If we find we weren't quite ready for such a leap, we can pull ourselves back in, knock the dust off, and prepare or train some more.

It would be nice if we were equipped with a timer that beeped to let us know when we're ready to act on the next phase of our journey. With an open mind, however, we can learn as much from our setbacks as we do our successes. When we take action, we may advance in the direction we want to go, or we learn some more. Either way, we are making forward progress. Embrace your journey. Challenge yourself. Surrender the outcome. Get the lessons. Live—and learn to love the process. I'm back in incubation mode, but I'll be dancing again in no time at all!

February 27   My Small Part of the Tapestry

There are a few circumstances in my life that with today's vision, I don't have a clue how it's all going to turn out—not even a hint or a glimpse of how things will evolve. It makes me think of a large tapestry, where I'm not privy to the whole design. I am only responsible for working on the small area I've been assigned at the present moment. All I can see is my part of the tapestry, and only the back of it, which is the messy side. Loose strings hang here and there and I can't get a vision for how my part plays into the full masterpiece being made. Trust and faith are all I have to go on, so I keep doing the work in front of me, believing I'm doing it right and will continue to get guidance and correction along the way.

I could worry. I could get discouraged and quit. Will that give me the direction, certainty or vision I seek? Will giving up get me closer to, or further from, living a life on purpose? I would rather feel lost while continuing to trust and take the next right action, than to quit taking steps altogether. I don't know any road trips where you can see the end from the beginning. If you can, it's not much of a trip at all. Just for today, I'll keep heading in the right direction, putting my destination in the Master's hands.

February 28   Thankful for Lead Ponies

The best way to get me to do something is to show me someone who's ahead of me, doing it faster and better. I joke with my husband that he's often my lead pony anytime we're walking somewhere. Without thinking, I let him get a few paces in front of me, and then I keep step with him as my guide. I don't always have it in me to lead the way. Some days my absolute best is just keeping up. What good would a leader be if she didn't have a follower? The nice thing about a good marriage or business partnership is recognizing each person's strengths and limitations, and maximizing the synchronization of both parties' efforts. No wonder from preschool on, we've been graded on how well we play with others!

Cooperation and coordination of efforts are important at all ages and in most endeavors. Thankfully, we've all been given different skill sets, so individually we don't have to be all things to all people. Self-awareness is key. Knowing where I would excel is as important as being able to admit where I need help, or which tasks to delegate to someone more gifted in that area than myself. I am grateful for the give and take, the push and pull, the blended efforts in my life. Who acts as a lead pony in your life, prodding you forward, encouraging you, and showing you what is possible? Show them some gratitude today—in word or in deed. A lead pony is trained to guide others to excel beyond what they could do alone. They are other-centered, versus self-centered. I am certain they aren't thanked enough, but today we can do our best to let them know how much we value them.

February 29   Darkest Nights Reveal the Stars

I recently heard a quote I really like by Charles A. Beard, "When it gets dark enough, you can see the stars." I interpret this in several ways, but rather than expand on each one, I'll share the insights that came to me and let you consider the ones that jump out most.

- ❦ Even in dark circumstances, there can be bright spots.
- ❦ In the darkest hour, light will be provided to guide my way.
- ❦ The darkest of moments offer a spotlight for people to really shine their own light and stand out.
- ❦ Light needs a dark backdrop to really set it off.
- ❦ Look up when all you want to do is look down.

Words are wonderful, but there are times for silence too. I hear hope and inspiration when I sit still and ponder this quote. I hope you do too!

March

I discovered the secret of the sea in meditation upon a dewdrop.
*~ **Kahlil Gibran***

March 1   **Preparing the Soil (Soul)**

Today is beautiful, sunny. Chilly, but a gorgeous appetizer for the spring season that's right around the corner. There's so much behind-the-scenes action taking place right now, even though we can't see most of it. Trees are mustering all their energy to produce hundreds of thousands, and even millions of new buds all over the world! Tulips, daffodils and many other flower bulbs are pushing through the hard winter Earth to create a colorful display for us to enjoy. Grass seed sown last fall is doing what it does so our yards will produce thick, lush, brilliant fields of green.

What did you sow last fall? What are you fertilizing and watering today? What are you expectant of, anticipating? Are you creating a welcoming environment for new ideas to spring forth, and new or existing relationships to blossom? If I spend all my time watering my neighbor's flowers, will mine grow? Invest your time, energy and resources in what really matters. What's going to add value to your life? If I take care of me on all levels—emotional, spiritual and physical—my soil (soul) will stay fertile and rich and the resulting harvest will be bountiful with plenty to share!

March 2   **Brown Paper Packages**

A quote I ran across yesterday really stopped me in my tracks. In his book *Anam Cara: A Book of Celtic Wisdom*, John O'Donohue said, "Sometimes the urgency of our hunger blinds us to the fact we are already at the feast." Are you trying so hard to achieve X, to arrive at Y, or to find Z that you wouldn't even notice it when you achieved your goal? Are you looking for something to show up in a specific package, to the point you are rejecting the other gifts life is trying to give you?

So many of us pray and pray for things we already have, but don't see. You may have the best reality of anyone, but you don't perceive it that way. Perception beats reality every time. How else could what you're looking for show up? Look around because maybe it's already there. I am so grateful for life's wake-up calls. Get the lessons. Find the gift. OPEN the gift. Embrace all the gifts whether they are wrapped or unwrapped, in striped paper or polka dots. Open minds get more gifts to open!

March 3   Faith + Positivity = Winning Formula

Does prayer really work? Sometimes I wonder. It's confusing when I hear some people say we are not to pray for specific requests—that we should only pray for God's will. Why would we need to pray for God's will? If He is in charge, what else would He willfully choose to bring into being? If not His will, then whose? All this thought process has, at times, made me feel prayer is pointless, but I had an epiphany recently. We don't pray to change circumstances; we pray to change ourselves, our attitudes, and our outlook, and this humble, open-minded perspective miraculously manifests outcomes which are in sync with our highest good.

For me, praying acknowledges that I'm not in control of everything, nor am I responsible to fix every problem. Prayer says, "I can't, but I choose to believe You can, and I think I will let You." By choosing to believe I have an ally more powerful, capable and insightful than myself, I can relax and inhabit a greater degree of peace and serenity. The act of surrendering my cares and concerns allows me to go about my day, swapping worry for trust, and fear for joy!

My positive energy, aligned with my faith, allows good things to flow into my life. If you doubt the power of your energy, conduct an experiment. Go through one day growling at everyone and feeling negative about everything. (Seriously, don't do the whole day—maybe just ten minutes. You'll feel it fast!) Now go through the next day intentionally smiling at everyone while keeping a gratitude list, jotting down at least one thing you are thankful for every hour. Please share your answers with me and your fellow readers at www.findingthegift.com, although I already have a strong feeling how your experiment will turn out. While it's true, I don't always get what I want, I choose to believe I'll always get what I need, when I'm open to whatever that is. Prayer + surrender = serenity. It works!

March 4   Finding the Aahh, and Then the A-ha!

Beauty. Serenity. Ease. Tranquil probably most adequately summarizes how I feel, right this moment on an island in the Caribbean. Today is my eighth day in Punta Cana, Dominican Republic. Two days ago, I realized I didn't need to spend a large sum of money to chase this feeling of *aahh* as the breeze rustles my hair, brushes my skin and makes the palm trees whisper softly. It can be anywhere, at any time, or at least not too far away.

What is your *aahh*? One for me is nature, which is everywhere. I allow nine days to vacation and relax in the Caribbean, so why am I reluctant to allow a half day, two hours or even thirty minutes for pure leisure when I am at home? My soul needs the *aahh*. The *aahh* leads to the *a-ha*!" The *yes*! The, *I know what to do now!* The *aahh* is like a gentle breeze that soothes and caresses my innermost being. It provides the answers. It's the gasoline for tomorrow. It refuels my *why*.

Today, I'm full of *aahh* as I lounge poolside in a straw palapas (a shade hut on posts, mounted over a huge bed/couch complete with pillows). The sound of running water flows from a nearby fountain. Enchanted music is playing through speakers hidden throughout the tropical landscape. I will take the *aahh* home within me and replenish it frequently.

March 5   **Simple Pleasures**

Simple pleasures. We all need them. Often they're free for the taking, just waiting to be found. You know how it feels when you indulge... Delight! Wonder! Content! Serene! Comforted! Secure! Relaxing! Joyful! Your meter reading says FULL. It feels so good to practice a little self-care and yet I will let days go by—sometimes weeks—without it, when I could be indulging in a simple pleasure that fills me back up, and lets me know everything is okay, and in fact, PERFECT right at this very moment. When I indulge in a daily detour for joy, I'm also sending several very important messages to myself. I am important to me. My needs and wants are a priority. I matter, and I'm up to the task of nurturing my own soul—I don't have to wait for someone else to do it for me.

Do you have regular self-indulgences that delight you and feed your spirit? Need a hint? Light a candle. Listen to music. Catch a fish! Decorate a cake! Arrange some beautiful flowers. Take a walk. Feed a duck. Paint. Sing. Skip. Ride the grocery cart! Sit by the water. Put your toes in some sand. Climb a hill. Race your dog down the street. Make a child laugh. Laugh with them. Try a new recipe. Smile at a stranger. Take the long way home.

Hopefully several of those ideas are appealing to you, or I've got you thinking about what you personally like to do to make your soul sing. Will you commit to taking one small action (or a big one!) either today, or this week—something totally for pure delight and spiritual recharge? Maybe something you haven't done in years? The world is a scavenger hunt! Hidden everywhere are the little treasures that make our lives full. Get your bucket, dust it off if necessary and collect as many experiences as you can hold. Race ya!

March 6   Birds of Different Feathers

One touch of nature makes the whole world kin.
~ **William Shakespeare** ~

Field Trip! I'm at the park this morning, sitting on a bench overlooking Old Hickory Lake, surrounded by pigeons, ducks, geese, mallards, seagulls, and a new species I've never seen before—small black ducks with white beaks. A man to my left is having a good old time fishing. I see grandparents with their grandson here to feed the birds and ducks. I hear lots of geese honking and the smooth whir of the fishing rod every time it's cast into the water. Oh wow! He just caught one. He said it's the first fish of the season! Looks big to me. I took his picture for him, proudly displaying his catch, a four- or five-pound largemouth bass.

I'm just sitting. Writing. Observing. Watching the time pass for a change, instead of racing to stay ahead of the clock. Wow, the fisherman just got another one—a yellow striped bass. He's beaming, telling me now he's already got his money's worth for his fishing license. Happy to join in the excitement, the grandparents are letting their grandson see his fish.

Community. Belonging. I feel it satisfying a hunger I didn't even know I had today. I was already noticing how the different ducks and geese interact in their own little world. Usually birds of a feather flock together, but today each group appears to be accepting and co-existing with their fellows—setting the example for the rest of us! Oh sure, even with ducks and geese, there are skirmishes. That's life. But we need each other. It feels good to be reminded today that I have a need for community the same as I have for fresh air, a roof over my head, tasty food and reliable friends. I belong and it feels good. Find a way to prove to yourself today that you belong here too.

March 7   **Car Wash Metaphor**

I drove through the car wash this morning to get the remains of a wet winter off my car. Going through the different phases of the car wash, I felt as if I was experiencing everyday life in fast forward. We live life. Things get messy. Our outlook can become covered with a grimy film. We don't feel as shiny anymore. Less sparkle. The "droppings" of life land on us just because that's life, and some things (relationships, jobs, negative encounters) do leave a residual slime on us. Before you know it, we are a big, dirty, tired mess! The process of getting restored and polished back to our original state can sometimes feel like we're going to drown, or get beaten to death before we come out the other side, shiny and new again. But in the car wash I whizzed right on through all the cycles and came out the other side, able to see more clearly. I didn't even realize how dirty my "windshield" had gotten until it was cleaned! I am so thankful for the reminder that life is going to get messy at times and I need regular maintenance to make sure I get restored to where I feel and look my best. I can trust in the process and know without a doubt I will come out the other side refreshed, renewed and ready to do it again!

March 8   **Why Did *Her* Flowers Bloom First?**

I did a double take this morning when I noticed my neighbor already has flowers blooming. They are gorgeous! Immediately I thought, *Why haven't any of my flowers bloomed yet?* Sometimes it's so tempting to compare my experiences, my growth, and my life to my neighbor's or friend's. When I'm willing to stop the comparison game, I find my energy is always better spent being grateful for what I have, and taking the next right action toward those areas in my life I want to expand. We will all bloom (though probably at different times in our lives) if we keep planting our minds and our ideas in fertile soil and watering regularly.

For today I will think of one action I can take to get me closer to where I want to be. I will also think of five gifts I've been given over the last year as a result of the small, but consistent, efforts I have made. I will trust in my own perfect timing!

March 9   Anchor the Middle

Weather this time of year can change on a dime. Life can too. Someone told me once to anchor the middle. Don't let myself get too caught up in the highs or allow myself to completely plummet into the low lows. In other words, avoid the extremes. For me, in either case, it's about remaining grounded. I'm reminded of a seesaw. It will go up and down, but I want to stay toward the middle so my world isn't constantly going from one extreme to the other. I grew up with a fair amount of chaos, and it's easy to get addicted to euphoria and drama—good or bad.

When I first got this advice, it was at a time when I was all about trying to avoid the low lows. I didn't really understand the problem with high high's, though. Isn't *Woo Hoo!* always good? However, after practicing awareness around this idea, I found I do prefer a more balanced approach to daily living. Whether too high or too low, in either case I'm more vulnerable to external circumstances, and less able to remain centered and present. Happy and sad are appropriate and desired. Euphoric and suicidal—not so much. Be happy. Allow and even embrace sadness. Say thanks! The expression, "This too shall pass," goes both ways, but if I'm grounded, I can weather life's ups and downs with balance and grace.

March 10   Loving the Old, Exploring the New

We rescued a cat off the street several months ago. Jazzy is a very small, feisty female who survived one and a half years of homelessness on nothing but attitude. She didn't get along with our other animals at first, but she loved all their toys. Every toy our cats had long abandoned or never played with, Jasmine thought was the best toy ever. She would play all night long, and the next day, and the next with each newfound delight. Now, like the other cats, she isn't excited about most of them, and only continues to play with a few favorites.

I guess there are two lessons to be learned here. First: how quickly do we take new people, new jobs, and/or new surroundings for granted? A quick and easy way to rekindle some of that new and fresh enthusiasm we once had is to jot down some of our favorite first memories of them. What did we initially love so much about the people and things we value in our lives? What was different about them that we appreciated from the very beginning? Commit to re-notice and rediscover these, and express your gratitude verbally and in other ways to show how much you still care.

Second: we crave mystery, surprises, newness, fresh inspiration, challenge and unexpected outcomes. We need stimulation, something that lifts us out of the everyday routine. How and where can you give yourself a refreshing experience? Can you take ten dollars and go to a toy store to see what looks fun? When was the last time you sat down on a swing just to see how high you could go? Today, why not take a trip to the grocery store and discover something new and exciting to try? Download a recipe and challenge yourself to make it. Buy yourself a single flower every week. Go to the hardware store and look around for a small project you've been too intimidated to try. Visit an art gallery once a month. Try a new international wine every so often with friends. I think you get the picture. Love the old and bring in the new! And repeat.

March 11   Open the Door and Get Wet!

Do not be too timid and squeamish about your actions. All life is an experiment. The more experiments you make the better. What if they are a little course, and you may get your coat soiled or torn? What if you do fail, and get fairly rolled in the dirt once or twice. Up again, you shall never be so afraid of a tumble.
~ Ralph Waldo Emerson ~

A soft rain is falling outside and I am enjoying the sounds. It's strange—if I didn't look outside, I would be certain it was raining really hard. There's a constant whoosh sound, like that of steady rain. Looking out on my deck however, the rain is falling easy, and occasionally I hear a gentle tap-tap as it hits the window. The constant noise also makes me think it must be windy, but the trees aren't moving at all. From where I sit, and from what I hear, I cannot discern the truth. I would actually need to go outside to better connect what I'm hearing with what I'm seeing to get a clearer picture of what's really going on.

This makes me think about life. I can't stay inside my house (or my head,) my safe place, or my comfort zone and still get the full living experience. I can make some assumptions, but it all comes together when I actively engage and immerse myself in life and with people. We're not meant to live our lives through a window, trying to guess what life might be like. Open the door and say YES! to getting your feet wet!

March 12   Paradise Is Everywhere

You can take the people to paradise but there's no guarantee that paradise will get in the people. I'm in the tropical paradise of Playa del Carmen, Mexico. The gentle ocean breeze makes the palm trees sway, tropical drinks are brought to me upon request, and in just a little while, I'll get a massage on the white sandy beach, surrounded by turquoise water. The only thing that has changed is my environment. I am still happy or sad, lonely or content, rich or poor. True paradise cannot be found simply by boarding a plane. (Yes, it can feel good for a few days to escape into vacation la la land, but I'm talking about something lasting.) Real paradise is an internal sense that life is good—better than I deserve. Where my heart is full and I could not ask for more. When I feel fulfilled in every way, at least in a particular moment. What is one small thing you can do today to bring more paradise into your life? Quit waiting for that dream vacation to make you happy and start creating your dream life at home, right now.

March 13   I Am Not That Different

Still on vacation, I look around here at the beach at the thousands of footprints in the sand. Hundreds of thousands of people have walked this path before us. Hundreds of thousands will walk it after us. We are not so unique in our lives, but our egos tell us otherwise— from one extreme to the other:

- ❦ I'm special.
- ❦ The rules don't apply to me.
- ❦ I'm better than so and so.
- ❦ I'm glad I don't have to live like them.
- ❦ I hurt more.
- ❦ I have less.
- ❦ I have more troubles than anyone else.
- ❦ Why did that have to happen to me?
- ❦ Life isn't fair.
- ❦ Life is hard.

None of us are saying anything new that hasn't been said for centuries before! When I view myself as separate, as better or worse than everyone else, I am missing the enormous serenity of community that is mine when I view myself as one of my fellow men. One of all those who have come before me, and all who will come after. I am just one of the entire human race. How is that for a bigger perspective?! Our problems are not unique. We just have to get the lessons and move on to the next one. Enjoy every second of this precious, brief time we have here on earth. Love out loud. Say grace (*Thank you*) and amen (*This is plenty*). Stop whining and start singing! Embrace what we love and let the rest go! Open our hearts. Open our minds. Open our arms. Life doesn't have to be so complicated.

March 14   Pushing Past the Safe Zone

> *What great thing would you attempt*
> *if you knew you could not fail?*
> **~ Robert H. Schuller ~**

Buoys tell you where it's safe to swim, but does that mean you should NEVER go past the buoys? I don't think so. We all need a little excitement, some adventure at times. Someone has to push beyond the boundaries—the status quo—to discover new territory, new inventions, or new physical capabilities. When one proves it's possible, all believe, and the buoys of life get moved out a little further.

This morning, the tide is coming in with such a surge that it took me a while to even spot the buoys. *They were there yesterday? Do they bring them in at night and they just haven't put them back out yet?* No, when I look intently I can see them. I guess the translation for life is that the safe zone may not always be easy to spot. We have to follow our intuition and be expectant that the teachers, the guidelines, or the light house will appear along our path. If we don't look for them, we might not see them, even when they're right in front of us. If we do intently search, we'll find they've been there all along. Look around! Take the help and guidance that's being offered. Occasionally push past the ropes—the boundaries! Get out of your comfort zone and try something new. Live a little. Heck, live a lot! Explore new waters. You can't gain sight of a new shore until you lose sight of the one you know. Have courage and go for it whenever prompted. You might not end up exactly where you planned, but I bet the journey will be worth it!

March 15   Someone's Got My Back

I'm still on vacation, halfway through, so I've only got a few more days left to enjoy my time at the beach. Hmmm… Actually, let me rephrase that. Wow, I have *half* of my vacation remaining! Yes, that feels much better. Perspective is key! (Okay, great, but that's not the lesson for the day—just a bonus.)

As usual, I cautiously opened my journal this morning, not having a clue what to write about, but trusting something would come to me. As I grabbed for my pen, I looked up and noticed one of the resort workers filling up a trash bag at the edge of the ocean. He has filled up three or four so far, and I wondered what it could be. I stood up to get a better look and saw him with his head bent over, grabbing up a line of seaweed leftover by the morning tide. Ouch, that must be backbreaking work—nasty work by hand—grabbing chunks of seaweed and stuffing it into trash bags. And why? So most people won't ever have to see it. It's not even 8 a.m. When the majority of beach dwellers arrive, the worker will be long gone (along with the row of seaweed) with no evidence to show he did this service for us.

I am a very spiritual person. I know what I believe, and for me, belief is a choice. Faith is a choice. The more faith I have, the better I feel. For instance, I choose to believe that someone has my back. That my God is taking care to improve my surroundings, to better my day, my life—even if some days that's as simple as making it more beautiful for me. What if, before you ever wake up, you believed someone is working to make your day better? How good does that feel, to believe it's true? How would you approach life if you were to believe that? More grateful? More trusting? More loved? When things are tough, imagine someone has made an effort to soften the lesson as much as they could, without removing the opportunity for growth. How does that make you feel? Nurtured? Protected?

We may never know for sure how much we are cared for, but I choose to believe it's a lot! Today, I will look for evidence. When I find a parking space right up front, I will smile and say *Thanks!* When I almost drop and break something, but don't, I will smile and say *Thanks*. When I get that call delivering bad news, I will be grateful it wasn't worse. When I see the sun peeking through on a cloudy day—even if just for a second—I will smile and say *Thanks*. When a butterfly crosses my path, I will be reminded of new life. I will enjoy these sacred moments—and smile and say *Thanks*. Today I will let myself believe someone has my back. That I'm cared for; that I am worth being cared for.

March 16   Life Like Water

Water is the driving force of all nature.
~ **Leonardo da Vinci** ~

Water is healing, restorative, tranquil, and reflective. From a small trickle, to a deafening roar. Violent. Powerful. Peaceful. All of the above. Today is our last full day at the beach. I took a walk along the ocean this morning and marveled at one of my favorite aspects of nature—water. Water is everything, from one spectrum to the other. It is pushing and pulling at the same time, with opposing currents existing simultaneously, and with tides going out and coming back in rhythmically. Water is consistent, and yet frequently moving. It is gentle enough to refresh, and forceful enough to erode rock over time. Water can flow over, around, under or through most obstacles. (It's difficult to stop the flow of water, short of building a dam.)

Water is life. Life is water. Everything is possible. We will experience both ends of the spectrum (in life) and everything in between. Will we allow our circumstances to dam us up? Or will we be persistent, resilient and embrace the flow? My posture, my attitude towards life makes or breaks me. A wave can lift me up and carry me, or if I'm fighting and rigid, it can knock me over. I'm going to trust the waves of life to carry me where I need to go. I will trust their reflections to show me what I need to learn. I might even let myself splash around a bit and have some fun!

March 17   **No Place Like Home**

We came back from Mexico late last night. It's amazing what a change of scenery can do for your perspective—while you're there, yes, but even when you return. It is so true, there's no place like home. To be gone long enough to see my home through fresh eyes is such a gift. I love the little piece of paradise I call home, and I love it even more when I have been away. I also love my pets and I'm always so glad to get home to them after vacation.

It was dark yesterday when we arrived home, so we didn't really get to fully appreciate being home until this morning. Waking up in our bed with sunshine pouring in from multiple windows—heavenly. Letting the dog out and seeing (for the first time in a week) the gorgeous hills behind our house, and the cows across the street—breathtaking. A week has passed but it seems more like a month. Wow, it's great to be home.

We left the heat running while we were away and when we returned, the house was super hot (thanks to warmer days) so we had to get the AC cranking! I feel so excited to think the warm Mexico air followed us home and winter is gone! Winter is a necessary reprieve from life as I know it—from outdoor life, especially. Without winter, I would not be able to fully appreciate the return of warmer temperatures, green grass, full trees and endless color! Going from winter to spring is sort of like returning from vacation and getting to experience the home you love all over again! Contrast and absence makes everything more wonderful!

March 18   **Balance Between To-Do's**

Rest is not idleness, and to lie sometimes on the
grass under trees on a summer's day, listening to the
murmur of the water, or watching the clouds float
across the sky, is by no means a waste of time.
~ John Lubbock ~

We are back from vacation with laundry piled high. My oil change light just came on. I have over two hundred unread e-mails. I have texts to reply to. It's time to schedule the pets for their annual checkups. Photography orders are backed up. I need to balance our checkbook and schedule bill payments for the first of the month. My son needs a book from the library. My husband needs me to find a receipt. And the list goes on and on! Slight variations exist between lives, but the pull to DO, DO, DO and then do MORE is there for all of us. How we handle the pull is the difference between stress and serenity, good health and high blood pressure. Balance. Intention. These are the skills I long to master. Just raising my awareness to the need for balance and intention moves me one step closer to achieving more of that in my daily life.

Today as I look at all the to-do's on my list, while I'm still spinning from yesterday's full schedule, I question if I really have time to sit outside and meditate. I can't afford not to, so here I am. Like magic, the second I sit down and feel the sun on my face, the moment I slow my breath and take in a big, deep inhale of fresh air, I am calmed in a way unlike anything else. The sun is warm and soothing, and the birds are chirping and singing to each other. The trees are slightly swaying to an easy breeze. I find peace, balance and intention. My meter is reset. At this moment, nothing on my to do list is more important than maintaining my serenity and carrying my peaceful state into the rest of my day. I'm going to pluck a blade of grass to keep with me today as a reminder of this moment. The blade of grass will also serve as encouragement to "take five" whenever I feel my meter needs an adjustment back to baseline. Fortunately, immersion into nature in some way or another is available twenty-four hours a day. Now that fits my schedule!

March 19   Stillness Especially in Busy Times

All men's miseries derive from not
being able to sit quiet in a room alone.
~ Blaise Pascal ~

I read something this morning that reminded me of the saying, "Go with the flow." I go with the flow all the time, but sometimes it feels more like a level four rapid! Sitting out here on the deck overlooking a gorgeous, calm spring morning, I observe birds singing, cats bathing, cows grazing and bees buzzing. An occasional car passes by. Everything else is still. The trees are not moving. An empty swing set stands ready but motionless. Balance. Knowing when to flow and when to be still. I get so busy with multiple projects and after running at a hectic pace, I find it challenging to seek stillness again, because the idea of being still feels so unproductive. Now in this moment, when I've taken the time to just be and breathe, it feels vital. I cannot afford to avoid stillness, especially when I'm busy. Imagine if I went up to the tree in front of me and we could understand each other? If I pleaded and shouted, urging it to grow faster, would that help rush it along? Of course not. Today I will do what needs to be done and look for a flow to follow. When the flow says halt and be still, I will listen.

March 20   **Algebra At Work in Daily Life**

Remember thinking during certain classes in high school, *Why do I need to learn this? I'll never use it!* Well, good news! Understanding the basic algebra formula $[A + B = C]$ can help me understand how important my attitude is in every circumstance and every relationship. Some things are constant and we can't change them. Other things are variable, but we are powerless over many of those situations as well. The one thing we can always change is our attitude. If my attitude represents "A" in the equation, then no matter what "B" is, I will always impact the outcome, which is C. Remember $[A + B = C]$. If I am struggling with a coworker (B), my attitude (A) can change the outcome of our interaction (C). If I'm facing a really challenging time or circumstance (B), my attitude and my acceptance, or lack of it (A), can impact my serenity (C) throughout the ordeal.

I have always been a math and formula person, so please indulge me if you are not—I love it when things can be simplified! The bottom line is that any time YOU are part of an equation, YOU can impact the solution. I find much hope in this, for so many things seem beyond our control. When we can maintain control of our attitudes, we can embrace our power and choose an active role in our lives, no matter what is going on. What equation do you want to see changed in your life? Be intentional about what value you bring to "A". Play with it and "C" (see) what you can change.

March 21   **Worrying For Nothing**

There are very few monsters who
warrant the fear we have of them.
~ Andre Gide ~

We woke to snowfall this morning. Usually schools in our area are quick to close at the slightest indication of treacherous roads. Here in the South, we have very hilly roads and aren't adequately prepared to deal with occasional snow and ice. We all have a tendency to think the world will stop when we begin to see snowfall. It's a really big deal when we have serious wintry conditions, so our fears are founded in truth, but most of the time it still never amounts to anything. We joke about everyone running to the grocery when snow is forecasted, but the stores do run out of bread and milk because of our panic. Today the snow is melting as soon as it hits the ground. I am reminded of the saying that a dog's bark is worse than his bite.

What else do we allow ourselves to get all worked up over? Things that at first seem like they're going to be a really big deal, but then usually nothing happens? Based on our past experiences, some situations do warrant caution and planning. Much of what we worry about, though, never materializes. Buy the "bread and milk" if it makes you feel more prepared, but remember all the other times you worried and panicked over nothing. Take it all in stride. Remember if it does "snow" (whatever that may look like in your life), it isn't the end of the world. In summary, most of what we think is going to be big and terrible only looks that way—it often does nothing more than scare us. A little bit of trust and surrender can go a long way. And if the "big and terrible" do happen, they will bring blessings as well, if we are open to seeing them. Either way, it's all good. Enjoy the moment for what is true right now.

March 22   Winds of Change

March winds can be so fierce! It's a gorgeous, sunny day, but the wind is howling and whistling, bending the trees with its strength! My cats are usually happy to go outside, but not when the wind is this intense. I also like to hide *inside*, when I feel the winds of change tossing me around. Whether I'm hiding or not, I can't stop time and I can't stop change. And how boring would life be if we never experienced anything new? If we never grew? If we never had anything different to anticipate? Just as March winds go hand in hand with a spring in full bloom, today I will accept not just the gifts, but the changes that come my way, knowing they, too, will lead me to a life of variety and color. I will also be grateful for exactly what I have today, so I might be blessed to give and receive more tomorrow.

March 23   Pack Light, Make Room For Gifts

This is a perfect moment! I indulged in sleeping late on this very rainy morning. Now sitting in my writing chair, I am enjoying the continuous sound of heavy rainfall, and the sight of my sleeping cats and dog all around me. As the earth gets a bath, I also feel cleansed of all worries, resentments and fears. In their absence, I feel content, forgiving and courageous. Everything feels fresh and clean, and I can breathe deeply—unshackled from all the mind and heart clutter I've allowed to build up.

Look around. What can you find that is perfect about this moment? Close your eyes—what do you hear? Rainfall? Peaceful silence? Distant chatter? The steady hum of traffic or maybe the occasional birdsong? Let your intentional mindfulness reassure you this moment is perfect. With each deep breath, let your soul be quieted from the troubles of yesterday and the worries of tomorrow. In this moment, you are free of all you were carrying. What you pick back up is a choice. Pack light, my friend! Make room for all the good stuff you will encounter today.

March 24   Like Attracts Like

"Don't join an easy crowd; you won't grow. Go where the expectations and the demands to perform are high." ~
Jim Rohn ~

I recently attended a conference for entrepreneurs and the keynote speaker said, "If you're the smartest person in the room, you need to go to another room!" John C. Maxwell shares a similar idea in his book, *The 15 Invaluable Laws of Growth.* If we want to keep growing in any capacity (spiritual, emotional, financial, cultural, etc.), we need to be around other people who are on a common path of growth. We also need to seek out people who are further down the road than we are. We need to be stimulated and challenged, and also encouraged to keep going.

Many motivational speakers and authors talk about the fact that our income will be similar to the five people we hang around the most. I think it's also safe to say that our spiritual and personal development will be indicative of the people we surround ourselves with. Hang out with people who have what you want, who live like you want to live, and who share the same values and goals. You will become more like your role models, who will probably be doing the same thing—gleaning wisdom from the people they aspire to become more alike.

Put yourself in an environment where you can grow. And, be open to mentor those who are coming up behind you, while continuing to be mentored by those ahead of you. Give and you shall receive. This is an abundant world, and with the right intentions and integrity, we are all limitless in who we can become and what we can achieve—with a little help from our friends.

March 25   Chameleons Need Masks; We Don't

The biggest part we will ever play on the stage of life is ourselves, but how often do we choose surroundings that allow us to blend in rather than stand out? There are many examples of camouflage in nature, where animals, fish and insects use their ability to blend in to their advantage: polar bears in snow; leopards in the jungle; and praying mantis on a tree. Some are even lucky enough to be able to change colors. The arctic fox is bluish white in the winter, but his warmer summer color blends in nicely with rocks and plants. The chameleon of course is iconic for its ability to change colors in certain situations as needed.

What about you? Are you able to be your authentic self most of the time or do you tend to hide behind a mask, saying and doing whatever you think other people need or expect of you? Does your mask change colors, depending on the group you're with, to try to fit in? A survival technique some of us may have learned growing up is to keep our opinions and feelings to ourselves to avoid rocking the boat or upsetting anyone. Maybe we even learned that challenging accepted beliefs was not a wise move. Unfortunately, such survival techniques can become a habit long after they are no longer needed. Coping strategies that helped us in a previous situation may actually hurt us if we continue to practice them now. Sometimes we can bury our thoughts, feelings and preferences so long that we forget what they are! Being free to be yourself is a true gift. Living an authentic life allows love and creativity to flow as intended. The good news is, you've already got the part! Take off that mask and cheers to you being the best, most honest portrayal of you that anyone has ever seen!

March 26   **Answers Are in the Ink**

Spring is coming and bringing with it, lots of growth in nature *and* in us! Seeds which were planted in the fall are starting to produce beautiful flowers. The ideas that have been percolating in our minds all winter are bubbling up to the surface now, with newfound clarity and maybe even a plan of action. I can feel change in the air and beneath the ground—a palpable tension between the way it's been, and the way it's going to be. Stop a moment—can you feel it too? In every spring, a shift is inevitable! As the earth bears new life and new fruits, so shall we. What have you planted for this spring? What ideas and goals are about to hatch in your life? If you were too busy or stressed out last fall to plant anything new, don't worry, I bet God put a few things in the ground for you! You'll just have to do some digging to see what it is.

Journaling is such a great way to connect with the answers you already have, but haven't fully accessed yet. If you're in the middle of a transition and still waiting for more direction, journal about what you're good at, what you enjoy and what your dream life looks like. I love to help clients discover their next steps in my coaching program, so they can create *A Life Worth Having*. Here are some additional questions I discuss with clients to reveal clues about their future:

❦ What do people like to hear you talk about?
❦ What are you most passionate about?
❦ Who do you like to help?
❦ What secret wish do you have?

The answers are in the ink so start (or recommit to) regular journaling to get them out! Also—take a walk and see what nature has to tell you. Slow down, look around and listen! Your spring is coming, but remember, your flowers might come disguised as something else, so be open to unexpected gifts.

March 27　　　　Shortcut to Spiritual Connection

It's a glorious morning to return to my deck after months and months of retreating indoors for the winter! If I close my eyes, I could easily be on an island somewhere. It's sixty degrees and balmy. The sun is shining, a gentle breeze dances through my hair, and the birds are all singing a symphony together. Being in nature is my shortcut to a spiritual connection. If I were to write Cliffnotes for how to get connected spiritually, I would tell readers to go outside and smell, look and listen. Then I would tell them to close their eyes and listen some more, and to BREATHE—in and out slowly.

There are numerous ways to feel connected spiritually but my fastest shortcut, personally, is an immersion in nature, especially in the morning when the day is new and my mind is uncluttered. After the long winter inside, I feel like a woman in the desert who just found an oasis! I am thirsty and could drink for days! We can fall into a drought spiritually and not even realize the full extent of it until we experience a clear connection again. As we get re-centered, we suddenly realize what we have been missing. Like talking to an old friend, today I'm picking right back up where I left off—connected, calm and grateful.

March 28　　　　Spiritual Connection is Critical

Your inner voice is the voice of divinity. To hear it, we need to be in solitude, even in crowded places.
~ A. R. Rahman ~

I am enjoying a preview of spring on my deck this morning, crisp but just warm enough to be outside. It's early and the sun is shining brightly from the east, casting long shadows through the trees. As the sun moves closer to the center of the sky, the shadows cast will be almost nonexistent with the light directly overhead. For the last week or so, I have been less connected spiritually (although yesterday was a huge step in the right direction). The result is longer shadows—less clarity, less peace, less inspiration and guidance. When a spiritual connection is at the center of my life, the shadows are reduced significantly because the light is directly over me (and inside me). I feel bathed in peace, light and love in every direction.

Like anything worth achieving, spiritual connection requires effort on my part, and that starts with making myself available. On a regular basis, I must do whatever is necessary to get and stay connected. For me, that starts with quiet time alone every day. A willingness to be still. An intention to stop doing and just be. To become fully present and engaged in the moment. It is here where I get centered again that the light is the brightest and the shadows disappear. Today I wish you lots of light and connection!

March 29   Sunny Side Up Please

My taste of spring was short-lived! Today it's overcast and in the forties again, too cold for the deck this morning. It's okay, all signs of spring tell me it's coming! My daffodils and tulips are finally starting to come out of the ground—they're in my front yard, which is shielded from the sun for most of the day. My neighbors' daffodils along the side of her house are already in full bloom. Positioning is everything! When everything else is equal, light can make a world of difference. I recently read *The Magic of Thinking Big,* by David Schwartz, which states that when a company's supervisors are discussing who to promote for an opening, likability is the first thing discussed and probably even more important than skill.

They need someone who can get along with their peers and upper management, and who can motivate and inspire their employees to work hard. Skill can be acquired but a sunny disposition is harder to develop for someone who doesn't have it (and probably doesn't recognize they need it). Let's be the people who bring light to others. We will strive to brighten the people and circumstances around us and watch our lives bloom in the process. Maybe we'll even encourage those who usually spend most of their time in shadows to join us.

March 30   Pruning Always Brings New Growth

Everything has seasons, and we have to
be able to recognize when something's time has
passed and be able to move into the next season.
Everything that is alive requires pruning as
well, which is a great metaphor for endings.
~ Henry Cloud ~

We have several very large palm trees in our sunroom. I always prolong pruning off an entire branch that is dying because it still serves a purpose (sort of) to balance out the pot visually. I'm afraid to cut it off because it will leave a big void and I imagine it will take *forever* to grow another one. I made a decision, in what seems like just a few weeks ago, to finally get rid of the dead branches, because hanging on to them meant postponing the growth of their beautiful, new replacements. Besides, once they are dying and brown, they are only going to get worse. It isn't like there's hope of bringing them back to life. So I cut all the dead away at the expense of the rest of the plant looking pretty empty and imbalanced. Today I noticed most of them have already recovered and are flourishing. Some already have new, six-foot branches opening up with more on the way!

Pruning is a metaphor I write about often because it is just that powerful. We can't hear it enough! We are often so afraid of letting go— of something, someone, maybe some job that isn't working— that we will cling to the dying branches. The thought of the void seems so much worse than the death itself. Invariably though, when we let go of what's not working and what is draining our energy and resources, we make room for new growth. Usually it's so much better than we could've imagined! We wonder why we waited so long?

Today, let's get honest with the person who may have the hardest time hearing this—ourselves. Is there a person or situation in our lives that is beyond restoration? Are we clinging to dying branches for fear it will take *forever* to replace them, when in reality, it would probably improve or feel better much faster than we might think? Decisions made out of fear are seldom the best path for me. Have courage. Do what you know needs to be done. Let go and watch your new life branch out in no time at all!

March 31   Time in the Hallway

Many religions are not in agreement about what is celebrated during Easter (if they celebrate it at all), but today I want to discuss the idea of dying and being resurrected. Of burying the old self so the new self can arise. It is scary sometimes to let go of our old ways to become something new. If we are hanging onto Mr. Wrong, for instance, we may have a tough time meeting Mr. Right until we make room for him. Or maybe it's time to let go of that dream that just isn't working out? At times it's necessary to close one door, even before we know which door will open next. The time we spend in the hallway waiting for the next door to open may feel like *forever*, but it's never really that long in the big picture! Have the courage to let go of someone or something when you become clear it's not what you want (and you keep hitting a brick wall that isn't budging). Maybe it's not meant to be and forcing things won't change that.

Embrace your time in the hallway! It can teach us a lot about ourselves, and we will discover clarity and intention we were unable to see when we were in the thick of things. We will grow in the hallway. As we grow, we make room for the new. At just the right time, the new door will open and we will see why everything happened as it did. Find the flow. You'll know it because it's like night and day compared to the non-flow. Let go. Be still. Spend some time meditating and growing in the hallway. When the door opens, embrace the new path but until then, please know, *this too shall pass*. Enjoy every moment, learn your lessons and be open to where it leads you. Change is inevitable and can always be for my good.

April

Have courage for the great sorrows of life and patience for the small ones; and when you have laboriously accomplished your daily task, go to sleep in peace. God is awake.

*~ **Victor Hugo***

The world is ugly and I hate everything in it. *April Fools*! Some days are such a gift! The weather is perfect. The birds are singing. All the best songs come on the radio, and I hit all the green lights. Today feels like it's going to be one of those days! This morning it's sunny outside and I feel sunny inside. I appreciate my life. I am blessed. I am pausing to take inventory of all of my treasures—tangible and intangible. The unexpected blessings, my relationships, personal growth, dreams coming true, and goals coming to fruition. I open my heart and shout, *Thanks*! I can even do a Happy Dance and yell *WOO HOO! THANK YOU!* Try it right now. Yes, you! Get up, do a Happy Dance and yell at the top of your lungs... *Woo-Hoo!* I promise you'll feel happy and grateful if you do this with a sincere heart, and you'll brighten the moment for anyone who sees or hears you— once they realize you've not gone crazy. (This does tend to scare cats, just giving you a head's up.)

I believe the more I say thanks and show gratitude for what I already have, the more I'll be given to say thanks and be grateful for. Gratitude is the seed for increase in all areas of my life (like relationships, health, and finances), and increase allows me to touch more lives in a positive way. You can't feel bad when you're expressing gratitude, especially if you're bold enough to do the Happy Dance! If you don't feel all that grateful today, perfect! Do the dance anyway—you need it more than anyone.

Happy Dance Challenge: take inventory of your blessings, dance and yell *Woo Hoo*! Then please send me a note at www.findingthegift.com to tell me what the Happy Dance did for you.

April 2   Let it Rain

Let the rain kiss you. Let the rain beat upon your head
with silver liquid drops. Let the rain sing you a lullaby.
~ Langston Hughes ~

The smell of rain is in the air bringing with it a quiet
knowing, a calm acceptance and a sense of surrender.
Mother Nature has an agenda all her own, and as nature
yields to her, so will I. For me, a rainy day feels like a
natural pause, a comma in the unfolding of life. Slowly
the raindrops are beginning to fall. Tiny drops from
heaven to cleanse and nourish the earth. I could push
through with all the many to-do's on my list, completely
ignoring the natural shift in energy all around me, but
instead, I will let the rainy day nurture my own spiritual
refreshing too. (Remember, by spiritual, I am referring to
the essence of you. Your brilliant, wonderful soul—just
as you were in the womb and still are, under all the layers
life has heaped upon you since you got here.)

Rainfall is really quite magical, serving an important
role in nature that's needed but not always welcomed (at
least not by two-legged creatures). Sometimes the
raindrops (or storms) in my life can feel like an
inconvenience, a delay or a forced alteration of my plans.
From a place of gratitude, I can trust that rain storms are
necessary for my growth and well-being, and I accept
what they offer me—a time to pause, regroup and
sometimes, redirect my energy and focus. If I never take
a spiritual time-out, I may not be tapping into all the
possibilities brewing around me. For today, I welcome
the smell of oncoming rain—in nature and in my life—
and I will take its cue to go inside and check in with my
spirit. If April showers bring May flowers, what will your
garden grow?

April 3   The Sun is Always There, So Is the Screen

While meditating and staring out my window up into the cloudy sky, I saw a tiny break of blue, showing just a hint of sun after days and days of April showers. Suddenly, my eyes involuntarily refocused on the window screen, instead of looking straight through it like usual. That's two powerful lessons in one mindful moment.

First, no matter what's happening in my world, there's always sun above the clouds, and I don't have to feel alone or hopeless in the midst of chaos or less-than-sunny days. I can rest assured that clouds are temporary, but the sun is constant, and the time I spend in the absence of light doesn't mean it's not there. Being reminded the sun is just out of sight helps me see past the clouds in my life as well. Nothing lasts forever, and in due time, the sun will shine brightly again where we can actually see it and feel it.

I love applying this to the days I feel God (aka HP, Higher Power) is nowhere to be found. He hasn't gone anywhere either, but have I? It's easy to trust in God when everything is going well, but how about when they're not? These are the days I can build my faith, when it seems the sun is not shining on me. This visual really helps me to know He's always there too, even when it seems He's not. I'm sure He's just backstage preparing something wonderful for me, and in time, I'll know what it is.

Secondly, it's easy to let little things block my view of the grand picture. Once my eyes focused in on the window screen, I found it difficult to see beyond it again, but once I changed my sight back to outside, I had a difficult time getting my eyes to transition back to the screen. The point is we can choose what we decide to focus on, even if it feels challenging at first to look beyond the screens in everyday life (distractions, small stuff, obstacles). These things will always be there, tempting me to shift perspective and lose sight of what's really important. Today, I will see the big picture and I hope you choose to do the same.

April 4   Growth Behind the Scenes

I have two trees in my backyard which are always the last to produce leaves in the spring. The trees in the woods behind them all seem to develop and grow leaves while these two remain bare. Every year, I start to wonder if they are dead. I watch them for promising buds, but I never seem to notice any signs of life until magically, they burst forth with full foliage almost overnight.

Even when I can't see evidence of growth and change in the trees, or in my life, major activity is happening within me and around me. I can't rush the process. Once I take whatever action I need to take, my job is to surrender the outcome and the timing, and just let it happen naturally.

Some change happens quicker than others, but everything I need (not everything I want) shows up in my life at the exact right time. The trees bloom, year after year, and no one has to worry to make that happen. Today I am reminded to trust and hope for things still unseen, exercising patience and enjoying some serenity too.

April 5   Nature as a Role Model

All's right with the world—ALWAYS. If you're not sure, just step outside and observe nature. Look. Listen. Smell. Everyone's doing their job. We're okay.

I love this quote by Sidney Lovett, "Every now and again take a good look at something not made with hands—a mountain, a star, the turn of a stream. There will come to you wisdom and patience and solace, and above all, the assurance that you are not alone in this world."

When I step outside in the mornings and feel the routine order of the birds, squirrels or even pesky bees, a peace comes over me. I actually feel a bit envious. Life, for them, is doing what they were created to do, no questions asked, and each makes a wonderful contribution to the whole. Even the trees and grass have seasonal rhythm, which assures us that everything is working properly, right on schedule.

I don't know if we're really that different, but we sure can complicate things. All too easily, we can lose sight of what we were put on this earth to do (what talents, giftings, and skills we inherently have, and what contributions we're meant to make), paying more attention to worry, lack, and pace.

Quick checklist: What makes you happy? Are you doing enough of that? Are you contributing to something that benefits someone or something other than yourself? If not, how could you find a way to do that? Do you have enough structure and order to help you function at your best? What changes or small disciplines could help? If you need to be reminded what an easy, natural flow looks like, use nature and her creatures as your role models.

April 6   **Spiritual Metaphors of Trees**

My huge, backyard tree is like my higher power, who I call God. The big branches are like arms, always outstretched, welcoming, beckoning me to come closer. I watch birds and squirrels land and climb on the tree. They stay awhile and take refuge whenever they need to, and sometimes they just hang out because it feels right. They are free to leave so they go and come back again, anytime they need to be close to Him.

Endlessly entertained, I can watch for hours as the squirrels run through the trees, jumping from one branch to another, sometimes very precariously when they land on the skinnier limbs which easily give under their weight. The closer the squirrel gets to the trunk of the tree, the more solid is his foundation, and the steadier the limb. When he gets far from the trunk, or, pardon the pun, *out on a limb*, the squirrel is less steady and the branch is unstable. I'm reminded to stay close to my spiritual center if I want to remain grounded and in touch with my support.

Leaves are like life in God's hands. They bloom in varying shapes and sizes. I'm watching a strong wind whip them around but the tree (God) doesn't let go of them. He holds them through all the seasons, snow, rain, scorching sun. Only at the very end of life does He let the physical being go, and embraces them into the earth where they originated. Many times, the storms in my life should have plucked me right off the branch, but somehow they didn't. I'm very grateful for what I can learn from trees and grateful I can climb up into my higher power's arms any time I choose to.

April 7   More Lessons from Trees

Why not go out on a limb? Isn't that where the fruit is?
~ **Frank Scully** ~

Sticking with the tree metaphor: while it's sometimes good to stay close to a supportive, strong foundation, I don't believe we should avoid all risk. Dare to be the top branch! Dare to climb the tree all the way up! Yes, the branches get smaller and will be more susceptible to strong winds, but the view is worth it. The top of the tree is still well-supported and anchored by a solid trunk.

We all have different callings and everyone's role in life is valuable. If you were born with the drive to pursue greatness, a unique perspective, or new discoveries that take you beyond average, go for it! Live your life! Venture beyond the comfort zone in the middle of the tree and push yourself higher to whatever it is you're striving for. As long as you maintain a constant connection to the trunk of the tree—your solid base—you will sway with the wind without breaking, and you will always return to center.

April 8   When Rest is a Four-Letter Word

Take rest; a field that has rested gives a beautiful crop.
~ Ovid ~

The trees in my backyard are perfectly still this morning, and after several days of dancing in the wind, the leaves are quiet. The lesson? Rest between winds. Relish the calm. Be still. Just ... be. Life throws enough storms at us regularly, so when we get a moment of calm, it's good to embrace it and allow (maybe even enjoy) a season of rest.

I'm speaking loudly to myself on this one. I have avoided rest and calm most of my life. If there isn't a storm around me, I know how to make one! Or if I'm not stirring up trouble, I can sure stir up some busyness to deal with the uncomfortable feelings I often get when everything's a little too quiet.

For me, resting and sitting still are foreign concepts, and the need to be productive has often been overly attached to my worth. The good news? Recognizing my resistance to rest is the first step to gaining the willingness to make different choices and embrace quiet seasons. Finally, I'm beginning to see how time wasted, is not wasted time, but a useful period of restoration and rejuvenation. In that sense, resting is an important part of productivity and re-creation—*recreation, duh!*—which I hope to allow myself to indulge in more often. If this hits home with you, I challenge us both to look for an opportunity to be still today, to rest and recharge.

April 9   Holding on to Crumbs

I set out for a much-needed walk today, after spending too many rainy days inside. Staring up at the overcast, cloudy sky, I saw a tiny piece of blue breaking through. The wind was strong and the clouds were moving swiftly, but as I walked, I desperately kept my focus hanging on that tiny piece of blue hope. After days of rain and gloominess, a sliver of clear sky seemed like the only beacon of beauty I could see at the time—my reminder of sunny days to come.

Despite my unwillingness to change my focus, the clouds kept moving and finally I shifted my gaze. To my surprise, I saw a much larger patch of blue looming across the entire horizon! Sometimes I hold onto tidbits of good—the crumbs—fearing that's all there is, and all I'm ever going to get. By narrowing my perspective, I nearly missed a much bigger gift just waiting to be discovered. Today I will open my eyes wider, and trust that my Higher Power wants to provide blessings for me, beyond what I can even imagine!

April 10   Daring to Hope

Hope begins in the dark, the stubborn hope that if you just show up and try to do the right thing, the dawn will come. You wait and watch and work: you don't give up.
~ Anne Lamott ~

After several days of dark clouds and rain, how beautiful it is to wake up and enjoy blue skies as far as I can see this morning! The sliver of blue yesterday gave way to a big chunk of blue, and overnight, all the remaining clouds vanished and the promise of a sunny day is now fully realized. I think I would've been very disappointed, and maybe even felt slightly cheated if it were pouring down rain again this morning, after getting a taste of sunshine yesterday.

How difficult is it to hope for a favorable outcome, when some of us have been disappointed too many times before? We know when we hope for sun after a week of rain we will eventually get it. Time has proven that over and over. What about other circumstances, when in the present moment, we see zero signs of things changing? How easy is hope and trust then?

For me, it depends on how often I have exercised my faith, recently and in the past. Faith is like a muscle that has to be used regularly to be strengthened. If I truly believe all things work for my good, I can draw comfort in difficult situations, especially if I've taken notice of how other problems in the past did finally work out. It might not always happen the way I'd hoped or expected, but usually in time, I will see the bigger picture and realize how I always got what I truly needed.

Occasionally I lose faith and hope too, but then a sliver of blue comes along to remind me, metaphorically, that my sunshine is on the way. Once again, I am reminded of the saying, "This too shall pass." And a new day begins.

April 11   Nature Inspires Everything

Is it possible everything we have ever learned or been inspired to do was rooted in nature? I am enjoying an early spring morning outside on the deck wrapped up in my favorite fuzzy blanket. How did we ever think to try to create a fabric this soft? How did we even aim for it or believe it was possible? Lambs, kittens and many other animals have shown us how furry and soft something could be. I just saw an airplane overhead as four or five birds also flew across the sky. If there were no flying birds or insects, would the human race ever have attempted flight? Would it have even occurred to us to work incessantly to find a way to get airborne? I don't know.

We have seasons, cycles, change, stability, evolution, wonder, long life, short life, easy living and harsh realities. The circle of life is full of ups and downs, new and old, life and death but we don't call it the circle of death. Life is simply living for as long as we have, and using our minds and gifts to make a contribution. Look at nature for inspiration and motivation. What are you capable of? What can you invent? Robert F. Kennedy declared, "Only those who dare to fail greatly can ever achieve greatly." Let's go make history!

April 12   Try It and See

How many times have we chased something, feeling so sure it's what we really want? Bumblebees are buzzing all around my deck and my dog, Goldie is driving herself crazy trying to catch one. She will see one who looks close enough to corner, and go at it, trying to trap the bumblebee, but it always escapes, leaving her snapping at the wind. I keep thinking if she ever catches one, it will be the first and last time! Maybe we need a big challenge to push us?

Striving toward a goal is admirable, but if we keep going after something (or someone) and it continues to elude us, maybe there's a good reason? Maybe there is an angel intervening on our behalf because what (who) we think we need or want isn't in our best interest? Maybe it's time to step back, get still, seek support, talk to friends, listen for guidance and go after something (or someone) else? Either way, it's all good. If you chase something, catch it and get stung, congratulations! That lesson is learned and now you can move on with certainty. You won't have to wonder any longer if it coulda, woulda, shoulda might have worked out. It didn't. Sometimes the only way we can move on is to try it out and see what happens. The truth will show itself sooner or later. And you will always, always, always have what you need to take the next step! Even when it doesn't feel like it, or look like it at the moment. It feels great knowing we can't make very many mistakes that can't be corrected or learned from. Jump and grow your wings on the way down!

April 13   **What the Buzzards Taught Me**

I just saw something I've never noticed before. (That happens a lot when I take the time to sit in nature without an agenda!) I'm watching six or eight large birds. Buzzards maybe? When they fly, they rarely flap their wings. Mostly they glide! Buzzards use the wind in their favor. When they get close enough to me, I can see them shake a little as they are balancing the angle of their wings with the current of the wind. Occasionally they flap their wings two to three times and it seems to take them up or down. Maybe they do it to steady themselves? Then they return to gliding. Buzzards have such a large wingspan that they can fly much longer just gliding, which is different than a small bird who does the opposite. When a small bird is flying, he flaps his wings most of the time and glides only occasionally. That's me, a small bird. As I grow spiritually and as I get better at life balance, I will be able to fly longer with less effort. I will be able to glide effortlessly through the winds of my life.

My wings (powered by God, my support system, self-care, daily rituals) will continue to expand as long as I put intention in the daily practices that yield growth. Those buzzards sure look like they're having lots of fun! I'm ready to give up the struggles that sometimes ground me and glide with them. Meanwhile, one day at a time, I will let my wings continue to grow, trusting one day soon I will soar with ease!

April 14   **Embracing Each Season of Life**

When did it happen? Overnight it seems everything green came alive. The grass has greened up and thickened. The trees are in full bloom. I can close my eyes and remember how barren everything looked just a month ago. Day after day, the skies were gray and lifeless. A week could have gone by before we saw the sun. The cold, damp weather kept me inside, but today the long dark winter is just a memory. It's funny how several days of sunshine and blue skies can make winter feel like it was many months ago, and yet I remember thinking back then, that spring would never arrive. One thing we can always count on is that time does not stand still and change is constant, whether we can see it or not.

When I'm in a tough situation, a scary transition or just having a bad day, I can remember back to other challenges that came and went, even though it felt like they would last forever. And when a perfect day or season comes along, I will embrace every second of it, because as much as I may want to hold onto all the good times, change comes in and shifts things around. It's not bad—actually contrast and variety are the secret sauce of life! If all we ever did was eat dessert, we would lose our full appreciation for it. (And it would be very unhealthy!) Whatever season of life you're in today, embrace it. Grow. Learn. Rejuvenate. Change is underway.

April 15   **Time to Recharge ... YOU!**

Recently I spent five days in Las Vegas. What a fun, exciting twenty-four-hour city! I attended an exhilarating convention, with activities from early morning to late at night, so balance was difficult to maintain. Today, back on my deck for the first time, I'm soaking up the stillness. With each long breath, I am drawing the soothing sounds and sights of nature deep inside me. Restoring. Replenishing. Back to home base. Back to where I operate most peacefully and efficiently. Just like our phones, laptops and other techno-wonders, we must recharge ourselves. The lower our battery gets, the longer we need to fully replenish ourselves back to a balanced state of being.

Today is dedicated to self-care, replenishment and allowing myself to slowly return to my usual daily routines. Laundry, unpacking. First things first. I can't do everything at once to catch up, so I will just start somewhere. My goals will be reasonable for today, given that I am plugged into my power source and committed to some down time while I recharge. It feels good to acknowledge I am a human being, not a human doing, and I need and deserve balance. Balance is the gift I give myself today, to get and stay present.

April 16   Want Mindfulness? Say "Blue"

*With mindfulness, you can establish yourself
in the present in order to touch the wonders of
life that are available in that moment.*
~ Thich Nhat Hanh ~

It's a gorgeous, sunny morning. Light breeze. Birds singing. Bumblebees buzzing. I am immersed in nature, but my mind is elsewhere. Thoughts keep popping into my head "necessitating" a quick call, an e-mail or a text, "right now, before I forget!" I have also stopped my morning time-out to quickly jot down a few other to-do reminders.

Presenteeism: you are there but you're not really there! I'm afraid that describes me more often than I care to admit. When my mind is racing and I'm having a challenging time letting go, I close my eyes and say the word, "Blue." Blue represents tranquility, sky, water and freedom. I repeat the word every time the worries of the day return, or just as the mind chatter begins again. I focus my hearing intently on sound and smell, whatever I can hear or smell at that very moment. If I can tap into my senses, I can get present and get out of my head. And I breathe. Breathe.

Today, be where you are. It is a choice. It is a discipline. Serenity awaits me in the present moment and once again, for today, I choose to unwrap the gift and be where I am.

April 17   Making Sunshine Out of Clouds

Today is cloudy, overly dark and chilly. Sometimes I really need a sunny day to lift my spirits. On a day like today, the heaviness in the air and the darkened skies serve to weigh me down, possibly exaggerating an already lower than normal mood. I woke up feeling tired and lacking inertia. On any given day, and in any situation, I can let external circumstances influence me positively or negatively. (I'm all about the positive influences!)

If I feel external circumstances bringing me down—work, relationships, weather, etc.—I have a choice. Today I choose to take action and let the feelings follow. For me that can mean a brisk walk or taking my body to the gym to move things around and sweat. Maybe turn on all the lights in the house to brighten things up, or turn some music on (or play an instrument if you know how!). At times, I need to get around a crowd at a lively coffee shop or go to the park. When I am dragging, for whatever reason, I choose to move my energy in the direction of life and positivity. The word "decision" means to cut off from. My entire day, my whole outlook will change just because of the small decision to cut myself away from the funky feelings I woke up with and fill myself up on the good stuff! Today, I choose to make my own sunshine. Join me?!

April 18   **Embrace the Now**

The past has flown away. The coming month and year do
not exist. Ours only is the present's tiny point.
~ **Mahmud Shabistari** ~

In true spring form and Tennessee fashion, our
weather has been most unpredictable. Cloudy and cold,
sunny and warm. I always find it interesting to wake up
to one kind of weather, which often sets the tone for my
day, only to have it changed completely in two hours or
less. I love sunshine! I'm good for an occasional rainy
day just to break things up, but give me sun and lots of it!
A few days ago I woke up to a gorgeous balmy day. I sat
outside and just let the sun flood my face, my body, my
heart. I really soaked it up. I went to the gym and when I
came out, it was colder and cloudy with a storm on the
way. I was so thankful I had taken the time earlier to
embrace the sunshine. We never know how long a good
thing will last. Wake up! Embrace it (him, her, them, the
cat, the job, the vacation—whatever IT is) and say,
Thanks!

April 19   **Volleying for Quality Relationships**

Conversation and relating to one another can be
compared to a game of tennis or ping-pong. Am I serving
zingers across the net, hoping to really burn my
opponent? How do they feel when they can't return it? If
they shut down, have I really won? If my opponent
begins to return the volley with zingers of their own, we
are now in a match to see who can beat the other down.
No matter who has the last word, nobody wins (unless
you're playing tennis).

My son is great at ping-pong. I like to play, but I'm no
match for him. It doesn't even feel like we're playing or
interacting when I'm on the receiving end of his serves,
unable to return them. My idea of fun is an engaging
volley of back and forth where both parties are actively

participating in the game, and it's more about the shared experience than scoring. (I recognize others enjoy being challenged in a match of comparable skill levels, and that's when my son needs to play his dad!)

With dialogue in relationships, it's not much of a conversation when one person is dominating. If that's the case, it's likely *no one* is listening. The silent partner has shut down and the talkative partner is learning nothing new, listening to the sound of their own voice. Be aware of all the conversations you have today. Practice active listening. Challenge yourself to learn something new about the people you encounter. Ask yourself whether or not you see others in a conversation as your opponent or as your equal? Ask yourself what you really want. To win? Or to truly relate and interact? Set your intentions and you will win at what really matters!

April 20   Comparing Your Insides to My Outsides

I had knee surgery just a few months ago. After six weeks, I had progressed to the point where I could walk normally without a limp. I could take stairs pretty well, but if you really stared at me, you might have noticed I was being extra cautious. My point is that you could no longer glance at me six-weeks post-surgery and know I was still hurt, and that my knee wasn't fully recovered yet. In other words, you would naturally have assumed I was fully-functioning (normal).

You may have pain in your own knee—or maybe your heart—and are comparing yourself to others who *look* normal. Maybe you feel like you're coming up a little short? You may even feel like you were handed a raw deal in life because everyone else *seems* to be happy and worry free, while you struggle. Countless times, people have made assumptions about me which were false. They were based incorrectly on what they assumed, or what I let others see, neither of which were the truth.

When I harbor envy, seasoned with a portion of self-pity, I'm going to attract more reasons to feel envy and self-pity. We all have pain. We all have disappointment. Healing myself is the best use of my energy, rather than comparing myself to others or dwelling on how I wish things were. Being grateful for everything exactly the way it is right now is crucial if I desire transformation. Focusing on how I want to feel, and affirming positive statements such as: *Growth IS happening in me*, or, *All things ARE working for my good,* will bring about the changes I desire. Remember, when you judge a book by the cover, you aren't getting the full story. Focus less on your neighbor or other lack, and just keep working on your own bestseller!

April 21   Envy is a Friend

Envy and jealousy just sound like bad words don't they? What if I told you they can help us discover clues about what's missing in our lives? It's true! In fact, taking an envy gauge of our lives can be a very useful tool. When we feel that familiar nudge of jealousy about someone or something, we need to pay attention to it, because we've just been given a clue—a puzzle piece to our soul. We can ask, *What really bothers me about that person or situation?* We can look deeper into why we feel threatened, and explore what envy is trying to tell us about ourselves. Once identified, we can take action to address that part of our soul that has a desire for something more or different.

For example, I used to feel envious of other women who could host a social gathering with grace, charm and ease. Being a great hostess may not be a big deal to some, but my envy told me it was a big deal to me. After identifying the longing, I decided to entertain more to get the practice I needed to become comfortable doing it. I have a lot of fun hosting events now and I've had people tell me I'm good at it. Jealousy woke me up to one of my giftings! Before the envy, I didn't even know I had that unfulfilled desire!

Envy can show us small puzzle pieces, or big ones, which can help us become more complete by digging a little deeper and finding a way to satisfy that unmet expression in us. I highly recommend Julia Cameron's *The Artist's Way* for anyone wanting to recover their authentic soul, whether or not you consider yourself an artist. In her book, she has an exercise called, "The Jealousy Map." I found this so insightful in my own life, and have a modified version of it in my coaching program, *A Life Worth Having.* Exploring envy is an invaluable way for people to uncover or recover something that's missing in their lives.

Make a list of various people you envy, as many as you can think of. Write down why you feel jealous. It might be the tiniest thing or it could be big—don't judge your answers. If someone comes to mind, you probably have a thorn that needs attention so write it down. What does he or she do better than you, or have that you don't, but wish you did? Be honest with yourself—have you resented them or criticized them, when really you were just envious and wanted to be more like them? Forgive yourself! The people who get on my nerves the most are usually my greatest teachers!

Doing this work helps me turn my resentment into gratitude toward them, and gain increased compassion for myself. Can you name what may have been holding you back, such as fear, self-doubt, or what others might think? Now, describe how you would like your life to be different, and come up with some immediate actions you can take to become more fulfilled in those areas. Again, start small. You're looking for tiny steps forward, out of jealousy, and into satisfying your authentic spiritual longings. No feelings of pain, disappointment or envy need to be in vain. When used as a key, these places of spiritual discomfort can unlock the door to your greater life.

April 22   Selective Focus

Better keep yourself clean and bright; you are the
window through which you must see the world.
~ George Bernard Shaw ~

I was at the gym this morning on an elliptical machine facing a wall of windows. Just outside the window, a beautiful spring scene begged to be noticed. A row of trees boasted a few remaining purple blooms making way for brilliant green foliage. The contrast was stunning! Suddenly my depth of field shortened, and I noticed all the big spots and smudges on the gym window in front of this tree. Once I became aware of the dirty window, my eyes had trouble focusing beyond the window, back to the beautiful tree.

With conscious effort, I could look beyond the spots and smudges, and once again enjoy the spring foliage and the beautiful day happening outside. Or, I could choose to stay distracted by the unclean window. The smudges made up about three percent of what was before my eyes. Why do some of us allow our focus to be on the three percent (the obstacles) instead of the ninety-seven percent (the beauty, the blessings)? Why do we struggle to focus on the good stuff, or tell ourselves we will enjoy what's good just as soon as all the obstacles are removed and the view (or life) is better? Today, focus on what's going well and what you have to be grateful for, and the imperfections will fade from your sight. Try it! It's difficult, if not impossible, to focus on both. Abundance or lack—where's your intentional focus going to be today?

April 23   You Were Born For This

I believe all of our talents and gifts (potential) are pre-wired into our DNA. Yet there are many we may never even discover. I just watched a group of young men give an amazing a cappella performance. How did they discover they could do that? I look around at the trees, bushes and flowers—even the grass. They are what they are. No doubts. No questions asked. Can you imagine a tree berating itself for being so tall, or for wishing it was more like a flower? It's easy to grow up influenced by all the should's and ought to's and "looking good" choices that make us ignore our inner voices, quietly reminding us who and what we are born to be and do. What do *you* like? What do *you* want? For so many of us, we can't answer that question because we silenced that voice so long ago. Take some time to think back to your interests as a kid. As mentioned before, I strongly recommend Julia Cameron's *The Artist's Way* as a guide back to the creative you. Let your true nature unfold. Better late than never!

April 24   Finding My Limits

Last week, I was in rehab for my knee surgery a few months ago, and the physical therapist started me with just ten minutes on an elliptical machine. I have now progressed to twenty minutes since then. I have missed my walks outside so much, and with the spring morning calling me, I decided I was ready to take a brisk twenty minute walk. I was on top of the world for six minutes before my knee started hurting. Unfortunately, I was six minutes from home and had to push myself to get back. My mind was flooded with life lessons!

First, sometimes we have to push through pain and obstacles and just keep our eyes focused on the finish line, moving forward one step at a time. I literally just kept putting one foot in front of the other (while my knee was screaming for me to stop), and kept telling myself, *I'm going to make it back home*. Secondly, it's okay to admit I have limits. Sometimes the only way to know what I'm capable of is to push my limits. I will either delight in accomplishing what I set out to do, or I will find out what my best is on any given day. Sometimes my best will vary if I'm tired, distracted, or have lack of nourishment or self-care. If I fall short of my expectations and previous abilities, I will celebrate that I still did my best on that day. When I continue to push my limits, I may fall short of the goal, but I will continue to grow in the process. I would rather overestimate myself and find my limits, than underestimate myself and never reach my full potential. I am not going to sit on the porch watching the world go by! Les Brown said, "Shoot for the moon. Even if you miss, you'll land among the stars." I'm good with that! Don Ward also says, "If you are going to doubt something, doubt your limits." If you think you can, you might be right. If you think you can't and never try, you are definitely right! Today is the day to take a shot. Either way, you win!

April 25   Hold On, The Gift Is Coming!

Summertime calls for a good old-fashioned picnic! Make up some sandwiches, pack some snacks and drinks, grab a blanket and a Frisbee and head to a nearby park, or in our case, the lake! On a whim, my husband and I did that on a weekday, just the two of us in the middle of the day to break up our routine. After eating lunch, skipping some rocks on the water and playing a little Frisbee, we lay back down on our blanket to stare up at the trees and the beautiful, blue sky to soak up some sun. As we grew still, we heard a very faint, but distinct buzzing all around us. We sat up to investigate and beyond our blanket in every direction were swarms of gnats! Busy gnats dismissing our intrusion and carrying on about their business of buzzing around the grass and wildflowers. Visually, it was easy to miss them and not notice all of their activity. If we hadn't heard them, we never would have seen them.

I felt encouraged to remember that even when I feel like nothing is happening in my life, when everything feels uncertain and on hold, activity and the buzz of life are still happening all around me. When it's time, I will see it. During the still times, I can rest assured that many things are happening for my good in the background and all around me. I don't have to fear being stuck in this place forever. Hold on—the gift is coming! It's just not quite ready to be revealed, but it will be worth my patience and faith. If I allow myself to slow down and tune in to me and to my circumstances, I might be able to see or hear some proof of what's taking place on my behalf. Even if I don't, I can trust it's still happening.

April 26   Afraid to Risk Losing A Dream

*A ship in harbor is safe, but that is
not what ships are built for.*
~ John A. Shedd ~

Why does an ostrich stick its head in the sand? I don't know, but why humans do it is a little easier to figure out. We may want something so much, but we don't go after it because if we fail, we'll lose our dream. We would rather stay comfortable on our cozy couches, dreaming, hoping, praying, wishing and asking ourselves, "Wonder what it would be like to do *that*?" When we should be asking ourselves, "How could I actually *do* that?" Followed by "I don't know exactly, but I think I'll try," and then taking a shot at it. Maybe that dream is all we have? Maybe our identity is so tightly wound up in that dream that we can't afford to lose it? Maybe we keep our heads in the sand about a job or relationship because we know deep down, it's not right, but we don't want to admit it, much less do anything about it. We disconnect from the part of us that knows the truth, so we don't have to get out of our comfort zones and take action. Once we do have awareness, it's very difficult to go back to blissful ignorance.

Awareness may lead to fear of the unknown, fear of loss, or fear of success. The cure for fear is always action! "I'm afraid!" Do it anyway. "I may fail!" Do it anyway, because either way you will grow. "What if it doesn't work?" It definitely won't work if you don't try, but what if it does? "Who will I be if my dream doesn't work out?" I don't know, but who are you now, with an unsung song in your heart?" We can't always know every possible outcome, but we can trust that everything—*everything* works together for our good, even if at the time, it doesn't feel like it. Have the courage to live your life! Resolve to take your shot! It may lead to something even better and bigger than you dreamed of! Personally, I would rather have my head in the clouds, trying different things, than buried in sand, trying nothing.

April 27   **Turn Negative Beliefs into Treasure**

How do I know I'm on the wrong path, or maybe on the right path, but capable of more? There are many clues we can look for. See if any of these seem familiar:
- ❤ I have an underlying sense of unfulfillment.
- ❤ I think about past dreams and wonder what my life would be like now if only I had _____.
- ❤ I am jealous of other people's success.
- ❤ I am often critical of people who are taking a shot and trying new things.
- ❤ I resent people who seem to be happy all the time.
- ❤ I complain about anything and everything.
- ❤ I sabotage my chances for advancement.
- ❤ I attempt to sabotage others because misery loves company.

✿ If people ask my opinion about their dream, I try to keep them safe from disappointment by telling them all the reasons it probably won't work.

UGH! So toxic! I'm frustrated just writing this, and I know it can't feel very good to read it, especially if any of these hit home with you. Our negative energy and actions, or inactions, are clues! They can serve as a treasure map if we will let them. In my coaching program, I created specific exercises to look at all the negative thoughts, beliefs and jealousies we each have, and use them to create a roadmap to the life we are destined to live. The goal isn't to eliminate all the toxins from our consciousness, but to use them very specifically to unlock the path to the *real* you. For today, observe your thoughts and actions, and begin to question what they may be trying to tell you. Be grateful for the guidance within.

April 28   Discovering Our Unique Purpose

In nature there is a reason and a place for everything, even if we don't know what it is. I'm outside on the deck, hoping spring is here to stay this time! A gnat just hovered beside me and I found myself asking myself, *why is he here? What purpose does he serve?* I don't have an answer! I have similarly wondered why we need mosquitoes, other insects, and even hyenas! As I watched the gnat for a moment, I realized something. I don't know why he's here, but HE does! We all have a place and a purpose. We were created to be great in our own, unique way. At times, WE may not even know for sure what we're supposed to be doing with our lives. Or we think we know, but after a time, we hit what feels like a dead end. The more I seek to know and understand myself and my spirit, the more clarity I attain toward knowing how I want to spend my time, and ultimately my life.

Over the years, I have utilized a lot of great books and techniques to uncover more of the real me. I've picked what I feel are the best of the best exercises for self-awareness, and now guide others in finding out who they really are, and where they want to go from here. I've been on the wrong path without knowing it, and I've been on the right path without fully recognizing where it was taking me. Now I know I'm on my *real* path! I see everything coming together from my past to support me and it feels like coming home. I am finding my place in the world. You are on your way too! You wouldn't be reading this book if you weren't. Wherever you are is part of the plan. Be grateful and trust. More will be revealed!

April 29   **The Power of Music**

Music is a higher revelation than all wisdom and philosophy. Music is the electrical soil in which the spirit lives, thinks and invents.
~ Ludwig van Beethoven ~

Today is dedicated to *my* piano man. What music are you listening to? What's playing in your head? Whether it's audible to anyone around you or not, we all have thoughts, music, or perhaps, conversations running through our minds much of the time. Can you imagine how you might walk while listening to slow, relaxing classical music through your headphones? Maybe casually, thoughtfully, or peacefully? What if you had rock 'n roll or pop playing (or anything else up tempo that really gets you moving)? Would you have more bounce in your step, maybe even more attitude? What if you were listening to something you hated, something dreary? Bleh—would you even have the energy to keep walking? It certainly wouldn't give you any additional energy and might take away some of what you already have.

Pay attention to what you're listening to, audible or not. Your state of mind is easily influenced by internal or external stimuli. In other words, be intentional and create your stride on purpose! Feed your mind, body and soul whatever it's craving, in the form of sound. I always ask myself when I go on a walk, exercise, or when I'm driving or cleaning, what do I need in that moment? Sometimes my spirit needs encouragement. Sometimes I'm just ready to jam and music helps raise my energy to the beat (which is especially helpful when I don't feel like exercising, or when I need cleaning mojo). Other times, I need silence or the sounds of nature to reconnect and get centered. I also use self-recorded affirmations to remind me how wonderful I am on days I don't feel so great. If you don't listen to music much, or even if you do, I encourage you to see how it might meet a specific need, or help you accomplish a task. Play around with different genres. Experiment with what you listen to and when. Add some variety. Music is transformative and can take us places we might not reach as easily on our own!

April 30   **Storms Make Us Stronger**

There are some things you learn
best in calm, and some in storm.
~ Willa Cather ~

It's late April and once again, I'm reminded of the saying, "April showers bring May flowers." I am writing this late in the evening and a huge storm just rolled in, which made me worry about my April flowers out in the storm. Begonias especially are so delicate. Then it occurred to me, yes, let them get pushed around a little by the wind and rain so they can get stronger than ever. I didn't ask for the storm, but as long as it's here, let's get some benefit from it.

Wow, so many parallels! I imagined the pretty little hanging basket full of flowers that never encountered wind or hard rain. The branches would never be tested. They would never have to grow stronger. They would never be challenged or forced to adapt. They would never be given the opportunity to bounce back, better and stronger than ever. That's what happens when we let a storm force us to grow ... we come back stronger and more beautiful than before. I'm not worried about my flowers anymore. Let the rain pour. Tomorrow morning they may look a little worse for the wear but come May, they will be a*may*zing! After all, it doesn't say April showers, bring April flowers, does it? Great things take time, yes, but often adversity as well. Embrace the storms of life. Your blooming season *will* follow!

May

Since we cannot change reality, let us change the eyes which see reality.
~ Nikos Kazantzakis

May 1   We Need Each Other

Staring upward into the large tree in my backyard, I noticed how each branch is connected to another branch, and that each group of branches is connected to yet another limb, and ultimately they're all connected to the trunk as a whole. The trunk couldn't provide the stability the tree needs without its strong root system firmly grounded deep in the earth. Just as the limbs branch out above ground, so do the roots below ground, branching out several feet in every direction to hold it steady. Each part makes an important contribution to the growth, beauty and stability of the tree. No one part is greater than the other, and it wouldn't be the same tree with anything missing.

This metaphor can apply to families, companies, churches, communities, schools, teams—anything where a successful, thriving experience is dependent on everyone doing their part. We inherently crave a sense of belonging—of community. We need each other, and we are needed, even when something inside may tell us differently. Celebrate the various roles each person plays in your life and in your community. Give thanks for their ability to do their part. Be glad you don't have to do and be everything. (I've tried that and it doesn't work!) Each of us together serves to enrich life for all of us, and together we create stability and serenity. Branch out!

May 2   Selective Serenity

Earlier this morning on my deck, all the harmonious nature sounds were completely drowned out by the sound of a loud stump grinder coming from my neighbor's house. At first I was disappointed, I mean, don't they know morning time is *sacred* and somewhere in some neighborhood book of etiquette, it must clearly state not to use a stump grinder till at least 11 a.m.? Thankfully, the gift of perspective paid me a visit and I realized that nothing had changed in my circumstances. The noise existed, yes, but my personal circumstances remained just as real, whether the machine was on or off.

Naturally, it was easy to become distracted by the noise and let my focus wander from my own existence and purpose, but I found if I concentrated on my task of being in the presence of nature, I could still hear the birds. I had a choice. I could hear whatever I chose to hear. (Hmmm ... this may be exactly the type of selective hearing husbands and teenagers have mastered!) This morning, the birds still chirped and sang for me, and all the noise was just noise and nothing more.

Are you facing some *noise* in your life today? Can you bring your focus back to what's important to you, letting the unwanted distractions fade into their proper place? Being able to focus is a discipline and it's okay to start small. See if you can clear your mind of anything other than what you are intending to do at this very moment. Try to hold that focus for sixty seconds. With practice, you and I will both gradually improve our ability to pay attention to what's most important and let the rest go.

May 3   Accept What's True Right Now

For here we are not afraid to follow
truth where ever it may lead.
~ Thomas Jefferson ~

A squirrel just appeared outside my window. He is scampering along a tree limb that hangs very close to my house. The movement caught the attention of Fancy, one of my cats. She is watching intently with curiosity, but also with the understanding she can't do anything right now, other than watch. Fancy is able to accept her reality: she is inside, the squirrel is outside, and they are not meant to engage—at least not today. Fancy is content to be where she is and accept the momentary gift of entertainment and intrigue.

Animals make it look so easy! I don't always embrace my circumstances with the same degree of humility and acceptance. I've spent hours, days, even months figuring out ways to achieve something that seems to elude me. The more I bump into brick walls now, the more I can recognize that an answer of *no*, or *not right now*, is ultimately protecting me from something and/or guiding me to what's best for me in the long run. Either way, Fancy just showed me how much more peace I can have by accepting present day reality, and enjoying all that I'm capable of enjoying, in this very moment. Acceptance doesn't mean I stop taking action for dreams and desired outcomes, but it does mean I recognize what's true right now and accept the gifts today offers me.

May 4   **Join the Team**

It's a beautiful, late spring morning and summer is right around the corner. The smell of honeysuckle and roses are thick in the air, and my spirit feels drunk on the sweetness. It's so fragrant and yet I must be thirty feet or more from the nearest honeysuckle bush. Smells are a powerful way to conjure up memory. Honeysuckle takes me back to second grade, playing on my first softball team. I cared more about eating honeysuckles and wild blackberries than playing ball! I wasn't a good player back then, but I loved being part of the team. For the first time in my life, I felt like I was part of something bigger than myself. I felt like I belonged, even though I was nowhere close to being the best player. In fact, I was a regular benchwarmer, but still valued as a team member. Win or lose, we did it together. Winning meant the whole team piled up in the back of the coach's pickup truck to ride to Dairy Queen for a frozen treat. Losing meant practicing harder to get 'em the next time.

Life can have lonely seasons, even when you're surrounded by plenty of people. Look for ways to plug in.

Put in some time to be part of something bigger than you, part of a group where you can celebrate victory and grow through temporary defeat. Our spirits crave fellowship, in the right amount—some of us need more, some less, depending on our personality. But we all benefit from a sense of community and belonging. If you don't already have one, find a "team" you can join where you are valued, regardless of your level of contribution. And don't be so concerned with "winning" that you miss the sweetness along the way. As the umpire says, "Play ball!" Have some fun today!

May 5   **Trees, Hats, and Masks**

Love takes off masks that we fear we cannot live
without and know we cannot live within.
~ **James A. Baldwin** ~

The branches of a tree grow out in all different directions. They touch, they overlap, and they split off into smaller branches. No two limbs are alike, and no two limbs have identical branches, but they are all part of the same tree. That tree is me; it's each of us. There are many facets to my life, and I always laugh when someone asks me what I do, because I wear so many hats! I used to be in corporate sales, so I understand what it means to be an employee, a salesperson, a boss, the client interface, and a co-worker. Today, I'm a creative—a photographer, writer and painter—while still being wife, Mom, daughter, sister, aunt, friend, business owner, coach, sponsor, sponsee, volunteer and member of a church family. I'm also a trauma survivor, which means I grew up learning to live fragmented, instead of integrated, and I have a tendency to divide myself and my life into parts. Because I had this terrified, insecure side of myself (and was secretly coping with my life using destructive behaviors like anorexia and bulimia), I learned to put on masks in order to do everything else. I became immersed in external appearance, perfectionism, achievement and control (the looking-good side) to make sure I was accepted and liked.

Sometimes I can still find myself putting on various roles like a costume, tweaking myself to suit each part, shifting in and out of different identities, and losing the real me in the shuffle. Thankfully, my awareness has grown in this area and I'm better able to recognize when I've slipped a mask on and need to come back to what's authentic and true. I'm learning to trust that the person I am is wonderful and most importantly, *she is enough.*

Today, I desire to be more fluid, more transparent—one self in all my daily endeavors and relationships, where the hat doesn't change who I am, it just decorates the real me! I encourage you to celebrate and embrace yourself too. All the wonderful and unique parts of you, knowing you also have one true identity, with many different branches and colorful hats. Wear them well, but always remember to be you!

May 6   **Love Means Let Go**

Today I read a meditation about butterflies—nothing new, but worthy of repeating and reflecting on it. If we hold a butterfly, it's possible we will rub off too much oil from their wings and they'll be unable to fly. We can catch one and keep it, but he won't be a butterfly anymore. If we really love someone, we need to love them loosely enough so they can still be who they are. Let them go when it's appropriate and let them return on their own.

This hit me like a ton of bricks today. My son recently turned sixteen and got his drivers license. Ironically, while his happiness and independence increased, my sense of being needed decreased. I am thrilled for him, but I also feel a sense of loss as he inches closer to adulthood.

Roles change and one event can mean the exact opposite to other individuals involved. Clinging to the past doesn't prevent change, and only serves to make it tougher to accept. I will let go and let life bring on the next chapter, knowing and trusting a great book is unfolding!

May 7　　　　　**A Harvest Requires Preparation**

Don't judge each day by the harvest you
reap but by the seeds that you plant.
~ Robert Louis Stevenson ~

How ready is your field for a new harvest? Our family is about to take our first mission trip. I'm nervous and excited. I was journaling about it earlier and wrote, "This could be the start of something big." But then I realized "the start" happened a long time ago, otherwise we wouldn't have chosen to book a trip to Guatemala for a working vacation.

The start is the start, not the harvest. New chapters begin with a vision, an awareness, a need or a desire for more. Then the field must be made ready—must be prepped. The soil must be tilled and broken down so it's better able to receive the seed, so that every particle of dirt is equal to the rest—level the playing field, literally. In life, I am no better than, and no worse than my neighbor. Together we can grow any vision. One speck of dirt can't do anything by itself. But a field that is ready can yield a bountiful crop. Prepping the field brings humility and community. Being "tilled" is surrendering to the greater good, asking, "How may I serve?" or saying, "Use me, I'm ready to serve." Long before the harvest, much work has been done. Today I'm grateful for all the work that's gone into making me who I am—the breaking down, the leveling of ego, the fertilization, the rain, the sunlight, and of course, time. No harvest can come without time, and it takes as long as it takes. Give gratitude today for wherever you are in the process. Celebrate everything, not just the harvest. Count it all as joy!

May 8   Fix it Right and Get the Lesson

While enjoying a morning walk, I saw an illustration for life and relationships in an unexpected way. Our streets have been in desperate need of the final topcoat of pavement. It has probably been five years or more since the preliminary layer was laid when the neighborhood was brand-new. Meanwhile, numerous potholes have formed as well as ruts and dips. They have been patched again and again and always wear away. Did they just come in and put the new layer over the existing one? No, they had to first smooth out and correct the existing layer before they could add on. Otherwise the roads would still be flawed and uneven.

When we go through things in life that rough us up a little—or a lot—we cannot ignore the damage that's been done, move on to the next thing and just hope for the best. Get the lesson, do the repair work and prime the surface for the next phase. When we don't, it's no wonder the same bumps and holes show up again and again.

Our timing is always just right. Maybe we need to keep hitting the same potholes until we are absolutely certain we are tired of them? Until we have had one too many jolts and we say, *enough*! Until we see that putting a temporary patch over them is just that … temporary. Where are the potholes in your life? What keeps tripping you up? Don't worry, you will pave the way to a smoother future when you are good and ready to move on!

May 9   **Friendships and Plants**

About thirteen years ago I met a friend who needed a place to stay for a week or two and I was able to provide that for her. Her name was Barbara. I don't even remember her last name or where she was from, or where she was going. She was in my life for a very short time, but she left me with something that will always make me think of her. She called it a Friendship plant—said you can't kill it. With neglect, it will look dead but with some water and TLC, it will come back to life and grow again. When I'm taking really good care of it, it even blooms with pretty white flowers. I have watered it too much and not enough. I have seen it blossom with many shoots and flowers and I have seen all evidence of life completely gone. At times there has been nothing but a pot of dirt.

This parallel to friendship has been a powerful reminder to me all these years. When I give it just enough attention, it thrives. If I smother it, I lose it. And if I neglect a friendship, it withers to nothing. Yet, when I start giving my plant (or my friendship) the care it needs, it often bounces right back as if nothing happened. This particular plant opens its leaves in the daytime and leans toward the sun. In the evening, it closes itself up for the night. Ha! A friendship with boundaries! I am blessed to have friends in my life who will always be there, even in times when life happens and we lose touch. I find this true for all my relationships: parents, siblings, even my husband. A little "water and sunshine" can go a long way. Make a small effort today to nurture a relationship that matters. Watch how quickly you can breathe new life into it!

May 10   Challenge Your Inner "Scaredy Cat"

The cave you fear to enter holds the treasure you seek.
~ Joseph Campbell ~

In our present home, we are blessed to have two upper decks. The sundeck has no steps, so I let the indoor cats go out and get some fresh air in the mornings, while I sit with my outdoor cat, Lucky and my dog, Goldie on the covered deck that leads down to the lower level. My next to youngest cat, Harvey, wandered off at five months old and disappeared for eight days. Miraculously we got him back, but he has been a "scaredy cat" ever since. Harvey likes to go out on the sundeck—well he likes the idea of it. After a few minutes though, he is standing by the door crying to get back inside. Today I brought him outside with me to sit in my lap while I write. He knows he is safe in his mama's lap. Harvey is looking all around and sniffing in every direction. Big sniffs! The kind where his head moves up and down with each deep inhale as he ponders all the new inviting smells available to him. We are just a short distance from the deck he usually gets access to. The smells must be the same in both places, but because of his fear, Harvey hasn't been able to fully appreciate the sights, sounds and smells all around him while on the other deck.

How true is that for all of us? How often do fear and anxiety prevent us from fully experiencing what is right in front of us? Instead of avoiding people and circumstances altogether, find a way to surround yourself with extra security and see if you can start venturing out of your comfort zone. Say yes to an invite and commit to stay for at least an hour. Take yourself on an experimental outing, something you have always wanted to do, but you were afraid to try. Honor your inner "scaredy cat." Although there is probably a good explanation for the fear, take the fear out for small walks so you can gradually increase your territory and realm of experiences. Trust. Live. The whole world is waiting to be seen, tasted, smelled, heard, touched and enjoyed!

May 11   **Thankful for Ordinary**

Gratitude can transform common days into thanksgivings, turn routine jobs into joy, and change ordinary opportunities into blessings.
~ William Arthur Ward ~

What a beautiful, ordinary day! The sky is overcast and gray. Birds are zooming by. Neighbors are doing chores. My animals and I are hanging out on the deck, just happy to be present and observe. Nothing spectacular is going on, yet I feel overwhelming gratitude for a pretty good, ordinary day. I will probably take myself and Goldie for a walk, and then get into some chores myself. Am I breathing? Then yes, today is a gift. Do I have the use of some or all of my senses? Then yes, today is a gift. Do I have love in my heart for anyone or anything? Then yes, today is a gift. Even without fireworks, presents, vacations, promotions, birthdays, anniversaries, weddings, births or anything else out of the ordinary, look around and see just how spectacular every-day life really is. Embrace the rhythm of routine, offering the opportunity to experience extraordinary serenity and security. It's already yours!

May 12   **Affordable Nature Fix**

Lush tropical trees swaying in the breeze. The sound of a waterfall spilling into a pool. The rhythm of the tide coming in and going out. Thanks to technology and the local nursery, we can have any or all of these in our lives on a daily basis. Yesterday we returned our two palms to the deck after keeping them inside all winter. Greenery adds instant life to any space—even if it's not real! These palms, purchased from the local hardware nursery are dancing in the breeze. I love watching their swaying shadows just as much. The deck instantly feels cozier, has an added privacy and just feels ten times more alive! Soon we will bring the fountain back outside as well. The sound of running water is soothing and can offer an instant source of meditation and relaxation. I have a white noise machine on my wish list—the ones with the optional sounds of nature like the ocean tide. I am calmed just by the thought of falling asleep or relaxing to the gentle lull of the tide whenever I wish. Enhance your space with the sights and sounds of nature. A little bit can go a long way to dramatically alter your access to nature-inspired relaxation, inspiration and a sense of well-being.

May 13   Start Living NOW

It's only 10:15 a.m. and today has been alternately filled with blue skies, fluffy-clouds, and bright sun light, AND completely cloudy and overcast—twice over! Now it looks like the rest of the day will be cloudy, with storms pending. Life can change on a dime. Just because I wake up to a sunny day or vice versa, it can completely change at any time.

The father of one of my sons friend's had a sudden massive heart attack and died two days ago, out of the blue. He was only fifty-one. I bet when he woke up that Sunday morning, he didn't know it would be his last, and neither did his family. There is so much tragedy in life we will never understand. Today I am reminded that even a long life is short, and a life abruptly ended is even shorter.

This is not a dress rehearsal. We don't know what the future holds, but we do have our say in today. Are you living the life you want to live? Are you saying what needs to be said? A real-life—whatever that means—is bound to be better than a pretend life, no matter how good a pretend life appears to be. Be honest with yourself. Take inventory of your life, where you live and work. Who's in it? What if today is your last day? What if you had ten years left? Stop waiting for X and start living for WHY. I recently read an unknown quote, "Life has no remote. Get up and change it yourself!" If you don't know where to begin, find a book club, a walking buddy, or a twelve step group. Branch out and experiment. Say what you like. Say what you want. Be open to the package it shows up in. Maybe it will look different than you expected, but it could offer more than you ever hope for or dreamed of. For me, I am going to enjoy this sunny/cloudy/sunny day for as long as I can.

May 14   Obstacle or Opportunity

I am convinced that life is 10% what happens to
me and 90% how I react to it. And so it is
with you...we are in charge of our attitudes.
~ Charles R. Swindoll ~

This morning I mixed up my routine a bit. I'm writing outside on my sundeck, with my three indoor cats as they get their morning air. This deck is off the upper level of the back of my house, so I am further into my backyard and a bit closer to the trees. I just noticed one off in the distance in the neighbor's yard. The tree is completely gone on one side. The top is there, the right side is there but the left side is clearly gone. It was probably struck by lightning. The tree next to it is full all the way around, top to bottom. It makes me wonder, why that tree?

It doesn't matter what happens to us in this life, what matters most is how we handle it and what we do with what we have. And also, how we perceive what we have and don't have, and what we have lost. The damaged tree stands just as tall and proud as the one next to it. It's still a tree and possibly the tallest one. At a time when it could have shriveled and died, it used the extra root power to go up! Life is life. How we feel about our life determines our perception of reality, not reality itself. How great a life do you have? Pretty awesome? Yes, I thought so. Me too!

May 15   **Getting Unstuck**

Someday monkey grass will rule the world! It spreads and spreads. Extreme heat and drought won't kill it. It takes a short nap in the winter and wakes up in the spring, ready to gain more ground every year. I need to get a handle on our front beds where the monkey grass has grown beyond thick and beautiful, and is now crowding all my other shrubs. It is going to take a shovel to accomplish the task and tame the monkey! I haven't mustered up the energy yet to get the shovel out and do the job right, but every so often, I will get in there and pull up a few wanderers. I know I'm not even making a dent in the problem, but it feels good to get my hands in the dirt and make a little effort. Until I get the motivation to do more, that's all I can do.

We have to stay stuck until we're good and ready to get unstuck. When we're done playing around with a problem, we'll solve it. We already know what we need to do and we can accept we are right where we're supposed to be, getting the lesson and building up the necessary drive to take action. Pretty soon we'll do it, and wonder why we waited so long! Usually, it's not as big of an issue as we made it out to be in our minds (and in our procrastination).

Make a list of what you're avoiding. Congratulations! Awareness and acknowledgment are the first steps. You are now on your way to getting it done! At some point, you'll starting thinking about how nice it will feel to just do it, and be free of the mounting pressure hanging over your head. (How many times have you carried tasks over from one to-do list to the next, and the next? Ugh! Me too!) When the payoff for avoidance and staying comfortable becomes overshadowed by the payoff for getting it done, the scales tip and suddenly you have more motivation to be unstuck than stuck. You will do what is necessary to feel better and improve your situation, enjoying a sense of accomplishment for finally taking action. No one can tell you when it's time. YOU are in the driver's seat. It's your life. You've got this!

May 16   Challenging Procrastination

Procrastination is the bad habit of putting off
until the day after tomorrow what should
have been done the day before yesterday.
~ Napoleon Hill ~

It's more difficult to start something than to stop it, and it's easier to continue something you have already begun, than start it from scratch. If I want to go on a walk, I have to decide to go on a walk, get dressed, put my shoes on and get the dog ready. Getting out the door is sometimes the hardest part! Once I'm already walking, I'm happy.

I have wanted to clean out my closet now that fall is here. The task seems way too daunting, way too big! I know once I make a decision to take that first step toward beginning the process, and then actually do it, all of a sudden, energy is in motion and the hurdle of starting has been overcome. Now I'm committed. I've started and it is so much easier to continue. One of Newton's laws of motion explains that once an object is in motion, it will stay in motion. Today I'm going to start by grabbing five summer tops and taking them to my spare closet. We'll see what happens after that!

What are you procrastinating about? Remember, it just comes down to making a decision and then taking the first action. Thankfully, you don't have to come up with enough energy and drive to complete the whole project! You just need enough momentum to start, and magically your perspective will change. It may help to set a time limit. Tell yourself you are going to give fifteen minutes to the project today to get it started. Often once I start, after fifteen minutes, I find I'm ready to give more. Make a decision and get going! The fulfillment of finally starting something you have put off far outweighs the self-created agony of postponement. You got this! Go ahead—I'll time you!

May 17   Renewed by Rain

What a perfect, beautiful, lazy, day to enjoy from my covered deck. It has been raining since yesterday—a soft, gentle rain with an abundance of soothing sounds. I hear the steady, hypnotic sound of raindrops falling, water rushing through the drain spouts and gutters, and cars driving by, splashing through puddles. Visually, the grass and trees seem to be getting greener by the minute! It feels like the earth is getting a bath—a huge drink of water. Replenishment. Renewal. Rebirth. Feels like a time out, and I'm letting the moment wash all over me too. My slate is clean. My soul is at peace. My heart is pure—full of love and empty of resentments. This moment is absolutely perfect. A place of harmony to recall again and again. In turn, I will share the love and peace I've been gifted with as I put down my pen and pick back up with my life and relationships. I am grateful and serene.

May 18   Stop Should-ing On Yourself

Nature has an inherent system of order. A natural flow. A nature flow! Wow. Light-bulb moment! It never occurred to me that the word 'natural' came from 'nature,' though it clearly makes sense. I long to experience a daily routine that feels as natural as the flow outside my window. I wrestle with the perfect flow instead. Perfect even sounds rigid and binding. I'm making progress and learning to trade in the "I should's" and instead, ask myself, *In this moment, what do I really want to do?* I usually have an answer immediately. The answer is there all along, but the should voice keeps muddying things up. Granted, sometimes what I want to do isn't always what I need to do, but my adult self can determine that. When I can mediate a balance between my wants and needs, and discern if there is any validity in the should voice, I can tap into my own natural flow and restore order and serenity.

May 19   Appreciating Mystery and Uncertainty

The true mystery of the world
is the visible, not the invisible.
~ Oscar Wilde ~

I feel a great sense of wonder and intrigue when the world is foggy outside. Mystery awaits! From a photographer's standpoint, country roads, hills, and pastures beg to be discovered in this mystical state of beauty. It's kind of like magic—we know there is a logical conclusion for not being able to see everything clearly (if at all), but it's fun to play along. Like a beautiful woman in a bathing suit, versus the beautiful woman in a bathing suit wrapped in a sheer cover-up—the hint of beauty is even more tantalizing. Adding to my excitement is the impermanence of the fog. If I wait two hours, it will all be gone, and all the mystery will be lifted. Everything will look normal again.

We crave the unexpected. We need a fair amount of uncertainty. How boring would life be if everything was predictable? Appreciate the suspended moments in time when you don't know what's going to happen or how things are going to turn out. Will you get the job? Is the house going to sell? Is it a boy or a girl? Is he or she *the one*? Relish the suspense. Learn to surrender the outcome and enjoy the moment. What is real right now? Enjoy that. I am going to jump in my car with my camera and chase the fog! See what I can see, and enjoy it while it lasts!

May 20   **Intentions and Boundaries**

Work when you're working and play when you are playing. If you're lucky, work is play! I am parked in a place I call, Foggy Cove, though it is not foggy today. The sun is shining, birds are singing and I even got to feed one duck. I asked him to go get some friends, because I have a whole stack of old buns, but he was swimming solo today. That duck isn't thinking about checking his e-mail so why should I? Many days I feel like I work all day simply because I stay plugged into my e-mail and attached to my phone every waking moment.

Today I'm experimenting with some new time and activity boundaries. Part of my day is dedicated to spiritual, emotional and physical health. When I'm in "growth and restoration mode," I will not check an email or answer my phone. True emergencies aside, most things can wait an hour or more. I'm going to clearly identify the work I intend to accomplish today, and set aside distractions to get it done. Most people have a "quitting time." That is a little trickier for those of us who work for ourselves. Often I feel compelled to always do one more thing. Even if I don't, I have a difficult time truly embracing "free time" (i.e. rest or recreation). I have known for a long time, intention and balance are the keys for me to live an amazing life. Awareness and maintaining a consciousness towards change does eventually bring about change. What I think about, I bring about. Today my intentions have manifested some small steps toward living my ideal day. Any progress at all is ... progress! I am shifting gears now. What are you going to do today, *intentionally?*

May 21   **Worry for Nothing**

Whenever I feel anxious or otherwise "off" on the inside, I can step back, or look outside and immerse myself in the calm, routine order happening in the world of nature. I might as well surrender my day, and this moment. My worrying cannot change anything. My life and this single day are going to unfold however they will unfold, regardless of how much I worry about how things are going to work out.

Take a deep breath. Breathe in the calm. Blow out the fear. Enjoy several deep breaths tell yourself uplifting and encouraging words. *I am at peace. I am surrounded by peace. I am cared for and loved. I let go of outcomes, and for this moment, I embrace the belief that I will experience exactly what I need, in the exact right timing.* Have a wonderful, worry-free day!

May 22   **Make Yourself Have Fun**

Nature is the host for many fun events. How much fun are you having lately? Do you even remember what you like to do for fun? Has your internal sense to be productive driven you so hard that your "fun quotient" is nonexistent? Can you even remember the last time you did something just for fun? Or maybe you only "have fun" one or two times a year? You call it an "official" outing and it's a really big deal. Come on—you deserve and need fun much more often than that!

Make a list right now of some fun activities that are available to you. In my area, I can canoe, hike, bike ride, go to the park, go bowling, have a picnic at the park, go zip lining, do cave exploring, go fishing, venture out on the lake with friends, have a campfire, play horseshoes, corn hole, or bocce ball, have a barbecue, go to a craft fair, or maybe a music fest. If these are the things on your list that you enjoy, it's time to do them more often. Fire the internal boss for the day and call in "WELL!" Set aside the time to go have some fun. You deserve it!

May 23   **When It's Safe to Shout** *Woo Hoo!*

This morning, I came out on the deck to journal and read, and receive my daily inspiration to share in this book. It's hard to receive guidance and be inspired when my mind is full of chatter. Sometimes it's very difficult for me to wipe the slate clean and leave my mind open to new ideas. To create focus, I decided to stare at a tree and think only of that tree. I saw the top branches lightly swaying in the breeze. There's not a lot of support at the top, but still, it doesn't topple over. Because the foundation is so secure, the top is free to sway any way the wind blows. It reminds me of a crowd cheering with their hands up in the air, waving *Woo Hoo*! Maybe that's what the top of the tree is shouting? It's safe to be a little crazy up there, because of all the support secured by the roots.

I imagine a kid sitting on top of their parent's shoulders, also yelling *Woo Hoo*! They can wave their arms, shout and feel safe while their parent has hold of them and won't let them fall. That's my child-self and adult-self working together. What a perfect balance between letting go (having some fun) while staying firmly grounded. Today I will be sure to look for the moment I can let go and shout, *Woo hoo*! knowing I am safe and secure in perfect balance between my wise adult-self and my fun-loving, spirited child.

May 24   **Morning Medicine**

Good morning, world! I am up and out on the deck early today. I love the quiet, undisturbed morning energy, with the undercurrent of a brand-new day bubbling up to the surface. Birds are in full song. Grass is glazed over with dew. At this moment, my day can be anything I want it to be. I may not be able to control everything that happens, and I may have appointments, work and other prior commitments demanding my time, but I'm in charge of how I feel about it. If I start my day with inspiration, meditation and quiet contemplation, I'm able to set the tone for the rest of my day. A state of wonder, peace and gratitude is a great place to begin! I hope you're taking your morning medicine every day too! (When I skip a day, I can usually tell.) Imagine if we all did this? When enough people start a daily practice of *Finding the Gift*, together we will build a kinder, more inspired world.

May 25   The Right Vehicle Makes the Difference

Yesterday, I attempted to take my first power walk since having my knee surgery about two and a half months ago. I realized about six minutes into it, I was not ready for fast walking yet, and had to limp back home. I had worked up to a ten-minute elliptical workout during physical therapy, and really thought I was ready to take things to the next level. I still felt restless and in need of physical exertion (a great, natural stress-reliever), so I headed to the gym instead. While six minutes of walking was too much for my knee, I was thrilled to be able to go thirty-six minutes on the elliptical machine. I was ready for more—I just needed to change "vehicles" to get there.

Are you where you want to be in your life, or are you at least headed in the right direction? What vehicle are you using to get there? Are you limping your way, or flying? If I wanted to go to Europe from the US, the best car in the world would still be the wrong vehicle. Look at your life and where you say you want to go. Be honest— if you keep doing what you're doing, will you get there? In this lifetime? Are you enjoying the ride or is it painful and slow? Take an honest assessment of the road you're on and the vehicles you're using to reach your goals.

What is going well and what needs to change? What could you *start* doing? What could you *stop* doing? It's always a good idea to take time out to look at the map of your life, see where you're at, and what you'll need for the next leg of the journey. Be willing to change vehicles when necessary, and don't be afraid to stop and ask for directions if you start to feel lost. Bon voyage!

May 26   Music Makes it Better

Life seems to go on without
effort when I am filled with music."
~ George Eliot ~

It feels so good to finally get back in the gym after my knee surgery. My body craves movement, physical exertion and release. Years ago, I got away from listening to upbeat music during my workouts, and started reading books or listening to audio affirmations instead. Recently I brought my iPod in and played one of my son's party mixes during an elliptical workout. I brought a lot more energy to that workout, because of what I was listening to! The pounding beat fueled me to a much greater level of exertion. Thirty minutes were going to pass either way, but I packed more in that time period than in one hour of using the same equipment, while reading a book. And when the time was up, I kept going! I wanted more!

I wondered how I could use music in other areas of my life to increase my performance and my level of enthusiastic participation. Music is one of many treats for my spirit. It can add life and energy to a room. It can instantly change the mood, the ambience, the vibe of the moment. When I need to raise my energy, or if I need to relax, I can create a playlist to help me do that. Music is a resource available to most of us. Let it take you where you need to go, and help you get there faster.

This year, the weather has had a hard time deciding to transition from winter to spring, with summer nowhere in sight. While last May, we were thrust into early summer with record highs, this year is very different. For every nice spring day, we've had two to four really cold winter days, and of course plenty of rain. When the time is right, we will have a lasting transition to summer, but no one can rush the seasons. It will happen naturally, as nature runs its course.

Have you ever tried to force a life decision? You believe intellectually it's in your best interest, based on what you think will happen, but you're torn because your heart says, *No!* or *Not now!* I knew a young couple in love who decided they should break up because change was imminent in both of their lives, which *might* cause them to break up. They were so afraid of a breakup happening in the future that they were going to go ahead and break up *now* (and hurt now) to prevent the possibility of hurting later.

Making decisions based on fear or worry is usually not our best thinking. Life has a way of letting us know when it's time to make a change, either internally or circumstantially. Maybe we're no longer in love with our significant other, our job or something about our life anymore? Maybe we're restless, unsettled, unfulfilled and we feel an unexplainable urge to go in a different direction? To the other extreme, some of us may prolong taking any action until we have the whole script written, and we have it all worked out to the last detail. Life could happen the way we plan, but more often than not, we will have to take action without knowing how it's all going to work out. Trust your gut and follow your intuition. Stop overthinking and over analyzing your life. (Ouch, I'm really preaching to myself on that one!) Don't let fear and worry force premature change. Keep putting one foot in front of the other, until clarity comes. Just walk it out. Make plans, but also allow for them to change. Quit torturing yourself with worries and what if's. All the answers will appear when it's time. Enjoy the good times, especially when they're still good!

May 28   Bounce to Your Own Beat

Have you ever noticed how someone wearing earphones is clearly on a different wavelength than you are? You can be side-by-side in the same room, but be miles apart, having two very different experiences. I have been on both sides of that situation. When I observe someone using headphones, I may witness an extra bounce in their step, intense focus, or an easy smile as they bob their head to their rhythm of choice. Sometimes I'm guilty of judging their free expression or find myself thinking they're weird, but it's because I don't hear what they are hearing, so their actions seem out of place. When I'm the person listening to great music no one else can hear, I don't care what anyone thinks! I might even walk with a little more sass in my step because I'm loving my music and I know they are missing out. My passion supersedes my need to conform and seek approval.

How true is this in life? Maybe we have a dream our families and friends think is weird? They can't see what we see or hear we hear, so of course they don't get it! Surround yourself with people who do! Keep bouncing to your own rhythm and you will attract others in your life who like the same music. Be true to you and the support will come. Whichever side of the music you find yourself on today, celebrate diversity. Celebrate that we all march to different drums and that makes the world a much more interesting place! Turn it up when you hear your favorite song and let the music play!

Human nature makes us wish for what we don't have. Women with natural curly hair would give anything for straight hair, and women with straight hair think it would be amazing to have curls they didn't have to work for. Some men may look at each other and think, *I could be more confident, rich, and good-looking if I had his life, his wife and his money.* (For the record, judging someone else's outside by your insides is never an accurate assessment. They may feel just like you on the inside, and think the same things about you and your life—but that's another topic.)

We pray for the warm sun to come back after multiple rainy days and when it does, we may soon complain about the heat. I've been waiting and anticipating the return of warmer weather for so long, and now that it's here, I have already caught myself thinking, *Wow—it's HOT! Can we dial it back down a little?* In every moment, we're living a dream life—a moment someone prayed for. Change will come soon enough and you may wish this day was here again. Age, health and weight are perfect examples. Were we satisfied with how we looked and felt ten years ago? Maybe, maybe not. Many of us probably wished for more and better back then too. And ten years from now, we will wish we were back in today, with this body, at this age, with our current level of mobility and health. In everything, be grateful. Celebrate the uniqueness of today. Focus on what's good about it. Think back to a time when you wished and prayed for what you do have today—when you would have been so thrilled to achieve it. Congratulations! You did it! The goal isn't to have everything we want, but to want everything we have. Think of five things you have today that you didn't have in the past, but hoped someday you would. A spouse? No spouse? More money? Less stress?

More clarity? Self peace? Acceptance? Find the gifts—they're all around you!

May 30   **The Greatest Show on Earth**

Get outside. Watch the sunrise.
Watch the sunset. How does that make you feel?
Does it make you feel big or tiny? Because
there's something good about feeling both.
~ Amy Grant ~

A choir of birds woke me up at 5:10 a.m. this morning. I tossed and turned for a while until it became clear my mind would not settle back down, so I decided I might as well get up to see the sunrise. I crept outside, armed with my writer's tools and sat down expectantly. I'm so glad I did! I feel like the first person to arrive at a concert. I've got a front row seat and I'm waiting for the show to begin. The preshow is already fabulous: birds are singing loudly, and a ribbon of fog dances across the grass and through the trees. The sky is beginning to turn amber along the horizon, where any minute, the star of the show will appear! I just changed seats to get a better angle.

It's funny to think this "show" happens every day. It's free, but many of us sleep right through it or don't bother to watch. Magic fills the air and I wonder why I've waited so long since the last time I watched a sunrise. I am grateful in this moment and my eyes are deadlocked on the sky, waiting for the sun. It's going to come up right behind my neighbor's house. The clouds are illuminated with light from the glow. Here it comes! Here it comes! Imagine facing every day just as expectantly? We have a front row seat to the greatest show on earth—our lives. Every detail has been carefully woven in to make it a must-see event. Every day, new puzzle pieces fall into place. Are you watching? Life isn't always a sunrise moment, though, because stories have to build.

The characters rise and fall, and rise again. Wake up, get a front-row seat and be ready for your life. It's already great!

May 31   **Find the Flow**

A few days ago, my husband and I returned from an exhilarating conference, where we met the team of people and fellow travelers embarking with us on our next journey of growth and purpose. We received much insight and clarity, and came home excited about where we are headed. A day of airports and travel can leave me restless and needing a release, so after unpacking I decided to take my dog for a walk. About ten minutes into our walk, my breathing was in sync again, my serenity had returned, and I felt grounded again. I looked up and realized I was walking in step to the movement of the clouds! As I moved, the heavens were moving with me.

Have you ever felt that feeling, where all the stars are aligned and you are truly in the flow? Where everything is going your way, doors open, help appears, resources are abundant and the whole world is saying, *Yes* to you?

In that moment, I felt that Heaven was going to meet me every step of the way. I didn't even feel like I was walking anymore, I was gliding and being carried along by the clouds. Life is meant to be lived in sync with who you are and what you're passionate about.

Be honest—are you in the flow or trying to swim against the current? Somewhere inside, you know the truth. Let that voice get louder and carry you downstream with greater ease.

June

There is a guidance for each of us, and by lowly listening we shall hear the right word ... Place yourself in the middle of the stream of power and wisdom which flows into your life. Then, without effort, you are impelled to truth and to perfect contentment.

~ Ralph Waldo Emerson

June 1   **Surfing Lessons: Part One**

After watching a movie last night about a surfer, I saw distinct correlations with how we live. Life is the ocean, the waves are challenges, and I'm the surfer. Sometimes the ocean (life) is very calm—we all need cyclical reprieves to allow us to rest and grow into the next set of waves. However, if things were calm and unchanging all the time, I would likely get bored from a lack of stimulation and challenge. Yes, thankfully the waves bring variation, surprise and excitement—we couldn't surf without them, and living would be terribly uneventful without change and challenges to keep things interesting.

My time surfing will be fun and rewarding, provided I have a good board (solid foundation, fine-tuned coping tools, and self-awareness), as well as a coachable attitude and an adventurous spirit. If I'm trying to surf on a heavy suitcase full of (emotional) baggage, I'm going to sink every time. When the really big waves come, I'll have a better chance of staying upright, as long as I'm standing on the right surface. Self-confidence, love, acceptance and forgiveness help me stand. Resentment, fear and negativity pull me down. With a firm foundation, chaotic waves don't have to knock me over. If we strive to build a life where we can maintain solid footing, regardless of what's happening around us, we will enjoy excitement, fun, peace, challenge, inspiration, and growth. Personally, I aspire to spend my time sailing across the ocean rather than wiping out and drinking salt water on a regular basis. I've done enough of that! Cheers to us gliding through our day today, cutting in and out of the waves, and having a blast!

June 2   Surfing Lessons Part Two: Coachability

Be coachable! Using the surfing example, if you find yourself going under a lot or just not getting the smooth ride you want, be open to someone who is further down the path than you. The real test of an open mind is listening to other possibilities, even when things already seem to be working just fine. If someone tells you about a new idea, or method, or activity, is it in your nature to automatically shoot it down just because you've never heard of it? That sure has described me a lot, but I'm working to be more open-minded. Remember the saying, "If it ain't broke—don't fix it!" Well guess what, sometimes it isn't broken, but it could be better and we just don't know it, or are not willing to admit it. The point is to be open to ideas and suggestions from others—to listen and learn from someone else who's been there and found an alternative. We don't have to act on every idea that comes our way, but begin the habit of changing from, "Nah—that won't work," to "Wow—I wonder if there *could* be a better way?" and "Hmmm, maybe I'll look into that." Our minds are like parachutes—they work better when they're open! Find one new idea to entertain today, and aim to stretch your mind and your world just a little more every day!

June 3   Personal Growth—A Worthy Experiment

My son was conducting an experiment for school using a big block of ice. With the faucet running as hot as possible, he watched as the water burrowed a hole straight through the ice, while the rest of the block remained frozen. The heat didn't spread all around and melt the whole block as he expected.

I see the hot water as the road for personal transformation and growth. It's always available, but I have to go to it and be open to change. We each have to do our own work; I'm not able to do it for someone else. It's possible for me to have a breakthrough, change from frozen to fluid, while the people closest to me stay unchanged (frozen).

Another interesting thing I noticed about my son's experiment was that the size of the hole made by the water was about twice as large as the actual stream driving through the block of ice, meaning the reach was wider than the initial contact. It's true—those closest to us will likely be touched in some way by our growth (even if it's just because we're easier to be around!). I may inspire someone to grow and change with me, or I might find the relationship changes as I shift into a new place and the other person stays where they were. That may feel like a loss, and rightfully so, but if I really want to keep growing, I may need to seek out other people who also have a burning desire to be the whole, authentic person they were created to be.

Are you with the right crowd—people who have what you want? (I'm not speaking of possessions.) People who are living their lives in a way you aspire to? Or those who can at least support your personal endeavors? We can't change people who don't want to change, but they may decide to pursue their own growth at a later time that's more right for them. Unfortunately, some of the family and friends closest to us may have a hard time accepting the new us, and may try to sabotage our growth so everything can stay the same in the relationship. Living life frozen may not seem great to them, but it is familiar.

You have to know what you know, and know what you want. Listen and trust your inner guidance. I don't know of anything worth having that didn't offer tough challenges and choices along the way. Go through your transformations and trust that when you come out on the other side, things may be different, but they will be even better than you could have imagined. The people meant to support you and/or grow with you will be there, cheering you on!

June 4   Adequate Sleep—Optimum Performance

Sleep is the best meditation.
~ Dalai Lama ~

The idea of sleep has always fascinated me. We are designed so magnificently, for instance if we cut ourselves, we heal automatically. When we eat, food goes in, nutrients are used and waste comes out. Why, then, were we created with a glitch in our endurance that requires us to lie down and lose consciousness for nearly a third of our day? Practically 33% of our lives are spent asleep, allowing us the means to recharge, much like a battery. I feel certain we could have been created to never need rest.

How many of us would buy a mobile phone that has to spend a third of the time on the charger? Or any device that has to charge eight hours in order to run for sixteen hours? And yet, possibly the most sophisticated creation of all time—the human body—was built needing significant downtime. Even in the sixteen hours awake, part of that time is needed to unwind, relax, and take it easy. The point is this: rest and restoration are critical to a high-functioning and satisfying life.

Are you following your manufacturer's guidelines for optimum performance? How many of you ignore the warning signs (like mounting stress, frequent illness, and daily fatigue) alerting you that you only have 15% battery left, 10%, 5%, and then you crash? Most devices now don't recommend a complete drain of the battery before re-charging, and we certainly function better without letting ourselves get too low. Watch for the low battery indicators on a daily basis, and you can have a long life!

I am not a teacher, but an awakener.
~ Robert Frost ~

If you aren't asleep (dead), but you aren't awake (alive), what are you? Comfortable. Average. Mediocre. As good as it gets mentality. Tolerant. *A significant portion of the population.* I have been working to be a better "me" since my teens. At seventeen, I knew I didn't want to live like a drone or be a slave to anything. Maybe even earlier, because at age nine I resolved to live a life very different than the way my parents lived. I would never divorce. I would never live paycheck to paycheck. I had my first job at eleven, delivering fliers door-to-door for $25 a week. That was big money at the time! I worked fifty hours a week between two jobs at the age of fifteen, while maintaining a 4.0 grade point average.

I have had a fire burning inside me for as long as I can remember, pushing me for more. For better. For all that is possible. I made plenty of mistakes! I have been married to Mr. Right, Mr. Wrong and Mr. Right at the wrong time! I have been a workaholic and a do-aholic! I have often neglected myself and my spiritual needs. Through it all, I have grown in awareness. I have learned from some mistakes, but others? Well, I had to practice them a few more times to get the lessons they offered. I am nowhere near where I'm going to be, yet I am miles from where I began. The fire continues to burn strong! I am awake! I am trying to wake up my neighbors—my friends, my community, my world. You *can* have more. Things *can* be better! Everything is possible! Are you willing to get uncomfortable to truly taste all of life's gifts? To die, knowing you really LIVED? I am. Come join me. There's always room for one more!

June 6   Cats Make Better Teachers Than Students

Look deep into nature, and then you
will understand everything better.
~ **Albert Einstein** ~

Cats have no worries, so why should I? They trust their needs will be provided for in a timely manner, and I trust that mine will too. Although that may be an oversimplification, I can look back in hindsight and say without a doubt, my needs have always been met at just the right time. Don't get me wrong, I usually have other ideas about when and how those needs should be met, but eventually, I see why things played out the way they did.

As they say, hindsight is always 20/20 and insight is great, but I think it's important to take that a step further. I believe it's beneficial to look in the rearview mirror and express gratitude for the trials, because of where they brought us. Of course, with situations like a serious illness, tragedy or death, these things will always remain a mystery and for those times, I choose to trust I'll be gently guided to a better place, even if I never fully understand why something bad had to happen.

We can learn a lot from observing our feline friends. My cats really know how to rest and relax, how to have fun, and how to enjoy mystery and play. Just to broaden their horizons, I tried to teach them some of my own philosophies a while back. I showed them about over-achievement through high stress, that being serious is more admirable than being silly, why it's important to figure everything out as fast as possible, how rest is for sissies, and to strive to burn both ends of the candle to the point they forget what fun would even feel like. Strangely enough, my cats weren't interested in learning these new tricks and apparently, are quite content remaining the teachers. Thankfully, after years of missing the secrets of life they've been trying to show me, I'm finally becoming a better student of them. If you don't have a cat of your own to teach you these things, my husband will gladly offer you one of ours (but he's not serious).

June 7   Accepting Winds of Change

This morning, the wind is playing hide-and-seek. Still, without a sound, and then a gentle rustle of the leaves. Still again, and then a mighty rush, twisting the leaves in all directions, causing the treetops to sway. In this dance, the wind makes me think of change. Sometimes it's so subtle, I don't even realize it's happening until one day, circumstances seem to have shifted, seemingly overnight. The wait is over and a new phase of life begins. Other times, the winds of change spin me in all different directions and I hang on for dear life, waiting to see where I'll end up. In those moments, there's no denying that something big is about to give way, and I long for the peace on the other side of the forceful wind.

How foolish and futile would it be for a leaf to attempt to resist the wind? To decide it's more powerful, in control, and unwilling to be moved, even though every other leaf on the tree dances with joyful surrender? When I think I'm better or worse than others (i.e. *special,* whether from arrogance or self-pity), I create a block to my inherent need to belong. I am not unlike everyone else, and insisting that I'm unique and immune to the forces of nature and life only serves to create distance from, rather than community with, my peers. Today I want to blend in, participate, and run carefree with the wind, accepting my place in the dance of life.

Sitting here with the ability to see all sides of the wind, I recognize the beauty in each transition. I appreciate the sounds of each phase with complete stillness and silence. A gentle rustle starting softly, climaxing, and then returning to silence. And the powerful sound of wind rattling every last leaf on the tree. Life offers variety for beauty, for unpredictability, for adventure, for growth and to instill gratitude. What good would memories be if they were all the same? Live and let live.

June 8   Seize the Moment

How can it possibly be sunny, with fluffy clouds to my left and yet, to my right I see dark, ugly clouds threatening rain? I've probably seen this before, though not very often. It's surreal—like standing in the middle of two very contrasting possibilities. Perhaps it's a reminder to seize the moment and be grateful. To enjoy the sunny, blue skies without depending on their permanency for my well-being. And to know if it starts storming, it's only temporary.

Maybe it's also a rare opportunity to see both ends of a cycle, a bird's eye view providing perspective on the impermanence of things, and the guarantee of change. In life, expansion and contraction are constantly in motion. Opportunities open up, and doors close. Relationships begin and end. As a baby is born, another soul is laid to rest. Spring and fall are very different seasons, in nature and in life.

Mindfulness reminds all of us to slow down, pause, and become aware of everything exactly as it is in this very moment. There will not be another one like it, and without intention, we can miss it. Gratitude tells us to give thanks for whatever we find when we take time to observe our life. Can you identify something wonderful—inside you or around you—right now, right here, even as you read this? What if we could all see things, not as good or bad, but simply here and now, and when that changes, we accept the next gift life offers (even if it's disguised inside an obstacle)? If we viewed everything we experienced without judgment, how freeing would that feel? Today, I hope you have a wonderful moment, and then go ahead, have another one!

In the midst of upheaval and uncertainty, I can always count on the soothing sounds of my backyard to woo me back to center. This morning I had the unusual opportunity to observe a fly up close. Its wings were surprisingly beautiful with intricate markings, fluorescent when the sun reflected on them just right, and they provided rapid speed for escape when I ventured too close. I've never considered a fly to be beautiful before, or worth a second glance, but I'm reminded every creature and every person are beautiful and interesting in their own way.

Not long ago, I watched an interview with acclaimed actor, Dustin Hoffman, regarding his experience becoming a woman for the movie *Tootsie*. He wanted them to make him up as a beautiful woman but was told they already did the best they could do. He knew what an interesting person he was on the inside, beneath the wig and the dress, and tearfully, he expressed a profound sadness, realizing how many interesting women he personally had missed getting to know, simply because they didn't measure up to society's standard of female beauty.

We are so much more than our external package. We're all uniquely beautiful and interesting in more ways than we each realize, and we've been given everything we need to thrive. Today, thank your strong body, your able heart, and your wise mind for carrying you through each day. Exercise your unique thoughts and talents to reveal your true worth and create lasting impact. (Contact me at www.findingthegift.com to learn more about The Body Project, the most evidenced-based body image program available, impacting more than 200,000 lives so far.)

June 10   **Turn Your Chair**

My patio furniture had gotten moved around so I randomly moved the chairs back to the general area where they belonged, but I didn't really pay attention to which direction my seat was facing. When I sat down this morning, I looked up and saw a beautiful, red-leafed tree in my neighbor's yard. I don't ever remember seeing it before! It was peacefully waving in the wind, cheerfully saying hello! I stared in utter amazement. How could I have never noticed this beautiful red tree, especially among all the green surrounding it? My chair was simply turned about seventy degrees to the left.

How many times do I miss the beauty and wonder this world has to offer by focusing on the familiar, by doing the same things over and over in the same manner, and by remaining in my comfort zone? My life has often consisted of extreme behavior and thinking: all or nothing, black or white, good or bad. Today I don't have to do a 180 or make a complete turnaround to alter my experience. A gentle turn can offer a different point of view, while staying grounded within. Open your eyes! Turn your chair! See, and say, W*ow*!

June 11   **It's Closer Than You Think**

This morning I'm struck by a curiously small gap in the thick line of trees that surround my backyard. Just a tiny patch that promises a clearing, before encountering even more trees in the distance behind it. I recently walked with my son beyond the trees to finally see for myself what it was like back there. When I moved in six years ago, I was told there was a creek not too far into the woods. My son explored it right away, and found it to be a favorite destination of the other neighborhood boys. Loaded with snacks and drinks, they always took a break in their favorite spot overlooking the water. I wanted to see this creek for myself but I was put off by the thick brush I would have to navigate to get there. Fear of poison ivy, scratchy branches, bug bites and the unknown added to my resistance to take the short journey.

Earlier this spring, while the foliage was minimal, I decided it was finally time for me to dare to go beyond my tree line and go on an adventure with my son. He led me in and out, over and under and around numerous trees, twigs, and wayward limbs. My trepidation gave way to anticipation and excitement! We navigated the last of the brush and came to a beautiful clearing with rolling hills and a peaceful stream. My first thought was, *I've been praying for and dreaming about a house on the water and I've had it all along!* The creek was much more than the trickle I had expected. We sat down in my son's favorite spot and ate our peanut butter and jelly sandwiches, which he had thoughtfully made for us. My eyes feasted on my surroundings. I marveled that this was right in my own backyard and I never knew the beauty that lay just beyond the brush and the comfortable familiar tree line I had accepted as *far enough.* Venture out! Take risks! Dare to dream! You may be closer than you think.

June 12   **Fleeting Moments**

I stepped onto my deck this afternoon to show my son the clearing I noticed the morning before, which brought back sweet memories and the promise that our next great adventure was waiting for us. The clearing was gone, disappeared, out of sight! I strained my eyes to look through the immediate trees just before me. Nothing. All I could see were branches and leaves—no clearing. I looked to the left at my neighbor's red-leafed tree, which had grabbed my attention, as it danced and waved in the wind. Now it was still, barely visible, and the branches close to the trunk bore no leaves and seemed almost dead. I was puzzled by each view, and gave thanks for the moments of brilliance each had blessed me with. I felt so happy to have been able to see the red-leafed tree and the clearing illuminated in a different light, which made it stand out for a brief time. I felt grateful that on my heart-filled path, I do see fleeting moments of beauty, which in the past I would have missed. Stop to appreciate what you have when you have it.

June 13   Know What I Know

Rushing to my deck this morning, I immediately looked for the clearing again. Right before me, it dazzled in the sun just like the first time I saw it. I looked to the left for the red-leafed tree. Glistening in the morning sun, beautiful and full of life, the tree gently waved at me once more. Sometimes I guess we just need to have the right light to see something. Maybe the light is circumstantial? Maybe it's an expectant attitude, a positive outlook? Some days, perhaps the light is just right and our vision depends on how open our eyes are, and which direction they're looking.

I gained another piece of insight this morning regarding trust and "knowing what I know." When I've seen or experienced goodness, and one day it disappears from sight, I can trust it will return. Also, I need to have faith when I experience something to be true, but for some reason the truth becomes hidden momentarily. (In this case, it was the difference of afternoon, versus morning sunlight.) Know what I know. Stop asking myself if I'm crazy, and doubting the truth. Trust that once again the truth will be revealed. Keep looking forward. A man once said, "The truth shall set you free." Wise man.

June 14   Two-Mile Long To-Do List

Overwhelmed by anxiety and a two-mile long to-do list, I stepped outside to take refuge in the rhythmic sights and sounds all around me, and immediately my worries started to lessen. The morning is full of activity: chattering squirrels hopping from tree to tree looking for breakfast; various birds singing a medley of songs; and the sun is rising to shine on us all.

My cares are put into perspective as I'm reminded the sun goes up and the sun goes down, and I can only do so much in the time between. I have to balance the human doing with the human being, or all my joy is overshadowed by tasks. Tomorrow will be here soon enough, and I'll have the same opportunity to cross a few more things off my list.

Lately, I've tried changing my language to feel more empowered, and it works! I'm giving myself less should's and have to's, and more wants. What do I want to do today? I could say, *I have to* ... but the truth is, I choose my life and I choose what I do each day. Even if it's something I really don't want to do, I'm choosing to do that over the consequences of choosing not to do that. Right now, get quiet and discern what your wants and priorities truly are. Breathe. Relax. Everything else can wait!

June 15   Removing Dead Branches

As a teenager, I was first introduced to the Twelve Steps of Overeaters Anonymous, while pursuing recovery from anorexia and bulimia. (OA welcomes all forms of eating disorders.) Along with the physical and mental health treatment I received, I found step work to be immensely helpful. In addition to working through my eating disorder, the steps also helped with how I functioned in life, and why I developed a problem with food in the first place. Today's entry reminds me of steps six and seven, where we are required to look at our personal shortcomings, also known as character defects, and ask for them to be removed. Much like "pruning!"

Several neighbors have recently trimmed or cut down trees that have died, or grown too large so close to their homes. In my backyard this morning, I noticed one of my favorite trees has some dead limbs, and that if it decided to fall my way, it would destroy my deck and damage my home. Additionally, my next-door neighbors have a Bradford pear tree between our houses, which they planted many years ago. While I greatly appreciate its beauty through the seasons and the privacy it provides, it has grown to be a massive tree, fifteen to twenty feet higher than my roof, and only ten feet from my house. If a storm were to take it down, or if age or health became a problem and it fell, this tree could damage my house as well.

These large trees have transitioned from being purely beneficial—offering shade, beauty, and privacy—to being somewhat of a threat to my home and thus, my well-being. Much like the survival skills I initially developed to navigate a chaotic childhood, these traits are more often a detriment to me now. My frequent use of people-pleasing, rage, guilt, fear, shame, control, blame, dissociation, overachieving, pride, and manipulation (all of which I needed to stay alive), have turned into liabilities, which threaten my quality of life and those around me.

When life sends storms, and I resort to using my old ways of coping, these character defects serve as a threat to my peace and my relationships. I've been working on releasing behaviors that no longer serve me or give me life. I've asked God to remove the ones that are stubborn and resistant, or that are out of my reach. Rumor has it when you prune often, your foliage will grow back fuller than before, improving the overall health, beauty and resiliency of the tree, bush or plant. I'm grateful today that I'm aware of my dead or obtrusive branches. I have been given tools to prune them and a loving Caretaker to

161

oversee and assist my efforts toward a healthier, more vibrant life.

June 16   Creating an Environment for Growth

We have a gorgeous Japanese Maple hybrid in our front landscaping bed. I noticed at least a year ago that a big bushy growth was slowly rising up through the Maple's delicate, drooping leaves. I thought it was a weed at first, but when I looked closer and saw that this "weed" was growing directly out of our tree, I left it alone. I guessed maybe all of the tree's foliage first grew in bushy and green, and then somehow turned into the beautiful delicate leaf style and color of the rest of the tree. (If you know trees, I know you are laughing at me right about now!)

This year, the unsightly growth was bigger than ever, covering up our pretty tree. After doing some research and consulting a landscaping professional, I figured out what was happening. The Japanese Maple lace-leaf is a hybrid plant, created by grafting the hybrid variety onto the root stock of a standard Japanese Maple. The root stock provides the foundation for the hybrid, but often a branch will begin to grow below the graft, from the root stock itself, with foliage from the original tree. In my case, it was an unsightly blob of green leaves—very different from the delicate, burgundy red leaves of my hybrid lace leaf. I had to prune the unwanted branch away so the hybrid could flourish. I also moved some overgrown neighboring shrubs to another bed to give our tree the room it needed to fully blossom and expand.

My past is my "root stock," my foundation, where I came from. It serves to hold me up and support the personal growth and beauty I now seek. With conscious effort, I can graft in a completely new life pattern. With consistent self-development, I can transform my past into something very beautiful and special. If old ways begin to crop up again, left unattended, they can completely cover up all of the "new me." Circumstances and relationships can crowd the "new me" as well. With attention and intention, I can take action and prune back what is unwanted to once again reveal the beautiful transformation that is me. How are you doing? Are you dominated by original root stock or is the "new you" flourishing? Are you crowding someone else from being seen? Are you the Japanese lace leaf struggling to expand? Take an honest look. Prune what is hindering you. Distance yourself from what is limiting you from fully expanding. Recognize who and what you were meant to be and let yourself blossom!

June 17   Forgiveness Sets Me Free

To forgive is to set a prisoner free and
discover that the prisoner was you.
~ Lewis B. Smedes ~

Every day I have a choice. I have things in my life I can be angry and resentful about, but I also have many things to be grateful for. It's difficult, if not impossible to feel both simultaneously. I'm enjoying an amazing early summer day with abundant sunshine and a gentle breeze. I have some flowerpots I want to fill and I'm looking forward to the trip to the nursery. On the other hand, my mind keeps wandering into internal conversations I would really like to have with two people. Oops ... there's another one! Actually there's three people I'd really like to give a peace of my mind. In each case, I have a legitimate reason to be angry and resentful. But who is being hurt and disturbed by all these imaginary conversations? ME!

I once heard the definition of forgiveness is giving up the "right" to be angry. I'm not admitting I wasn't wronged, or that it wasn't a big deal. I am, however, choosing not to let it take me out of the moment, and ruin my chance to enjoy the present. In this moment, I'm going to accept the fact that what's done is done. I will recognize that we're all human, and we all make mistakes and do or say things that in hindsight we probably wish we hadn't done or said. I am going to allow my mind to fully embrace this gorgeous day and allow gratitude to penetrate my whole self. Gratitude feels a lot better than anger and resentment. Each of those situations will work themselves out and I can choose in the future to avoid putting myself in a place where I could experience the same unwanted actions by these particular individuals. I love the question, "Am I a victim or a volunteer?" I can choose not to "volunteer" for more of the same unwanted behaviors from others, especially if these behaviors are a pattern instead of a one-time occurrence. Today, this very moment, I give myself over to what is happening right now. For me that is a beautiful summer day unfolding with a chance to dig in the dirt and create something beautiful! What are you willing to let go of so you can embrace this moment? Just for today? What can you do to generate feelings of love, creativity, gratitude, generosity, kindness, contentment or anything else that just makes you feel good? The choice is yours! I hope you will be good to yourself starting right ... NOW!

June 18   **Small Decisions Add Up**

I'm reading a great book called, *The Slight Edge* by Jeff Olson and I'm listening to the audio version as well. As I was watering my freshly-planted summer pots this morning, I noticed one plant was sticking up too high and wasn't firmly planted in the dirt. It still looked good, but it was only a matter of time before it would die if I didn't get it further down in the dirt with the rest of the plants. I could wait till tomorrow or the next day and it would still look good, but that's short-term thinking.

We laid new sod to patch some dead spots, and I didn't feel like turning on the sprinkler this morning. I looked at it and thought, *It looks okay, one day of not watering won't hurt.* My life, my health, my relationships, my wealth—everything may look okay today, but the small decisions, the small disciplines I do or don't do, matter. They all add up over time. Today I will view small decisions and small efforts as part of my big dreams, goals and life intentions. Today my values and aspirations will be evident and congruent with all my choices, big and small.

June 19   **You're the Parent Now**

What a beautiful sunny summer morning—perfect for a walk. Lately, we've been seeing baby bunnies in one area I typically pass by, and yesterday, I saw a doe and the smallest fawn I have ever seen. As I approached, the doe froze and then took off. Within seconds her baby followed obediently. Naturally. Mamas and their babies are a joy to watch! I had only seen the baby bunnies on my previous walks but today, I saw the mama bunny lying dead in the road, and I felt so sad! She got them as far as she could and now they have to fend for themselves, the best they know how.

Lots of us have issues with our parents. There are things we wish had been different, ways we would have preferred to be treated. Our parents are no different than those in the wild. They do their absolute best, given the circumstances, and all they know, and all they were taught. When there are gaps, we have to take over where they left off. We can sit around and feel sorry for ourselves or we can take the time to listen and nurture the parts in us that need attention. What do we need today? Love? The quickest way to feel love is to show love to someone else. Safety? Friendship? Recreation? Be the parent (to yourself) that you've always wanted. It's never too late to start loving and caring for the most important person in your life—YOU!

June 20   Careful What You Wish For

If you can dream it, you can do it.
~ Walt Disney ~

We are negotiating the sale of our home. I thought this was what I wanted, but I'm having mixed feelings as I sit out here enjoying my amazing view. It's funny how clarity suddenly shows up after we say what we want and then actually get it! Maybe it's not what we want after all? I am leaning heavily on intuition, trust and spiritual guidance. I'm choosing to believe the only reason this house will sell is because there's something even better waiting for us. It's easy to get too comfortable and fear change. We may stay in a home, a job or a relationship because it's good enough, and we don't believe things could possibly be any better, though secretly we dream of more. For me, I long for even more land, my own forest to roam, a body of water to gaze at frequently. What else would complete the vision of my ideal home? Don't be afraid to ask yourself, *What else*? Name it. Say it. It's safe to speak your dreams. Careful what you wish for—it might actually come true!

June 21   You Hold the Pruning Shears

We did some yard work yesterday, and my job was pruning bushes. I like that job because the results are immediately visible and satisfying! We have some bushes on the side of the house that had gotten pretty big. A few months ago, I trimmed them way back, but in just two weeks, several branches shot up six or eight inches and looked hideous! After all that work I did, I was going to have to trim them again! This shrub is pleasing to the eye now, but the same shrub would be totally unruly if left alone, with no guidance, help or care.

Pruning offers several metaphors for me about spiritual guidance. As the one doing the pruning, I'm shaping and guiding the shrub in a way I feel is appealing and also functional. Wouldn't it be easy if someone else was responsible for my life's pruning? The truth is, I hold the shears. When tuned into myself and my spirit, I can discern my ideal shape. I can take an otherwise unruly self and guide it into a growth pattern that best suits me, and makes me a blessing to be around. Also with regular pruning, my growth rate is far greater than when I just let everything go. Sure, there's still subtle growth happening in me even then, but it's slow and not purposeful. Life might be okay for a while, and then all of a sudden chaos emerges, and massive corrective action is required to get back on course. It's definitely easier in the long run to remain intentional about my life, and my growth. It's also okay to ask for help, because sometimes we can't "reach it" all by ourselves, or our judgment isn't clear and we need a second opinion. Guidance is all around. The shears are available. Pick one area of your life that is stagnant and give it some attention today!

June 22   **Take a Trip Home**

My neighbors are gone on vacation, and this morning, I see my cat, Lucky, wandering around by their pool. It dawned on me that many of us could have a great vacation right at home! Because home is where we live, it's easy to take our surroundings for granted. What if we took a day to see our home and the city we live in through the eyes of someone on vacation? What would we do? Where would we visit? What would we "write home" about? What would we want to visit again in the future?

Today, take the time to see your home and hometown through the eyes of someone seeing it all for the first time. Explore! Break out of your routine! Rediscover why you chose to live there in the first place. I bet it's still as special now as it was then. What could you do to make your home more like a retreat? Buy an island-scented candle. Listen to music with the flavor of places you would like to visit. Light a special candle at the dinner table. Make room for a hammock. Offer up a prayer of gratitude for the corner of the world you choose to call Home. There's no place else like it!

June 23   **Find Your Happy Place**

Sun and water are two of the most powerful forces in the world. When channeled properly, the sun can produce as much solar energy as we desire to use. A body of water can float the biggest ship man can build. When I immerse myself in sun or water, I can feel all of my stress completely melt away.

Today I'm at the park getting the benefits of both. The sun is warm and embracing me. My eyes are feasting on the expansive lake before me. Gentle waves from distant boats are rolling along. I'm almost oblivious to the traffic going by, just forty feet from where I sit. I close my eyes, take a deep breath and let myself sink down into this moment of bliss and retreat. I can let it all go. What I decide to pick back up and take with me is a choice. For right now, I'm enjoying my lightened load. Where do you let it all go? The gym? The park? The bath? A favorite chair? We all need peace and tranquility, and a safe place to set aside our worries and fears, our work, and our responsibilities to others. Find your happy place. I'm going to enjoy more of mine right now!

Blessed is the influence of one true,
loving human soul on another.
~ George Eliot ~

Yesterday, while at the park enjoying a gorgeous summer day and my surroundings, I found myself thinking, *Can it get any better than this?* Then along came a mama mallard with seven precious ducklings. They stopped to take a break five feet from the bench where I was sitting, overlooking the lake. I wondered, *How does a mama with no arms keep up with seven babies?* Most of us would have our hands full with just one! She guided them with frequent quacks but mostly, she led by example and they followed suit.

Some of us were fortunate enough to have been taught well by our parents or caregivers. Others didn't get that same opportunity. Regardless of what you experienced growing up, and no matter how old you are now, mirroring someone else who has the life, work and relationships you want can provide much insight for attracting more of that in your own life. Socrates said, "The unexamined life is not worth living." Find a mentor. Take them out for coffee or lunch. Ask them some questions about how they got where they are. See if they have some tips for you, and if they are open to meeting with you again occasionally. Think they are too busy? Maybe. People make time for what is important to them and they may feel very honored by your request. You won't know if you don't ask! Tell yourself you are worth it—you are! And be ready to repay the favor down the road.

June 25   **Your Place in the Sun**

I've been a professional photographer since 2005. When I photograph people on a bright sunny day, I will often place them in the shade under a tree. Sun splotches leaking through the leaves are not usually flattering, so I'll ask them to move around until they don't feel any light on their face. This is a foreign concept for most people—to tune into whether or not the sun is on their face. They have to tap into an awareness of something they usually wouldn't think about. That's mindfulness lesson number one.

On a broader scale, it's also good to develop an awareness of the "sun" in your life. Is it shining on you, or are you caught in the shadows? You can start by asking yourself how you feel. Are you happy, fulfilled, or at least headed in the right direction? Or have things gotten a bit "splotchy?" Maybe you need to move things around a little bit, until you're more aligned with the desires of your heart.

I believe there is a place in the "sun" for all of us. A place where we can be authentically and wonderfully us, using our giftings and talents as creation intended. Learn to recognize and acknowledge light on your face, light in your life. Give thanks for the glow and the flow. During times in the shade, remember the sunlight is often just a few steps or turns away. Keep adjusting and you'll feel it again. In everything, give thanks!

June 26   Be the Real You

*If a man happens to find himself ... he has a mansion
which he can inhabit with dignity all the days of his life.*
~ James Michener ~

Taking a walk with Goldie today, I noticed she was definitely in hunting mode. Although I couldn't detect it, there must have been an inviting smell of baby bunnies in the air, or maybe field mice. She was single-focused, constantly sniffing and scanning the fields. That's right—be a hunter, Goldie! You're not just a house dog—you're a hunter!

Say who you are and be that! Because the only person whose opinion actually matters is YOURS! You're not just a dad, mom, student, employee, etc.! You are multi-faceted! Find and allow your full self-expression to rise to the surface. You may already know what that looks like, or maybe you're just beginning to have a hint of who you were created to be. And it's possible you feel clueless about your real identity, because your heart has been buried for such a long time, but not to worry! There are many great books and programs out there to help. I've listed some of my favorite books in the back, if you need some suggestions. Today is your day! Stop living undercover and start being the REAL you!

June 27   **Morning Walks Start the Day Right**

I have always been delighted at the prospect of a new day, a fresh try, one more start, with perhaps a bit of magic waiting somewhere behind the morning.
~ J. B. Priestley ~

I have recently started enjoying my early morning walks again, thanks to my continued healing after knee surgery several months ago. The pulse or the vibe in the air is different in the morning, as compared to other times. I can sense the day rising, and it is full of hope and possibility.

Walking in the morning is such a natural way to jumpstart a day full of gratitude and appreciation for everything in my life, exactly the way it is. I can lay down whatever I choose not to carry over from yesterday. My slate is clean and each day is a fresh start. Getting off on the right foot by hitting the pavement for twenty minutes in the morning sets the pace of my day. Walking through life in rhythm with gratitude, hope and wonder feels great! And the best part is—it's free. Enjoy!

June 28   **Tea for Two?**

We live in a world full of opposing beliefs and contradictions. We differ in the areas of religion, how to parent, and our financial philosophies, just to name a few. I love remembering there is probably an element of truth in all things. Even if I don't personally support a way of thinking, I aspire to remember that I can view every person and every belief as my teacher. I can glean some lesson or degree of wisdom from everyone and everything I encounter. I have to remind myself that people with opposing beliefs feel just as passionate, and just as convicted in what they choose to believe as I do. And it's their right to take a stand for what they believe in, just as much as it is mine.

My neighbor recently told me his grandma used to just nod and say, "Well, that's not my cup of tea." I love that! We don't have to judge each other's choices. We each get to decide what IS our cup of tea and live accordingly. Today, suspend judgment and criticism of people who are different from you and celebrate diversity and variety— the spices of life, remembering that love, tolerance and compassion are universal truths we can all share together.

June 29   When I Prioritize Me, I Will Be Free

When we truly care for ourselves, it becomes possible to care far more profoundly about other people. The more alert and sensitive we are to our own needs, the more living and generous we can be toward others.
~ Eda LeShan ~

Is compulsive behavior robbing you of joy? Do you say, "That's it! I'm *not* going to do this anymore!" Or, "Starting tomorrow, I'm going to do *this* every day!" But then the next time you're faced with the choice, you act against your intentions? I believe we all have specific areas in our lives where we struggle to do (or not do) those things which keep us true to ourselves. Some examples may include: diet, exercise, smoking, biting fingernails, spending habits, and drug or alcohol use. Some other challenging behaviors may involve going back to unhealthy relationships, getting enough rest, standing up for yourself, not being consumed by worry, and cruising social media sites when we really need to be doing something else. (I'm guilty of several of those!)

We repeat self-destructive behavior again and again. Sometimes we switch vices or compulsive behavior/non-behaviors, but the end result is the same. All these unintentional behaviors performed (or not performed) repeatedly over time can leave us feeling so shameful that we no longer feel we made a mistake, but that we are a mistake. We become filled with self-hatred and self-doubt, lacking self-trust and short on hope that we can ever act in a way that reflects our true desires. How could we possibly allow the greatness we have inside us to be fully expressed with a dark cloud constantly hovering over a corner of our life?

When I prioritize me, I will be free! Too often, we are told to put others first. Care and compassion for others are great attributes to possess until they get out of proportion and lead to self-abandonment and self-neglect. We know when we're doing this to ourselves and inside, we rebel! The abandoned-self fights back to get our attention. Just like some children resort to acting out as the only way they know to get attention, part of us starts looking for ways to sabotage our happiness in order to get our attention. That part isn't getting authentic expression so it needs an outlet, a release, or a vice. Compulsive behaviors only provide a temporary escape though, leaving us with the original problem of self-abandonment, compounded now with shame and self-loathing. It becomes a vicious cycle. We act out again and again and have a temporary escape from feeling bad, but we ultimately feel worse, so unfortunately, we do it again, still seeking relief.

The only way I've ever been successful at breaking these destructive cycles is by making one seemingly insignificant decision to make a different choice, while praying for help to be relieved of the compulsion and to see through the seductive lie that doing this/not doing this will "fix me." I'm not vowing forever, just one right choice in that moment. Strangely enough, one right action can give me just enough of a self-esteem boost to make another right decision. All the while I'm reminding myself what I really want, what I really value, and what my true intentions are for my life and day-to-day living.

With each small, seemingly insignificant decision, self-trust begins to come back. Self-respect starts to return. All of me begins to rise up, united again in purpose and intention. The greatness inside me can be more freely expressed without the shackles of shame holding me back. When I prioritize me, I will be free! Cheers to your inner freedom today allowing full expression of all the goodness—the Godness—and the greatness inside you!

June 30   Prioritize Me to Be Free: Part Two

Make a list of the many parts of you who need expression. Perhaps a dancer, a painter, a creator, a lover, an angry teenager, a humanitarian, a wild and reckless adventure seeker, someone who likes to build things, or a curious wanderer. How can you treat them to safe expression today? Are there some parts of you who just need to be heard and acknowledged? Deep in a hidden corner of your soul, maybe you have some loneliness, sadness, disappointment, envy, anger or grief? These are all valued parts of you. If ignored, they may eventually rebel in an attempt to get your attention, or you may continue to experience an un-named longing, or a sense of unfulfillment.

When we honor and acknowledge all parts of us, we love ourselves more fully and have much more to offer the world around us and the people we care about. Acceptance is key. You cannot reject a part of you without consequence, anymore than you can cut off a limb and not miss it. I used to wish away the parts of myself I didn't like. With fantasy scissors, I would cut those parts out of my life forever. Now I have learned to recognize and acknowledge those parts of me. They are valid. They need to be heard. It doesn't mean I act upon every whim, it just means I listen to my needs, and I provide nurturing and reassurance to the voices inside— the fearful, rebellious, reckless, angry, and naïve pieces of me.

I offer comfort to the scared little girl. I acknowledge the angry teenager and provide a way for her safe expression. I can encourage the young adult in me, who still feels like she's trying to find her way in a big world. Tuned in to all of me, I offer guidance, wisdom and parenting as needed. Most of all, I offer love and acceptance to all the many wonderful parts of me. When I prioritize me, I will be free! Today, I hope you will stop to listen and say hello to all the valuable parts of you, so you, too, can take good care of your "selves" and learn to be free!

July

Nothing is either good or bad. It's thinking that makes it so.

~ **William Shakespeare**

July 1   Turning Work Into Fulfillment

Choose a job you love, and you will
never have to work a day in your life.
~ Confucius ~

The trees are calm and the birds are singing this morning. They're not worried about what's going to happen today, or next week, or next year. You would never hear a tree say, "Oh no, what if a tornado comes through here next month and rips me out of the ground!" They're also not trying to alter their existence and everything around them. They are content to do what they were created to do. In order for me to do the same, I need to be still long enough to know what that even looks like.

This morning I decided to complete a writing exercise to help me stop and think about what my purpose is—why I'm here. Facing the reality of being physically unable to continue in my current profession, I want to make sure this time around, I place a higher priority on personal fulfillment. I spent some time exploring what I was good at, both professionally and personally, and I listed the things I enjoy doing. Most importantly I noted what brings me passion and zest for life, because for too long, I worked solely for money, success and recognition. I achieved those things, but stress and dissatisfaction were always present. I didn't choose this transition, but I am grateful for the opportunity to find a new, more fulfilling path. When my life is aligned with what I was created for, joy and peace will be my constant companions, and worry will become a distant acquaintance.

July 2   Computer Lessons

My computer has been running slower and slower over the last several months. I knew something was wrong, but my anti-virus software didn't detect anything. Finally a friend suggested running an anti-spyware detector, which found several, severe spyware programs running constantly. I gained valuable insights from my computer that day!

When I have too much on my plate and too many things running in my head, I start dragging mentally. I'm overwhelmed by all the tasks constantly calling my name. I make a list in hopes to prioritize, but everything feels like urgent, and I sink further into paralysis. I was reminded by my dear, patient husband to just pick one or two things, and block out the chatter of everything else. Focus on what's right in front of me. I love the phrase "analysis paralysis." Nothing happens when I'm busy obsessing, and I need to close the extra "programs" running in my head. The quickest way to get a lot of tasks done is to do one task at a time, even when they're all of equal importance.

The second lesson my computer taught me relates to the spyware that was bogging my system down. Other people's "junk" had invaded my space, decreasing my efficiency and peace. In *Codependent No More*, Melanie Beattie says, "...God never gives people more than they can handle. That doesn't include codependents because they're handling stuff for at least four or five other people." If I'm worrying and obsessing about people or situations that don't belong to me, I'm trying to play God—a software I never received. When constantly updated and maintained, my recovery program—personal development—will catch things running on my hard drive that don't belong to me. I have the option to delete them at any time, and restore my sanity and serenity. When I find myself obsessing over outcomes, I release those thoughts and remember to surrender and trust. Take the actions that are mine to take and let go of the rest. My computer is running again at optimal performance, and I can too, with regular maintenance.

July 3   **Trust During the Storm**

For the last few days, a hurricane has been pounding the Florida coast and we've seen the spillover effect in our weather here. Last night at dinner, viewing the trees outside our window, I was speechless at the force whipping them around. It was both beautiful and fearful at the same time. I was reminded that my illusion of control over my life is just that—an illusion. Thankfully I am part of a much bigger plan than I could ever imagine or personally direct. My worries are quelled as I trust my provider to care for me.

In this instance, I clearly see I have no better alternative than to trust, for I am powerless over the winds of change. I welcome them. Otherwise I could not appreciate the peace and stillness of calmer times. The winds always lead me further along in my adventurous life to a better place, if not immediately, then after the storm. This morning, I'm thankful for the reprieve in the rain so I can enjoy my time on the deck. The wind is still very active, yet the sun has just broken through and my soul is warm. What a beautiful start to a new day!

July 4   **Outside the Box: Part One**

I woke up to a beautiful summer rain—the sound, the smell, the breeze. I came up with a way to stay dry and yet still immerse myself in nature for my morning time. I opened the door to my back deck and sat down on the floor, just inside. The air conditioning on, the door open, and the rain falling—just because I can! Yes, I know I'm letting the cold air out, but the benefit to me is far exceeding the cost of wasted air-conditioning.

I'm not sure if anyone ever told Maxey that cats don't like to get wet, and they certainly don't intentionally leave dry shelter voluntarily. He sat by me briefly at the open door, ready to start his morning adventure. After a few minutes of pondering, and perhaps encouraging himself, Maxey strolled out into the drizzle. He walked a few feet and started licking fresh water off our grill before taking off. I guess he decided quenching his thirst with summer rain was worth getting wet.

Fancy, a mostly indoor cat, definitely supports the notion that cats don't play in the rain! Or maybe she just doesn't like to get wet. When she saw Maxey head out for some fresh water, she timidly stepped out onto the covered edge of the deck. Very quickly she returned to the house—not her cup of tea. What is right for one of us, isn't necessarily right for the rest of us. Wait! Maybe it's a timing issue, because with the water down to a sprinkle, Fancy just ran back outside to drink some fresh water too. This reminds me to trust myself, be patient, and wait until my gut tells me to proceed. Now Maxey is back on the deck, soaking wet and content, while Fancy dances in the rain. Live your life without comparison and should's, and get outside the box when the situation calls for it. Today, dare to do something different, or a little outside the norm.

July 5   **Outside the Box: Part Two**

My husband just came into the room to find me lounging on the carpet, writing beside the open door to the back deck. I was as close as I could get to nature this morning, without getting soaked by rain. He laughed and asked me what in the world I was doing? I laughed too, and said I was just having my morning time—no further explanation required or given.

I once heard something that changed my life: adults announce and children explain. I now catch myself when I start to give long, lengthy explanations to justify my actions or to get validation from others. Instead, I shamelessly announce my intentions or actions and then stop talking. I'm open to comments, feedback or questions, but I don't have to voluntarily spew at the mouth to get someone else's approval of my every move.

I do think timing is key—knowing when to celebrate life and act child like (free from inhibition), and knowing when to boldly take the actions of a confident adult. Balance between both is essential for my soul and daily well-being. Life would be way too boring if we never let our "kids" out to play! Well, the rain has stopped and morning time is over. I shall smugly close the door to begin the tasks of the day. I challenge you to do one thing today without offering a voluntary justification of your actions. Tell yourself it's okay to do something a little different, and then enjoy your freedom of choice!

July 6   Peace Is a Choice

Gratitude can transform common days into thanksgivings, turn routine jobs into joy, and change ordinary opportunities into blessings.
~ William Arthur Ward ~

We moved a month ago and I'm sitting outside on my new deck, which backs up to numerous surrounding properties and the main road. I no longer have my beautiful forest of trees to gaze at, but somewhere in the distance I can hear some birds—when my neighbors AC unit is resting. While I loved my private deck surrounded by thick woods, this morning I realize peace comes from within. Only when I am content internally, can I be content and see the good in my environment and circumstances. My vision of nature has been altered due to our move, but I do have plenty to look at, if I choose to see it. Today I see peace and gratitude as a choice. I will look for and find some peace today.

July 7   Trust in the Path

Early this morning while my son had football practice, I decided to walk the path around the school. I remembered when they first created the walking trails and all the volunteer effort that went into clearing the area. I haven't been here since that first summer, and a lot has changed in such a short time. Everything has become overgrown with weeds, and the nice, neat edges originally created are now haphazard and random.

Our best intentions and plans can come to fruition, but without regular maintenance, and an ongoing desire to keep what we've attained—physical health, good relationships, or a positive mindset—things will slowly go back to the way they were. It reminds me of the saying, "We're either moving forward or backward." Rarely do things stay the same.

I set out this morning to walk the same path I'd walked two years before. Sometimes the way became less visible due to weeds, but I kept going, trusting my memory, and believing I would find my way. I observed the many obstacles—big weeds encroaching on the trail. I walked around them. Jumped over them. At times, I had to put forth a lot of energy just to stay on the path. Life can feel like that when it takes extra effort just to get through the day!

I reached one spot where the overgrowth was so thick that I actually stopped in my tracks for a moment, not sure I wanted to push through. The path was no longer visible at all and it really seemed like a dead end. I have reached places with goals, work and relationships where moving forward looked impossible. I either had to quit, or summon up the courage to press on. I hated to have to backtrack, Yelling, "I'm doing this!" I jumped in and ran much of the next bit through the thick brush, dodging flying beetles and wasps, and ignoring the fear of ticks and other insect bites. I knew if I could get through this section, I would be fine the rest of the way. Sometimes we just have to dive in and get through the tough stuff, knowing this part won't last forever. I did feel triumphant when I came out the other side and sure enough, I found the buried path was visible again, and I enjoyed the rest of my walk. If you don't quit before the miracle happens, your perseverance will be rewarded! Whatever you're walking through today, keep going!

July 8   Richer Than We Think

Ordinary riches can be stolen; real riches
cannot. In your soul are infinitely precious
things that cannot be taken from you.
~ Oscar Wilde ~

I'm in Colorado staying at my sister's house. She lives in an older neighborhood where all the houses are close together, separated by fences. Every house's footprint contains rich, unique character. I sense strong boundaries and individual pride, but there's also a very strong sense of cohabitation. This is mine, that is yours, but we're all getting along. Coexistence and acceptance, with a sense of ownership. Do you own your life or do the people, places and things in your life own you? Do you walk around with the spirit of much, or a spirit of lack? Being wealthy is so much more than having money in the bank. Do you feel wealthy? Rich? If not, what's missing? Are you sure? Look around your life, your home. You may have more wealth than you realize.

July 9   The Hike: Part One

Today we went hiking in the Colorado mountains, along Lost Lake Trail to be specific. Our hike up was everything you might expect on a great hike: seventy-two degrees, partly sunny skies, scenic views, breathtaking waterfalls and lush green foliage. At the top of the trail we found a beautiful, crisp lake nestled between the mountain peaks. Suddenly, a raindrop fell. Then another. Thunder rolled. Other than concern for my professional camera getting wet, I knew we were in for a magical, one-of-a-kind experience. Within five minutes, we started our descent amidst an all out thunderstorm with lightning. Solutions appeared for my camera bag so I could fully enjoy the adventure.

We had the pleasure of experiencing an amazing, scary yet thrilling encounter with nature as we raced down the mountain. Temperatures dropped to the point our fingers and toes grew numb. We were frozen, filthy and soaked to the bone when we finally reached our cars. No question, this was the best hike I have ever experienced. Why? Because it was the most memorable. We faced a challenge and we thrived. Status quo does not make you grow! Embrace everything that comes your way. See the silver lining. BE the silver lining. Be the one that says, "Hey, this isn't so bad! In fact, it's kinda cool!" Feel the magic. Find the gift. Let life show you how strong and capable you really are. Not every moment in life is great, but there are great moments in every life. Open your eyes to the unexpected gifts of today.

July 10   The Hike: Part Two

Our hike that started out warm and sunny drastically changed into rain, thunderstorm, lightning and plummeting temperatures. As we got colder and more soaked coming down the mountain, my legs and feet seemed less responsive. Some steps felt more like swimming as I tumbled forward, one foot after the other, luckily finding a solid foothold each time. I have a slight tear in my left knee that started screaming with intense pain at times. I thought about sitting down. My mind was filled with thoughts like, *I can't do this*! and *I can't go on!*

I coaxed myself to go a little bit further, just a little bit further, again and again. And with each decision to go another short stretch, I made it down that big mountain! Big tasks loom large. Impending change can seem impossible. Enduring a loss can feel unbearable. Take your focus off forever, next month or even tomorrow. You can do great things one step at a time, one moment at a time. Quit overwhelming yourself! Think of one small thing you can do today to get you closer to where you want to be. Take a rest when you need it, but get back up. Gently, slowly, steadily, surely, you will get there if you keep moving forward.

July 11   **The Hike: Part Three**

On my Colorado hike, I was with two of my siblings and three of our kids. On the way up, we came across a gorgeous waterfall surrounded by huge rocks. My brother had been there many times and he encouraged us to crawl down over the rocks to get closer to the falls. He led the way and we followed. A few times I got so far behind that I wasn't able to see the path taken by the person before me. It looked impossible, but because everyone had gone ahead, I knew it was doable. I pushed myself to catch up to them just on sheer faith that if they could do it, I would find a way as well.

There are times to lead and times to follow. Olympic records are continually broken as each competitor raises the belief in what is possible. Are you in a position to raise the bar? To pave the way for others? Do it. Can you stretch just a little bit more to personally achieve something someone else has already proven possible? Go for it. You may even encourage the next person to give it a shot. Visionaries need support and mankind needs visionaries. Embrace your role whatever that is today. Everyone is relevant.

July 12   **Guarding My Peace**

I got back really late last night from our wonderful family vacation in Colorado. Storms delayed our flight over an hour. It was 2 a.m. before I got into bed this morning. I had a wonderful time with family, however all the activities and late-night games finally caught up with me. Today was a day to relax and replenish. Midafternoon, I took a soothing bath. A bath in the middle of the day is one of the greatest luxuries to me!

An approaching storm began wildly blowing the tree outside my bathroom window. As I lay still, immersed in my warm, serene bath, I felt completely detached from the fierce wind nearly bending the tree in half. It felt like I was seeing two ends of the spectrum. Ultimate peace and serenity, versus a wicked storm.

The chaos couldn't touch me though. My peace was bulletproof, separated by thick, brick walls and glass. If I let my ears dip down into the water, my peace was even soundproof! It was amazing to watch a turbulent rainstorm bending trees and blowing debris just inches from me, as I soaked in quiet calm.

I aspire to walk in that quality of peace and serenity daily. Where no matter how much drama is going on around me, I am unmoved. Unfazed. My peace is guarded, airtight. No one, no thing or situation can knock me off kilter. How often have I sold my peace for pennies? How often have I given it away at the slightest nudge?

Today my balanced, grounded, calm state of being is my most prized possession. I will practice the self-care necessary on a daily basis to protect my most valuable asset—my well-being. Do you know what self-care rituals restore and replenish you? A bath? A walk? A cup of tea? Silent meditation? Music? Take inventory of your spiritual comforts and enjoy them on a regular basis—and especially when intensive care is needed.

July 13   Need Love? Give It Away

I saw something today that I've seen a hundred times, but today I saw it on a deeper level. Ha! That's what this whole book is about—uncovering truth right before our very eyes. My cat, Lucky frequently walks up to our dog, Goldie to nuzzle her as he walks by. Lucky will intentionally make several passes, brushing up each time on Goldie, who happily receives the gesture. Today it occurred to me that Lucky needed some love, so the natural way for him to meet his own need was to show love! Getting love was the byproduct of giving it. Animals are really instinctive and smart! As usual, we can learn a lot from them.

Be honest—how many of us sit around on a pity pot hoping someone will notice the sign on our forehead that says, "I need love," rather than taking the initiative to get our needs met? Let's remember the quickest and easiest way to receive love is to give it away! Look around today and see who might need a loving nudge!

July 14   Pruning Redirects Our Focus

I am out on the deck this morning and one of my palm trees caught my eye. It's very healthy but there's a dead limb I have needed to prune away. Just because one part dies, the rest doesn't have to. How often have I felt that life was over when a relationship or job or other significant chapter in my life ended? Now that the palm branch is dead and removed, more life can circulate through the living branches.

For a while, we may keep giving our energy to the parts of our lives that are dying. When we get the courage to prune those things away, we can pour that same energy into the pieces of our lives that are thriving, or could thrive with just a little more attention. What is dragging you down today or holding you back from living a fuller life? Where can you place your focus to bear more fruit? It's time to break away from the old parts that don't serve you anymore so the new can come through.

Yesterday I went on a walk. The sun was shining and summer was in full bloom. Colorful trees and flowers were everywhere, complemented by lush green grass. Somehow at first I didn't give much attention to all of that. I kept noticing what was wrong instead of what was right. I noticed chipped driveways and weeds, and anything else ripe for criticism. After about ten minutes, I realized what was happening and I remembered the whole point of the walk was to breathe, relax and generate a sense of appreciation and well-being. As soon as I clarified my intention, my attention completely changed. I noticed the brilliant pink blooms on a Crape Myrtle tree. I became aware of all the different colors of flowers I could see in one glance. I let my breath go deeper and I relaxed. My well-being increased.

Where is your focus right now? Is it making you feel good? Are you getting a desirable outcome for where you are placing your attention? Check how you're feeling. That will be your first clue as to whether or not you may want to change your focus and perspective. The exciting thing is we have a choice! Give two people the same life, same job, same relationships, same bank accounts, etc. and those two people could have two very different outlooks and dispositions. Sometimes the "funk" takes over us before we even know it. When we are ready to feel better, we can shift our focus and find a way to love our lives again.

Example is not the main thing in
influencing others. It is the only thing.
~ Albert Schweitzer ~

A really wonderful lady left this earth today. She would have been ninety-seven in one more month. She was friend to many, and also a wife, mother, sister, grandmother, great-grandmother and my neighbor! I never heard my elderly friend speak one cross word to anyone, or about anyone. She was always kind, gracious and uplifting to be around, and someone I aspire to be like. Even in her last days, I sensed her love, gratitude and concern for others, without one ounce of self-pity. What will people say about you when you're gone? Are you living a life worth remembering, and touching people in ways they will never forget? Are you pursuing your dreams and passions, and donating your time to others? Is there a small shift you can make in either direction? If you do what you're born to do, gifted to do, and you regularly give back in some way, you will be fulfilled and a blessing to many who come across your path. I will continue aspiring to be as influential to others, as Ms. Christine was to me, and to live an authentic life, spreading sunshine every step of the way. We can change the world, if we all start living our legacy, now.

July 17   **Self-Care Comes First**

When growing flowers and plants, it's important they are cared for consistently, especially after a major transition like being repotted. I can't flood them with water once a week or once a month and expect to have the same impact as watering them just the right amount at ideal intervals. Relationships vary as much as plants and flowers. Most need a little attention on a consistent basis. When in crisis mode, like my potted flowers in the heat of summer, some may require even more care than usual. Other plants like my indoor palms and Scheffleras prefer a weekly drink.

If I get busy and began to neglect my plants and flowers, I won't see the effects immediately after the first skipped-watering. There's a window of grace to allow me to get back on track, same with relationships. But if I let them go too far, I'll have to work especially hard, once I start putting forth effort to care for them again. Like before, I may not see results right away. I will need to keep providing the consistent care they need, and trust that even when they aren't immediately responsive, they will recover and flourish again. If I offer complete abandonment over an extended period of time, it's likely a plant will completely die. However I have found that plants, like people and relationships, are very resilient and if there is any life left at all, there is hope for full recovery.

Where is this more true than in the most important relationship of all? The one with myself! If I neglect myself physically, spiritually, emotionally, recreationally and socially—there really is no "me" but a shell of a person merely surviving day by day. Like a neglected flowering plant, I would be lucky to have any green leaves remaining, and certainly couldn't expect any blooms. Identify what part of you is deficient. Make a list of which activities, goodies and daily rituals will nurture the part of you that is neglected. If you're reading this, you are breathing and that means there is still hope! Do at least one loving thing for yourself today. Good relationships with others are the result of regular self-care. Water your own plants first! Then you will have much to share with others.

July 18   Can You See Me Now?

Argue for your limitations,
and sure enough, they're yours.
~ Richard Bach ~

Walking my dog the other day, I noticed for the first time something unusual about a pair of trees standing just five feet apart. The leaves of one intertwined with the branches of the other. Then I noticed the second one had branches, but no leaves at all—it was dead! It was standing there as an imposter! Many passersby wouldn't even notice. They would see the leaves of the other tree overlapping, and assume both trees were alive, just as I did for a moment.

I thought immediately about how many of us live as imposters. We say the right things and look the part, but we're empty inside. We may associate with successful, productive, joyful people but we only give lip service. We're faking our smiles and our comprehension, but our interactions are hollow. We aren't really living to the fullest. Maybe no one else will notice, but we know the truth. I hope if someone looks closely at you, they will see a thriving tree, but if not, please keep reading!

Unlike the dead tree, it's never too late to come back to life! Surrounding yourself with positive, powerful influence is a start. Ask yourself, *What do I really want?* And take a step in that direction. Too often we believe we're not smart enough, disciplined enough, maybe even not lucky enough. Cancel! Delete! Stop buying into those lies! In my coaching program, *A Life Worth Having*, I blast through these false self beliefs and help clients join me in learning to replace them with other beliefs—the real truth about ourselves. Then and only then can we really move forward. If you're reading this, the seed you grew from is still very much alive. It's time to stand on your own, with the branches of your life in full bloom!

July 19   **Creating A Life Worth Having**

I saw another metaphor in the trees I wrote about yesterday. One tree was completely dead, but standing so close to the live one, that unless you took a close look, you wouldn't really notice it didn't have any of its own leaves. We will mimic the behavior and attitudes of those closest to us. Our bank accounts, our relationships, our spiritual values will all be within close proximity to the people we spend the most time with. This can be a very good thing, depending on who we are surrounding ourselves with. Just like the example of the dead tree from yesterday's entry—even if we are not yet where we want to be, or we have strayed far from our original goals, we can now surround ourselves with who and what we aspire to be. Eventually we are going to become like them with enough effort, intention and time.

Birds of a feather flock together. Like attracts like. Who are you spending your time with? Do they have the life you want? Do they have the internal abundance you seek? Change your friends or *change* your friends. Some people are in your life for a reason, a season or a lifetime. Know the difference and spend time with them accordingly! Conversely, be the light to those around you. Give someone a hand up when they see in you what they want for themselves. Most of all, be conscious of the influences you are giving and receiving. You have a choice. Creating a life worth having is a very intentional, conscious process. I believe you can have, be, and do anything you want. Cheers to your intentional life!

July 20   **Heart Aches**

In my life's chain of events nothing was accidental.
Everything happened according to an inner need.
~ **Hannah Senesh** ~

Out on the deck, the rain is a soothing lullaby as it hits the metal gutters and runs through the drain spouts. What a beautiful, rhythmic melody. It feels like salve for the soul. For whatever reason, the last few days have been emotionally charged for me. I got in a tiff with someone close to me and my heart hurts, but I also have feelings of anger and indignation rising out of the pain because what happened was so senseless, and unnecessary. I think my pride hurts more than the actual injury. I wonder if that's where the phrase, "add insult to injury" comes from?

I believe everything happens for a reason and everything is working for my good. Some days it's a bit easier to see how anything good could possibly come from a particularly "not-fun" situation. Faith must take over and assure us that even though we can't see it in this moment, we *are* being loved, guided and cared for—even when it hurts. When this happens, offer your heart some extra TLC, apply salve for the soul—whatever that looks like for you. For me, an immersion in nature almost always helps. I trust that tomorrow I will feel better, and today I will continue to look for all the other reasons to feel grateful right now. I can also surrender the hurt and choose to let it go. When relationships hit a bump, I will forgive and let my heart become soft, loving and open again.

July 21   **Spot It, You Got It**

News flash! We don't have to like everyone or be liked by everyone! I always thought something needed fixing if two people didn't get along! If someone just plain rubs me the wrong way, more often than not, I'm getting a valuable clue about myself. Who does that person remind me of? Who else acts in the way that is bothering me so much? It could be someone from my past. OR ... it could be a part of me that I'm reminded of that I don't like very much. "Spot it, you got it" is a phrase I've heard a lot and can really relate to. When someone's behavior really gets under my skin, I can use that person or circumstance as a lesson. It's these people who can often teach me the most and help me grow to the next level of awareness about myself, if I'm willing to ask, "What are they showing me about myself?" In the meantime, the situation is real, and I can choose how to react. I can respect everyone. I can show compassion. And ... I don't have to hang around people I don't enjoy being around. Guess what? Not everyone will want to hang around me either. Can I accept that not everyone will like me or my ideas? In all situations and relationships, my goal is to learn more about myself, get the lessons and grant others dignity, compassion and respect. Today I won't rack my brain trying to figure out why someone doesn't just naturally like me, or why they don't act as friendly as I think they should. I am wonderfully me, seeking neither approval nor acceptance from anyone else but me and God, the two relationships who matter the most. My serenity is always available and worth preserving.

July 22   Being a *"Noticer"*

To acquire knowledge, one must study;
but to acquire wisdom, one must observe.
~ Marilyn vos Savant ~

Recently my family visited my sister and her family, and my six-week-old niece. I haven't been around a little baby in a very long time. My tendency was to continually entertain her and try to engage her. It was difficult at first to let her just hang out in her swing or her bouncy chair, but soon I noticed she was often very content to just look around and observe. Then it hit me—that's her place in life right now, to just take it all in. I am so used to "doing" that I felt like I was neglecting her if I just let her be.

My six-week-old niece reminded me to slow down, look around, gain appreciation and regularly just *be*. I do not need to constantly provide myself with activity and entertainment or distraction. Being still and being a *"Noticer"* (a must read by, Andy Andrews) can lead to a rich, fulfilling life. Today and every day, take at least one timeout to just … be.

July 23   What's Taking Root In Your Life?

I'm grateful to have been on multiple vacations for much of the last 45 days! Unfortunately, the weeds in my flower beds did not take a vacation. In life, as in flower beds, it is much easier to deal with weeds proactively, the minute they surface. By now, some of them have really thickened and taken root, and I wasn't able to just pull them out by hand as usual. I'm going to have to dig them up using more effort.

The longer I let something go unattended in my life, the harder I'll have to work to get things back in order. The same thought holds true for daily disciplines and good habits, but in a good way. When I first decide to start something, even the smallest temptation or interruption can derail me from my intention, because it hasn't really taken root yet. In other words, getting me off track is as easy as plucking a new weed from the ground. However, the longer I let that habit develop, and the more I repeat it, the stronger its roots take hold in my life and the harder it is for a little thing to deter me from my intentions.

A two-fold lesson: if you wait until the weeds of life *really* get your attention, you'll have a lot more work to do than if you proactively survey your life for them and take action as soon as you see the first sign of concern. On the flip side, by allowing good habits and disciplines to really take root through repetition, it will be less likely for everyday life to pluck you out of your routine and un-ground you from your true (and new) intentions. Plant what you want and weed the rest!

July 24   **"Expert" Advice**

There is a time to take counsel of your fears,
and there is a time to never listen to any fear.
~ George S. Patton ~

So little experience, so much opinion! I read something like that recently, and it made me think about those people we encounter in life who will encourage us to focus on the obstacles instead of the opportunities. On why it can't work, instead of how it could. Otherwise known as dream stealers, often the people we care about the most try to protect us from new, unknown experiences. Sometimes they will be right and we would do well to listen to them, allowing their life experiences and wisdom save us from making some big mistakes. However, it's very possible they will be wrong sometimes too—well-intentioned, but uninformed.

Fear of the unknown, or past failures can make someone else discourage me from pursuing my own dreams. When I buy someone's opinions, especially about big decisions, I buy their lifestyle. I buy their life, but only to the extent they have been successful and courageous, because I could end up with their limited beliefs too. Do they have what I want? If yes, then I need to do what they did and treat their guidance as golden wisdom. If not, I may instead want to find a more credible source to seek counsel from. I wouldn't ask a pessimist how to develop a positive attitude.

I wouldn't ask someone who makes wigs to teach me how to build a rocket. Still, we seek advice from unqualified "experts" all the time, and sadly, we let other people's fears, failures, and lack of information determine our next course of action. Don't let other people's opinions lead to your oppression. Get the truth! Explore the risk! Make your own informed decision, after doing your homework. Then trust your intuition and go for it! The person who falls and gets back up is always stronger than the one who never tries.

July 25   Daily Repetition? Just Do It!

We are what we repeatedly do.
Excellence, then, is not an act, but a habit.
~ Aristotle ~

We hear about overnight success and our brains know the truth—nothing happens *overnight.* Too often something in me still falls into delusional thinking and

197

expectation, not wanting to do the repetition of small steps consistently. I found myself wishing for an outcome today, but then feeling frustrated at the realization that I couldn't just *do* it. The only way to achieve this outcome is through small, daily repetition. But I want it now! Wow, how many times have I wanted to write a book in one day, or take a foreign language lesson, desiring mastery right at the onset? Too often! What's the saying? Good things take time! Living in a microwave, fast-food society, my inherent desire to pull up to the drive-thru window and have it my way is so much more appealing to me. But I have a choice. I can dismiss the urges, desires, dreams, and goals that are going to take longer than one day, or I can do one small thing today (and the next, and the next) to get me closer to my goal.

If I make it more about the journey rather than the ultimate outcome, I may be more inclined to take that small step. If I look for the joy in actually doing it, or if I think about what I can get out of it *today*—the reward solely in today's action—I may be more likely to just *do* it today. When I slow down long enough to enjoy myself in that activity, I may find the willingness to do it again tomorrow. What is a step you can take toward your goal today and even more importantly, what's the gift you can find in doing that today? When I adhere to daily disciplines, I find the Miracle Gro for my dreams and goals! Cheers to us all *Finding the Gift* by taking one small step today!

July 26   De-Clutter Your Closet/Your Life

Right up front, I'll admit today's lesson may be geared more for the female reader, but guys may be just as guilty of doing this too. I have spent a fortune saving money on clothes. Read that again. I have spent a fortune SAVING MONEY on clothes! The clearance racks call my name and draw me to the back of the store. I can buy ten things for the same cost of one regularly priced item. So I buy twenty! After starving myself from something I might really like, I binge on clearance, consignment, Goodwill, etc. and the end result is a closet stuffed with items I only half like. *But they were half price!* my inner saver cries out. Wall-to-wall, my closet contains pieces I never would've paid full price for because the fit isn't quite right, the color was a shade off from ideal, and overall, I don't feel like a million bucks when I'm wearing it!

I had an epiphany recently, after a big shopping spree taking an extra 66% off the already 30-80% off, marked-down price. (HUH? Exactly! Crazy math!) What if I were to treat my closet like a piece of high end real estate, where the only clothes that can live there are the best of the best? Best fit, favorite colors, and high likelihood of wearability.

When I look at clothes in the stores now, I think past the low price or awesome deal and I ask myself, does this fit my personal brand? Do I feel good in this? Will I wear it often? Does it deserve a place in my closet with my other favorite things? Branding, personal style and confidence is important, regardless of the price. We carry ourselves better when we feel confident in what we're wearing. We can make quicker decisions when we have fewer choices, or more obvious, "right" choices. De-clutter your closet and give your discards to people in need and that's a win-win situation. Let that be the first step to de-cluttering your home, your office, your life. Clutter is a creativity killer and you deserve space to think, be and create!

July 27   Walk Before Running Away From Home

Walks are good for taking a time out when I need to remove myself from a situation, or I feel creatively stumped by a problem or project and I need to go pound the pavement for a while. Usually a walk will suffice, but certain situations call for a hike because a walk is just not going to cut it. I threw an all-out hissy fit today when someone I love expressed their opinion that my behavior wasn't up to par for them this morning. Immediately, I decided to *run away from home*! I got dressed for a hike, packed a backpack with water and an energy bar (since I might be gone *forever*), pens, journal, and my camera, and I jumped in the car. It's funny how driving in the fast lane while blasting classic rock through the speakers can indulge my anger and eventually accelerate me past my frustration into exploring the hurt that lies beneath.

By the time I got to the state park for my hike, I was ready to journal about why my feelings were so hurt. I hiked up the mountain ridge with sadness and then came back down with acceptance. Now I'm sitting on a bench by the lake listening to birds and insects, and enjoying a calm spirit. *Nothing has changed but me.* No one has a perfect life and everyone goes through stuff. Today I'm grateful I know how to acknowledge and feel my feelings, do what it takes to work through them, say sorry when appropriate, and talk things out with the ones I love so I can forgive and release resentments and get back to my wonderful life.

July 28   Broccoli Builds Self-Esteem?

What type of fuel does your car need to run at its best? Most of us are very consistent with the fuel we put in our vehicles, but not so much when it comes to what we put in our bodies. Do you just eat everything randomly, or have you ever thought about what your values are when it comes nourishing your most precious, a priceless, and rare vehicle of all—you? Let's be honest, some of us treat our dogs better than we treat ourselves! (Sometimes we confuse the word treat with toxin!)

Remember the science experiment where you put a steak in a carbonated beverage and it dissolves in a matter of days? I'm not above having an occasional soda, but the message I want to convey here is intention. What do you want your body to look and feel like? Do your actions support your answer? "You are what you eat" is not a new concept. While good nutrition is important, to me the bigger issue above your nourishment is whether or not you're acting against your personal values.

When we intend to do one thing but do another, we can perpetuate feelings of shame, disappointment in ourselves, poor self-esteem, and lack of self-trust, maybe even self-hatred. If we load this gun every time we eat, how can we expect to feel great about ourselves with this incongruence hanging over us and everything else we do? Congruency is key. Let's strive to honor our values, and our integrity in all we do. Self-respect comes from the sum total of all our actions and nothing can be discounted, even if we tell ourselves it doesn't matter. For today, seek to notice where you feel genuine alignment with your values and where you might not. Awareness is the first step toward future change.

July 29   Journaling Helps Solve the Puzzle

I am a buyer of blank books. Kids find it interesting that I would buy a blank book. They say, 'Twenty-six dollars for a blank book! Why would you pay that?' The reason I pay twenty-six dollars is to challenge myself to find something worth twenty-six dollars to put in there. All my journals are private, but if you ever got hold of one of them, you wouldn't have to look very far to discover it is worth more than twenty-six dollars.
~ Jim Rohn ~

I will state many times in this book that I believe we have all the answers inside us. How accessible the answers are can be the tricky part! Do I take time to pray and meditate, which for me means opening up my spirit to listen for guidance and the answers to my prayers? I believe praying is my conscious self asking for help and affirming life the way I want it to be. I believe my spiritual source (God, Higher Power, Creator), is willing to show me the answers when I take time to meditate and listen. Some of us can sit still and reflect more easily than others. Not to worry! I hear from my spiritual source in several ways.

Journaling on a regular basis is a practice I highly recommend. Dump your brain onto paper like pieces of a puzzle. If I dump a 500 piece puzzle onto a table, it creates a great big mess. If I just let it sit there, the pieces are not going to put themselves together. Journaling for me is moving the pieces around. It's picking them up one by one, studying their shape and looking for ways to make it fit with another piece, then another and then another.

I may journal today and not think much about what I wrote. Three days from now, I may be doing another brain dump that triggers an "aha!" moment, based on something I wrote previously. I can also look for recurring themes in my writing. If I find myself repeatedly journaling the same hopes, wishes or pain, the need for change may become more obvious and clear to me. This exercise is more productive than leaving all those thoughts jumbled up in my head as nothing more than confusion. Take the pieces out and look at them. Name them. Give them a voice. In a whisper or sometimes a shout, you will hear them speaking wisdom, guidance and truth. Unlock the answers—they are waiting for you!

July 30   **Unlocking the Answers Within**

How do you allow yourself access to answers within? It may seem they are locked up, but you do hold the keys. In the previous entry, I shared how journaling is a fabulous way to work out the puzzles of life. Taking a walking meditation is also very helpful, as long as I intentionally focus on being present. It does me little good to obsess about a problem throughout my entire walk! Some other ways to turn off the noise of life and get present include: folding laundry, cooking, baking, painting (on a canvas or a bathroom wall). Anything inspirational or creative, sewing, taking a shower, scrap booking, driving in a very present state, washing a car, cleaning, playing golf, reading, and listening to music.

When I'm thoughtfully engaged and intentionally present, the channel is static-free and anything can become meditation, allowing answers to drift to the surface and become conscious thought. When I'm obsessing over yesterday or tomorrow, my consciousness is already saturated with thoughts. Essentially, the channel to my inner knowing is full of static and nothing else will get through. Today, look for ways you are already "meditating." If you're not "hearing" anything, try again. Intentionally tune into being present. Clear the static and just listen. You'll be able to solve more puzzles and walk in greater peace. Why? Because the answers ARE inside you, my friend. Use your keys!

July 31   Courage to See

Thinking more about the recent entries on meditation and keeping my channel clear and receptive, I'm reminded that sometimes I purposely jam the signal. It's true! I intentionally stay so busy going from project to project, keeping my to-do list never-ending, that I completely avoid getting in touch with myself, my thoughts and my feelings. It feels like I'm afraid to wander into the deep, dark forest, fearful of what I might see or hear, and even more scared of what I might have to do about what I find. If I keep my head in the sand, maybe I can avoid becoming responsible and taking action? Once we uncover something, it becomes harder to ignore.

Why do I do this? Fear of the unknown. Fear of change. Fear of obligation. Already overwhelmed. Whatever "it" is, is already true, whether I allow myself to see it or not. The answers to fear are courage and trust. From the Al-Anon program, "I will know how to handle situations that used to baffle me." I trust today that I can handle all facets of my life: my challenges, change, my talents, relationships, my calling(s), my vision, my blessings, abundance, commitments, and choices. Rarely is life so urgent that I must tackle everything at once anyway. Today I will make time to breathe easy, to give myself the gift of presence, and to do the next right thing. It will all work out, one day at a time.

August

Troubles are often the tools by which God fashions us for better things.
~ H. W. Beecher

August 1   **Spiritual Fuel: Musical Metaphors**

On some nights I still believe that a car with the gas
needle on empty can run about fifty more miles
if you have the right music very loud on the radio."
~ **Hunter S. Thompson** ~

Music can be a metaphor for spiritual fuel. We operate in life at different speeds and our energy needs vary, given the circumstance. Am I choosing the right fuel for what I'm trying to accomplish? Am I listening to relaxing music while trying to finish strong on a project? Am I going to bed with loud music pulsing through my head? Am I trying to run on fumes, using no fuel at all? Be congruent. Choose a tempo that fits the moment or season.

Of course, music can be a metaphor for influence and relationships. If you're in a period of life that is best served by positive upbeat "music," don't surround yourself with people who tend to be downers. Life can flow a lot easier when the external stimuli you allow yourself to be exposed to enhances your goals and feeds your spirit, as opposed to detracting and taking energy from you. Notice what "music" is influencing you today. People, places, things, sights, sounds, energy, movies, radio. You are the star of your show—choose your supporting cast and set the stage wisely. And remember, the right soundtrack is everything. With intentional alignment, your masterpiece will unfold with ease and be met with standing ovations. What are you fueling up on today? Congruency is the key to efficiency and purpose! Fill 'er up!

August 2   **Hiking Path Metaphors: Part One**

There are many different types of paths. Each path has ups and downs, figuratively, and sometimes literally too. A narrow path is easily defined, and I don't have to deal with indecision or doubt. I've just got to go with it and trust. On the downside, a narrow path is very rigid, with few options. I can feel confined, wondering if I will fit through the small spaces. A wide path offers flexibility, freedom, and choice. There's room for play, and room for a wayward step or an error. A wide path doesn't dictate expectations, but provides a general direction to follow. How does your life feel right now? Are you on a narrow path or a wide one? There's no right answer—the question is whether or not it's working for you.

Taking a hidden path can be scary. The beginning is visible, but then it appears to drop off, or it takes an unexpected turn leading out of sight with no indication of where it will go. Hidden paths require complete trust, with a hint of caution. I have learned to approach what appears to be the end with hesitancy, yet expectant that the next path will appear, and it always does. My perspective doesn't allow me to see the connecting trail until just a few steps before I reach it.

If you're on a path filled with uncertainty today, may you be filled with an extra dose of faith and trust that a connection will be made visible just when you need it.

August 3   **Hiking Path Metaphors: Part Two**

When I have a higher perspective and can see a path for miles, I approach with comfort and confidence. There it is, start to finish. I will start here and I will end there. I can tell the journey looks interesting, with lots of twists and turns, but since I can see it in its entirety, I have more trust. The beginning and ending is defined, even though I don't know exactly how everything will unfold along the way, or how I will navigate every turn. I'm not guaranteed to never trip or fall, but I know how to get up, learn, and keep moving forward. I feel this is similar to entering college, getting married or becoming a parent. We can imagine the big picture but we don't know exactly how it's all going to go. If you can see a path in front of you that looks and feels right, go for it! Trust you'll be given everything you need along the way.

Going uphill is harder, but more comfortable for me than going downhill. I take each step with intention. I feel more in control and can pace myself better. Going down can be scary, especially if the way is steep. Pacing becomes more difficult to control, making it harder to choose solid footing. To be safe, I take smaller strides. I equate going uphill to climbing toward a goal, as compared to achieving a goal and running with it (downhill). Sometimes when I get what I want, suddenly everything can seem to happen too fast. Even if it's good stuff, personally, it takes practice for me to go with the flow and trust I'll be okay. I've always had more fear of success than failure. I also think I'm more comfortable fighting for something than enjoying the peaceful attainment after the struggle, but I'm working on that.

For now—I see the path directly before me and take one small, intentional step, and I trust my next step will be guided. I'm reminded that hiking and life aren't about arriving, but embracing the path we're on, the blessings *and* the lessons. It's encouraging to remember we're free to change paths if we need more safety, more certainty, or maybe the opposite—more adventure and excitement. If I can't change paths immediately, I will find the gift right where I am. Today I will enjoy the journey, rest when needed, help others along the way, and frequently look up to enjoy the view!

August 4   Trust the Path Will Become Clear

I haven't written in a while and I'm astounded to see that today, two full years later, this entry for August is in sync with my last August entry. Wow … God *is* writing this book … not me.

We recently returned from a fabulous vacation in Cancun. The resort was huge with lots of winding sidewalks. It took a while to learn the best routes to where we wanted to go. One day I was trying to determine the quickest way to get back to the lobby from our room several buildings away. Because of my viewpoint and some small hills, the sidewalk I was on appeared to vanish for a stretch and reappear exactly where I needed to come out. I decided to stick with it and soon came to a fork. The path to the right was fully visible, which was great, except it wasn't going to take me where I wanted to go! I could see where the fork to the left came out way up ahead, but it looked like it ended in lush vegetation, and didn't appear to run all the way through. I kept walking and trusted that the way would become clear as I got closer. Sure enough, as I moved along, more of the path was revealed as my perspective changed, and I ended up exactly where I needed to be.

Sometimes we can't see how we're going to get from point A to point B. As we walk forward in faith, hope and trust, the path becomes visible. Sometimes, just enough vision is revealed for only the next few steps. We will encounter forks in the road. Some are opportunities to confirm where we really want to go, and how committed we are to get there. Other forks may show us alternatives we hadn't even considered or dreamed of, and they may be the right choice at that moment. With an open heart and mind, and a willingness to ask for directions, we will find our way! Are you on the path you want to be on? If you look ahead five years, are you moving closer to your goals or further away? Take a break to evaluate. It's never too late to get back on track or change direction altogether!

Be daring, be different, be impractical, be anything
that will assert integrity of purpose and imaginative
vision against the play-it-safers, the creatures
of the commonplace, the slaves of the ordinary.
~ **Cecil Beaton** ~

What happens when you come to a fork in the road and your next step isn't clear? What if you look far ahead in both directions and just can't be certain which path is best for you? I like the simple advice I received once from my recovery community when I felt really stuck—make a decision and go with it until more is revealed. I have used that a lot.

Sometimes the minute I decide what action to take, I feel relief and conviction that my choice was right. Other times, I know immediately I made the wrong choice, and guess what? I can change my mind! The only thing I know that is not reversible is death. If you're still alive, you can always change course.

Evaluate where you are, but don't let fear keep you frozen. Making no decision can be right for a time, but eventually, any decision is better than paralysis. Motion creates motion. Change is not always comfortable. I'm not sure I have ever experienced growth that wasn't accompanied by a level of discomfort. In fact, my degree of discomfort is often directly proportional with how much growth I'm experiencing. If you're going through a tough situation, get the lessons! We don't grow when we are comfy couch dwellers. We grow when we're engaged and taking chances. When we make mistakes. Saying the wrong thing can possibly lead to a more useful discussion than if we hold our thoughts inside and always play it safe. It's okay to make mistakes! Stop worrying about playing it safe and just play it! You'll figure out your next step if you keep putting one foot in front of the other, while paying attention to how you feel. Self-honesty on our journey is critical as we choose our path, and a great source of internal guidance. Go ahead—take a risk!

August 6   Challenging Old Beliefs

What is more mortifying than to feel you've missed
the Plum for want of courage to shake the Tree?
~ **Logan Pearsall Smith** ~

Today I woke to an amazing thunderstorm with heavy rains. A perfect day for sleeping in! I love our covered deck on days like today. I gathered my things for reading and writing outside and brought my cat, Harvey to sit with me. I'm not sure he's ever been outside during a thunderstorm. He was naturally concerned and extremely alert. I wondered if he was looking up at me periodically to see if I was as concerned as he was. It felt like every time he checked with me and saw that I was not disturbed, he could adjust his natural assessment from, *This is scary*, to *Hmmm, this is new and different, but it seems like I'm safe*. As long as his safety remained in check, Harvey was open-minded to looking around and observing this new experience.

We all develop beliefs in childhood about what is good and bad, what is safe or unsafe, and what is scary or not. When was the last time you challenged yourself to look at a situation differently? Consider the possibility that maybe you're holding onto an idea that isn't based on truth. Some of our inherent beliefs do still have validity today, but others may not.

I read somewhere recently to start saying, "Yes" more often, instead of automatically saying, "No." If someone asks you to attend a social event that seems beyond your comfort level, commit to go anyway. Give yourself permission to leave after one hour if you aren't enjoying the experience. Safety is always important, but so is stretching beyond our comfort zones and common beliefs. Do it with care and awareness and the world, as you know it, will start to expand. Go outside and let the rain fall on your face every now and then, leaving your umbrella behind! Maybe you *won't* catch a cold? Challenge your old beliefs. Stretch yourself. Fun and freedom await!

August 7   Hand-Me-Down Beliefs

My pastor tells this story occasionally and sharing it here seems fitting, since we're challenging old beliefs. A mom is in the kitchen frying up a ham, while her eight-year old daughter watches. When she sees her mother cut off the end of the ham before throwing it in the pan, the young girl asked, "Mom, why do you have to cut the end off?" Her mom replied, "That's a good question. I've just always done it because my mom used to do that. Let's call her and ask." So they called the grandma, who gave the same answer, "I don't really know. My mother always did it, so I did too." They all decided to ask the great-grandma on their next visit. Next Sunday, they asked her, "Why did you always cut the end of the ham off before frying it?" and great-grandma said, "My pan was too small."

Maybe it's time to challenge old thinking and try something new. Pick one old belief to hold up to the light and see if it's still relevant today. Do one thing to push yourself a little outside your comfort zone, or your usual M.O. Even if it's just taking a different route to work, or making a new recipe, there's a big world waiting for you—venture out!

August 8   Reality is Real

I'm enjoying a nice, quiet, cloudy day—a perfect setting to go inside myself to observe and reflect. I have been seeking direction and peace on a particular issue that has been in limbo for quite some time. Our house has been on the market now for eight months. We really want to sell it, but we aren't seeing any activity and are getting tired of trying to keep it ready to show at a moment's notice. Yesterday we received a pretty concrete answer— even if we did find a buyer, it wouldn't appraise anywhere close to what we paid for it, so they wouldn't get financing anyway. We would have to drop the price by twenty percent to even have a chance. Or wait a year or more and try again.

Don't you hate it when you pray and journal, looking for guidance and then you get it, but it's not the answer you hoped for? Now I want to say to God, "Are you sure? Hey, no rush! Take some more time to think about it." In the end, self-honesty is a big part of my journey. Being willing to stay in reality full-time is the path I choose today. Better to make decisions based on truth rather than fantasy. Like it or not, reality is real, so I might as well choose to face it. Hiding my head in the sand like an ostrich doesn't change anything, just makes me less prepared to make good decisions. Today I am thankful for answers, even when they aren't what I wanted to hear. I now have good, solid information and can put my focus, time and attention on how to make this new reality my friend. I can proceed in a different direction, grounded in truth. Clarity is a gift and today I receive it with gratitude.

August 9   Rhythm and Roll

Today is the first day our son goes back to school. (And all the mothers let out a cheer!) We have seasons of the year and seasons of our lives. My son will be a junior in high school, so the school year/summer seasons and what that means to a home with children will look different for us in a few more years. For now, I am relishing the idea of going back to a routine. I'm up earlier today to take care of me before everyone else gets up. I may have to call the Army out here to get our son up after a summer of bedtimes long past midnight, and sleeping till noon.

Our bodies crave rhythm! Our souls need some routine. We need a balance between the expected and unexpected. Too much of either is not a satisfying life. Too much routine leads to boredom and stagnation. Too much uncertainty can lead to a steady state of insecurity, doubt and fear. We do need uncertainty in our lives to keep us on our game. To challenge us. To satisfy the human need to be curious, to be surprised. We love movies because we don't know what's going to happen. Some even make us sit on the edge of our seats to see how it will end! Imagine living our lives with that much tension every day? Everything in moderation, and so today I celebrate the balance a school routine imposes on my family. What rhythms do you cherish? What beat are you marching to? Take a moment to consider if you have a healthy balance of the expected and the unexpected in your life. Are you too comfortable? Too scattered or anxious? Too serious? Mix it up till it feels good to you! You'll know.

August 10   Following Our Internal Clock

We all have an internal clock. Are you a morning person? A night owl? Are you trying to be both? I have at times, but that can quickly turn into serious sleep deprivation! It's tough because I love to be up before everyone else to have my quiet time, but I also occasionally enjoy staying up into the wee hours of the night to be alone with my creativity and the part of me who can focus and knock out a deadline. Clearly I can't do both all the time, and I know which schedule is more ideal for my overall well-being.

I thrive on my internal clock during the day as well. Today I made my list of to do's and put a star by the ones that have to happen today, so my priorities are clear. The first two items on my agenda are "write" and "walk." Ideally those are both done early, but I got a late start today. I have to write before my mind gets too cluttered by the events of the day and before the chatter in my head increases. While I prefer to take an early walk before it gets too hot, I know I am *more* likely to take a walk later, than I am to write later in the day. I usually won't write once my "primetime" is missed. Knowing my internal rhythms helps me function better.

Most days, are you working *with* your internal clock or against it? When are you most inspired? What time of day does your body like to exercise, eat, sleep? What do you know about yourself in this regard? Do you have routines that optimize your clarity, your mental and physical energy? Is your sleep quality the same from 10 p.m. to 6 a.m. as it is from midnight to 8 a.m.? Mine isn't! If you don't already, get to know your rhythms. Experiment and make mental note of your findings. Find the ways to show up as the best YOU!

August 11   Turn Down the Chaos

*People have a hard time letting go of
their suffering. Out of a fear of the unknown,
they prefer suffering that is familiar.*
~ Thich Nhat Hanh ~

Recently, I wrote about the need for uncertainty in our lives—to a degree, anyway. We crave mystery, surprise and anticipation. I grew up with more than my share of uncertainty. Normal life to me included a steady infusion of chaos and drama, contributing to a constant sense of insecurity. I think we crave what we know, what we're used to and comfortable with. Even if it's not great, it is familiar. To keep chaos in our lives (which generates that frequent adrenaline rush some of us have grown accustomed to), we may regularly do the following: pay bills late even if the money is in the bank, find reasons to pick arguments, run late all the time, look for faults in others, complain about anything/everything, choose love and work relationships with people who also need chaos, change jobs and residences frequently, and neglect our basic self-care including having enough fun and rest. I'm guilty of some of these, and I'm sure there are many more ways people use chaos on a regular basis to feel alive.

Awareness is always the first step toward change. If you are content to participate or even create an abundance of chaos in your life, you are free to continue on that path. However, if this describes you and you're ready to let some or most of it go, congratulations! Now you have awareness and a desire for change! We can't stop a lifelong pattern overnight, but we can identify a starting place. There are several ways to reduce daily chaos. Instead of waiting for the last minute to leave, plan to leave fifteen minutes early. If you do arrive early, use that time to meditate, journal or read ten pages of a good book. Rather than finding faults, try to find one good quality in everyone you encounter and in every situation. Take a five-minute breather for every fifty-five minutes of work. What is one action you are willing to take today to feel more love, stability and serenity in your life? Small steps lead to big change!

August 12   Out of the Shadows

Fear makes the wolf bigger than he is.
~ German Proverb ~

Today is a warm sunny August morning, with lots of life already buzzing in the air. I have two thick, lush palm trees on our deck along the railing to the steps below. My outdoor cat, Lucky (who looks like a sleek miniature panther) loves to run up the steps, and with a flying leap, land in the midst of the palm branches falling across the rail. One afternoon, I happened to see him do this and the sun was angled just right, so that all I saw was his shadow. At first I was so startled! Shadows can be larger than life and for a split second, I thought something very large had jumped up on my deck! As soon as the light hit him coming out from the shadows, Lucky was right-sized again.

How often do we have situations, worries and fears in the shadows of our minds looming much larger than they really are? As long as we let them stay there, they will seem bigger than life, and bigger than any possible solution we can come up with—in the dark. Shine some light on them! Expose them! Talk about them, write about them and separate the truth from the exaggerations and distortions that our minds and emotions are projecting into them. I'm reminded of a Twelve-step recovery saying, "A problem shared, is a problem halved." Whatever the problem, it's usually not as big as we believe it is, and often, we are worrying or fearful of things which will never come to be.

Today, take at least one of those worries out of the shadows and shine some light on it. What is the truth today about that concern? Is your worry changing anything? Share it with a friend, say a prayer and let it go. If there's something you need to do, do it and surrender the rest. You can live in shadow or in light. I am thankful to know I have a choice. Reality is only as real as my perception of it in any given moment. Looking through light helps me see better!

August 13   Down Time IS Productive

I awoke today to a wonderful drizzle! It's darker outside than usual, inviting me to stay in my pajamas all day! I am not sure why on a cloudy, rainy, overcast day I'm more inclined to give myself a break? The voice inside that shouts, *Must get it done! Time is passing by!* and *Hurry up!* seems to be silenced on days like these when the sun is hiding. I am more able to give myself permission to relax a little, even to the point of indulgence and rebellion against all the times I wouldn't let myself take a break. Sometimes on days like today, I will allow myself to read and write for hours only to find it's time for lunch and I'm still in my PJs. I have done that before and then all of a sudden, the sun comes out and I feel exposed! Betrayed even. I cry, *Hey, I thought we had a deal? I was hiding under that cloud cover!* Today was going to be one of those days. I was going to be lazy, but then the sun popped out signaling my normal hours of operation have begun. Unfortunately, I'm jolted back to the reality that it's much later than I realized. That internal voice rises up and says, *Now you're waaay behind!* I take note of several lessons:

❧ The truth is always the truth. If it's noon, and I'm still in my PJs, that's true whether it's sunny or rainy. Even though I am under the illusion that it matters less on a rainy day, the truth is that time marches on and the day is ticking by. Even if no one else knows but me, it's still true. Oh how that can apply to all of our secrets!

❧ Everyone needs a lazy day now and then! Especially those of us who push ourselves and maintain a very busy schedule on a daily basis. We need some downtime with permission! Rain or shine.

❧ Downtime doesn't necessarily mean we are not being productive. Giving in to a need for a timeout, for fun, for lunch with a friend is necessary to recharge our batteries! We need times of non-productivity to fuel and stimulate our ability to be productive and creative.

Just because no one else sees it or no one else knows, the truth is the truth. A healthy balance between production and timeout is crucial to optimal performance, well-being, serenity and contentment. C'est la vie!

Lucky just meowed like crazy outside, which is often his way of announcing he has delivered a "gift." Sure enough, with a little investigation, we have a very large, living frog under our outdoor coffee table. I went in to get something to rescue him and transport him from our two-story deck back to the safety of the grass. We've had many excited "gifts" run right off the deck to their deaths, so it was important to keep the rescue contained. When I went back outside, the frog was gone. He was nowhere to be found and not splattered on the ground below. Hmmm … maybe sometimes it's appropriate to let nature run its course? I definitely felt my need for uncertainty being met as I tiptoed around searching. That frog could hop out at me any second! My curiosity was piqued. Where was that frog!

Maybe I was indulging in chaos that wasn't mine—letting myself get sidetracked to jump in and get a little drama fix, all in the name of "helping." While all of the pearls of wisdom and metaphors of nature were filling my brain, I answered with, *But I just want to help that frog!* A noble thought, but often we need to step back and let others help themselves and give them a chance to be creative and solve their own problems.

Self-doubt began to set in. Maybe I didn't really see the frog? Maybe I was just crazy? And the nuggets of wisdom just kept coming! "Know what you know!" Well, I know there's a helpless frog somewhere on my deck, scared to death, and by gosh, I was going to find him! I decided to get help—always a good idea when we feel stumped and uncertain. I let my dog, Goldie, a very accomplished retriever, go out on the deck. She went crazy sniffing him out, so at least I was validated and convinced I hadn't imagined the frog. I checked in one last possible hiding place, and there he was—sitting still, pretending to be invisible. Can frogs give you warts, or is that one of those old beliefs from childhood? Just to be safe, I had a yellow plastic glove on one hand and a box in the other. Did I think he would comply and just hop in the box? Wishful thinking and another lesson: how many times before I finally accept that others cannot read my mind and automatically do what I think is best for them?

I went to capture him, and that sucker hopped all over like crazy. I bet he got three feet of air or more with each jump! Goldie went nuts! I screamed! I'm out in broad daylight in my PJs—now "everyone" knows I haven't been "productive" yet today, and it's 11 a.m. (Even though anything I have done or not done in PJs this morning is *exactly* what I needed to do today!) I put Goldie in the house and thanked her for her role in the rescue. After a little more excitement, I cornered the frog, got him in my box with an extra plastic bag for good measure, and safely released him back into the wild. I went to grab the hose thinking he might like a drink after all that excitement but when I returned, he had vanished. I think this time I will let him go, and release him to the father of all creatures. I also think I will get out of my PJs now!

August 15   Owning My Choices

The strongest principle of growth lies in human choice.
~ George Eliot ~

Some bushes will constantly need to be trimmed, and most weeds will return too quickly and need to be pulled, again. I can fight and rebel against this all I want, but my resistance is a waste of energy. Yes, it's a never-ending chore, but *only* if I want a beautifully-landscaped yard with clean, orderly beds and shapely trees and bushes. I do have a choice. I can let it all go. I don't have to prune bushes and pull weeds. How often do I forget this is optional, and it's only because I desire a certain outcome that I'm willing to put forth the effort?

In most cases, we do have choices in our lives, although at first glance it may not feel that way. With financial struggles, we may feel we have no options, but with some creativity, we can often find alternatives we hadn't considered before. Working is a necessary choice for many of us. We can choose to not work and live the consequences of that decision. In our families and relationships, we maintain communications with whomever we want. No one can "make" us do anything.

Take a good hard look, and I think you'll find there are alternatives for most situations. We may not like the alternatives, but they are there. Just like my yard work, my spiritual, physical and emotional well-being requires regular maintenance if I want to feel a certain way and experience health and growth. It never feels good to be backed into a corner. When you look close, you'll find you have choices, even if it's just changing your attitude and outlook. Owning your choices gives you ownership of your life. Taking personal accountability for where you are and where you're going is true freedom!

August 16   Accepting Others

The beginning of love is to let those we love be perfectly themselves and not to twist them to fit our own image.
~ Thomas Merton ~

"Have more pointless, non-productive fun." This is my latest assignment from a well-meaning friend who knows this is an area of my life that's out of balance. *Bubbles!* How much more pointless can you get? (Okay, go buy some bubbles, it's actually pretty fun!) I bought a tube with a very long wand, and as you wave it, it creates long, trailing bubbles that break off into regular ones. I have another wand that has a star shaped hole. Nope! The bubbles aren't star-shaped, but it was fun anticipating what they would look like. I'm guessing no matter what shape your bubble blower is, it's going to produce round bubbles. I see a key lesson in acceptance coming.

Accept people, places and things for whom and what they are and quit thinking, "If I try hard enough, I can change them." Bubbles are going to be round, and people are going to be people. The good news is I can always change myself and my circumstances. If a "circle" isn't what I like, it's time to move on. It doesn't make me or the "circle" good, bad, better or worse. It's just not a good fit, or at least not right now. (All relationships have challenges, so this isn't your permission slip to end a relationship just because everything isn't going your way.)

Have the courage to be brutally honest with yourself. Yes, that may mean taking action or making a tough choice. We don't have nine lives like our feline friends, so make this one count! Surround yourself with the people, places and things of your choosing, not someone else's. Absolutely don't settle for anything less than everything! And celebrate the "circles" you encounter along the way—somebody loves them just the way they are! I love the saying, "Live and let live!" Do your thing and let others do theirs, without your interference or attempts to change them. Personally, I've got my hands full working on me. Guess I'll go back to my bubbles now!

August 17   Food For Thought

Why do some plants and flowers close up at night and reopen every day? Protection, I suppose. Why do plants and flowers grow in the direction of the sun? We grow toward whatever is feeding us. When we look at some plants and flowers, it's more obvious in some than others how much they've been stretching toward the light to get those necessary nutrients. What are you leaning into? Is it providing nutrients? Life? If we could see the physical bend showing which way you are leaning, what would it point to? Are you leaning with intention or is it just anyway the wind blows? Are you bearing the fruit you desire? The fruit we bear is a direct reflection of what we've been feeding ourselves—our bodies, minds and spirits.

- ✖ Need more compassion for yourself or others? Feed on gratitude.
- ✖ Need more abundance? Fill up with service and giving.
- ✖ Need more peace? Chew on acceptance.
- ✖ Want forgiveness? Swallow your pride.
- ✖ Want love? Give it away and you'll have a never-ending feast.

We have many sources of life. Protect yourself from that which doesn't serve you, and lean into that which does. Get your share and watch your life blossom!

August 18   Go For It!

Yesterday I saw a cat bolt across five lanes of busy traffic at record speed. It was amazing and terrifying to witness! He didn't look left or right. He got in the zone and flew. While it seemed unexpected and frightening to me, obviously he had calculated the risks, waited for the right moment, and executed his plan without hesitation. It's true, many cats have done that and not made it. Well, guess what? At least fifty percent of small businesses fail in the first five years. Of those that make it, another fifty percent fail in the subsequent five years.

Even with those terrible odds, people muster up the courage every day to give their idea a try and start a business. With an alarming divorce rate, people still get married all the time. Yes you might fail, but what if you succeed? If you're not happy where you are, it's time to calculate the risks, create a plan, and move when the window of opportunity appears. It beats the alternative of staying trapped on the sidelines, gazing across the road to where you really want to be, wondering if you could make it.

The decision has to be iron cast. If the cat had taken the time to look over his shoulder, to focus more on the obstacles than on the prize, he would have lost precious timing and maybe even his life. He didn't stop midway to see what others thought of him either. At that moment, and throughout his run, he was focused on one thing—reaching his goal and what that would mean. He had a strong "why" which helped him defy the odds. I don't know who said it, but it's worth repeating: "Don't let people who have given up on their dreams talk you out of yours." I challenge you to leave your comfort zone and chase your dreams! Even if you don't get exactly what you started out seeking, I bet the journey will be worth it. Voltaire said, "Good is the enemy of Great!" Go for Great!

August 19   The Heat Is On

Our bodies are such amazing, complex systems, constantly regenerating and renewing themselves. A while back, I had surgery on my knee and in the acute healing process, this knee was very warm to the touch when compared to my healthy knee. I could literally feel how hard my body was working to heal itself. This brought to mind several sayings regarding transformation through heat and fire.

- ❦ "She has several irons in the fire."
- ❦ "He really brought the heat today!"
- ❦ "She's in hot water now!"
- ❦ "Nothing like a trial by fire."

When the "heat" shows up in our lives, whatever that looks like for each of us, it can be mildly (or extremely) uncomfortable. When we feel the temperature rising in our circumstances or relationships, we can trust that a transformation is taking place, or an opportunity for growth is at hand. Resistance is the opposite of acceptance, and only serves to make the struggle last longer or keep me from benefiting fully from an opportunity for change. I'm always better off asking, "What's my lesson here?" rather than "Why is this happening to me?"

Imagine metal trying to maintain its current shape when surrounded by fire? It would be pretty impossible for it to not be changed. If it's happening to you right now, get the lesson! Too often, the fires life throws at us seem scary and something we want to avoid, but if we're seeking and listening to the guidance inside, it's safe to trust we'll be cared for until we come out the other side. I choose to believe every circumstance is for our greater good.

August 20   **Bring On the Meltdown**

Are you feeling the heat today? At work? Maybe at home? Maybe the fire you're facing today is just a little fire, giving you the chance to refine such virtues as patience and trust, or surrender. Maybe you get to prove whether or not you can be grateful in all things and stay focused on what really matters when inconveniences pop up? Sometimes we face bigger fires and they're pushing us to do something we've known we've wanted or needed to do for a long time, but lacked the courage or the motivation. Now circumstances have intensified, and we finally have some added incentive to take appropriate action. At times, I've ignored my inner promptings and outer circumstances until the fire got so hot, it was obvious what my next move should be. I like that though—I feel like I can't really make a mistake! God has a way of bringing growth opportunities back around to teach me and take me to new and exciting places, even when it doesn't feel like that at the moment (and my feet are burning!).

Allow the silversmith of life to mold you and shape you when the temperatures get cranked up. Maybe a meltdown is exactly what you really need? Sometimes we need to let the "old" melt away so the "new" can emerge. When life's circumstances are at their hottest, the greatest work is being done in us. Trust in the process and know you'll come out better, stronger and more refined on the other side. Absolutely everything works for our good!

August 21   Annual Or Perennial?

Separate reeds are weak and easily broken; but bound together they are strong and hard to tear apart.
~ *The Midrash* ~

Resiliency may be one of the top secrets to a happy existence. Life happens and sometimes that looks or feels like getting knocked around, pushed off path, or hearing silence when I'm seeking answers and direction. Being resilient means I come back stronger than ever, no matter what has happened or how long I feel I've been underground in a season of uncertainty.

I planted six average-sized mums in my front flower bed last fall. About two months ago, I began to see some leafy green breaking through the ground primarily in one spot, with another little patch off to the side. *I planted six mums, so what's this?* I asked myself. I came so close to deciding the little one was a weed and was tempted to pull it out, but I decided to let it grow and see what happened. Now, I have one gigantic mum that is just starting to flower! It's huge! The big one and the small one merged together. What's even more astounding, I put six beautiful mums in the ground in November. Winter came and all six of them grew barren of any life. Spring arrived and they showed no sign of life. I could only wonder if they survived and would come back. All this time—ALL THIS TIME— the mums were pooling their resources and uniting together underground to burst back to life bigger, taller and more beautiful than ever before, except as one huge flowering bush. "We can do more together than we can ever do alone" has never been more evident than with these six mums.

Flowers that only bloom once are called annuals, but flowers that come back again and again are called perennials. Are you an annual or a perennial flower? Will you bloom once and that's it, or will you keep coming back season after season, no matter what? Did you or someone else tell you that you're an annual? That your time has passed? That you had one great season and that's it? Reject that lie! Cancel. Delete. The champions of life have figured out how to be perennials, to come back and bloom over multiple seasons and you can too. Resilience: taking what you're given and bouncing back better each and every time, adapting as necessary for you to thrive. It's never too late to allow your resilient spirit to blossom. It's time.

August 22   Balancing Our To Do Lists

What is the good of your stars and trees, your sunrise and the wind, if they do not enter into our daily lives?
~ E. M. Forster ~

On your Mark. Get set. Slow! Why are so many of us racing to a finish line that sits six feet underground? We all end up the same—dead—so what's the rush? Although this is a morbid thought, embracing the truth that none of us get out of here alive can liberate us! We can live our lives stressed out and rushing toward goal after goal, or we can slow down and take some interesting detours. We can fill up our to-do lists with endless tasks, or we can identify two or three daily outcomes to strive for and leave some breathing room for life to surprise us. My lists can go on and on and on. As soon as I check off five tasks, I think of ten more! My to-do lists are great for helping me prioritize what I need to be doing and where I should spend my effort. I just need to remember there is life beyond the list!

Maybe I will pencil in: sit outside under a covered deck in the middle of the summer rainstorm. Or how about: thirty minutes of daydreaming to conjure up a big adventure? Tomorrow I think I'll put on my list: waste time today, at least an hour or more with my best friend talking about nothing and everything. A good friend of mine used to say relationships grow when we waste time together. As a Do-aholic, I could think of nothing more absurd but I've come to know he is absolutely onto something. We say we need more balance in our lives. We can start by putting more balance in our lists and remembering, there is no gold medal to be the first one to finish this race.

August 23   Prune the Negative to Positively Grow

Got confusion? Got Chaos? I'm enjoying an unseasonably cool, seventy-degree August morning on my deck. My two potted palms just got my attention. I'm not sure when it happened but suddenly, they're a big hot mess! Each of them has some pronounced brown stalks which are almost completely dead, while at the same time, each one also has new shoots opening up. The branches causing unsightly chaos are so evident— I can tell exactly what needs to go so these plants can thrive and be beautiful. What if we could view our lives with such simple clarity and perspective? Unfortunately, it can be a lot less obvious what may need to go, if it's our own life we're talking about. It's clear what I need to do for the plant, so I'll get my pruning shears out and get to work. What remains will be a beautiful, thriving tree with all the branches existing in harmony once more.

I am able to step back and see the palms from a distance to make this accurate assessment. If I was *in* the pot, surrounded and immersed by all the stalks and leaves, I may have a harder time discerning what the trouble is. Maybe I wouldn't even think there was any trouble? Or I might focus on what I know is good in the pot (my life), while trying to ignore what's not particularly desirable or useful. Remember that thought as a little child, "If I can't see *you*, then maybe you can't see *me*?" The truth is the truth, whether we acknowledge it or not. Consult with friends, family and mentors when you feel confusion and chaos, or you suspect something may not be flowing quite right in your life. Seek objectivity, even when you think everything is going fine. Get regular input from someone who is neutral and can see your life from a distance. Frequently step back yourself, far enough to where you can get a bigger perspective of the whole. Journaling, praying, and meditating are some of the ways I seek perspective. Taking myself out of the situation for a day or two can also be very helpful, whenever possible.

I'm going to fix these palms right up. Are you ready to let go of some things yourself, and move forward with renewed clarity and pruned intentions? A word of caution: go easy. The rest of your life may look and feel a lot better with just a few, small tweaks. You will flourish by removing the negative and allowing more room for positive growth.

August 24   Good Unfolding

How did it happen? How did it go from excruciatingly hot, one-hundred-degree days to crisp, fall evenings and cool mornings? "Overnight?" I do love summer but by the end of it, I'm ready for a change. My lesson: even when I'm in the midst of intense heat (intense anything) for what feels like a long time, a shift is happening even though I don't see it. And one day after what seems like a never-ending period of discomfort, a change comes from nowhere. Out of the blue. But it didn't, and there was nothing accidental about it. Transition was happening all along and the sudden *evidence* of it makes it appear to have happened overnight.

I can trust my good is being worked out behind the scenes at all times. At the right moment, I will see the manifestation of all the blessings and lessons that have been prepared for me in the background. I find peace in believing I'm being cared for in a nurturing and intentional way, for my greater purpose. I choose to stay on track today and know that my good is unfolding all around me, all the time, even when I don't see anything.

August 25   Why NOT You?

It is not because things are difficult that we do not dare,
it is because we do not dare that they are difficult.
~ Seneca ~

Why *not* you? Extraordinary things happen for ordinary people all the time. Some people believe in their dreams and can allow themselves to hope for *A Life Worth Having*. They have faith and take action to realize their wildest dreams coming true. Other people have *other people syndrome*. They tell themselves that extraordinary dreams only come true for other people. They see themselves as incapable of anything truly great. Rather than hope and risk being disappointed, they don't even try. They tell themselves they are resigned to whatever life deals them, whatever comes easy, and that's as good as it gets for people like them. That's a bunch of hooey! And very sad.

I'm a shoot-for-the-stars kind of person and if I land on the moon, that's still exceptionally awesome! I will know I did my best. Don't get me wrong though, I have my share of fear, doubt and avoidance I must constantly work to overcome. I do allow myself to dream and that's what I hope to encourage you to do as well, if you don't already. When I share my dreams with friends, some are truly excited with me and for me. With others, I can see them shut down, avoid eye contact and check out of the conversation, because hopes and dreams make them uncomfortable. They don't allow themselves to hope and dream and they aren't able to say much when other people share theirs. These aren't the type of people to seek encouragement for a new dream or idea. Protect your hopes and dreams—they are precious!

So are you a dreamer, a believer, or do you struggle with *other people syndrome*? Right now this very minute, I'm telling you the only difference between those who DO and those who DON'T is BELIEF. Make a decision to believe you're as good and deserving as the next person and step up! Take a shot! Know that you deserve it and reach for the stars! The only person holding any of us back is the one we can look at in the mirror and change. Today's the day you start owning your destiny because anything is possible if you're willing to believe you are *already* extraordinary! Why NOT you?

August 26   Never Say Impossible

Do what you can, with what you have, where you are.
~ Theodore Roosevelt ~

This summer, I was fortunate to travel to Guatemala on a voluntourism trip, working with "Hug it Forward" and "DreamTrips" to build schools in remote areas. As we journeyed to several villages, we enjoyed incredible beauty driving through the mountains. On our first day, I was surprised to see villagers farming the sides of the mountains. The slope must have been at least forty-five degrees! It was nearly too steep to walk, much less till the soil, plant and harvest the crops. I guess nobody told them it was impossible!

The Guatemalans took what they were given and made it work. On mountain sides that farmers in other areas of the world wouldn't dream of working, the Guatemalan people are reaping huge crops. They believed it could be done, so they did it! Others saw it was possible so they joined them and planted their own crops. When you drive through Guatemala, you will not see much wasted land. If I drive through your life, what would I see? Are you utilizing all you have been given? What would you begin to cultivate if you believed it was possible? What would you attempt to do if you knew you couldn't fail? Success in anything isn't guaranteed, but failure to try yields the same result every time. Nada! Zero!

Believe in yourself. Believe in your neighbor when he or she is attempting the impossible. When one person succeeds, we all succeed because the borders of possibility have just been expanded for everyone. We won't conquer a mountain in one day, but today we can take one step in the right direction. Go ahead—show me what you're working with and what you can do with it!

August 27   **True Wealth**

While in Guatemala this summer helping to build a school, I learned several lessons. One of them was about perceived wealth. At first glance, it's easy to view those with a lack of material wealth or opportunity as poor and perhaps someone to pity. It may also be easy for someone to view and envy the next person as wealthy just because they appear to have a great life.

The truth is I know people who have money who are poor in personal fulfillment and relationships, and are full of fear and despair. I know people who have limited funds who are rich in laughter and family, in tradition and personal peace. My natural instinct was to feel bad for the impoverished communities in Guatemala, and I realized some of them may look at Americans with envy for our perceived wealth. After spending several days there, I realized in many cases the Guatemalans are richer than some of us will ever be. They are rich in family and community. They are abundant in traditions that ground them. As a people, they seem to know who they are and through hard work, are making the most out of all they've been given. They are rich in heritage and values.

The Guatemalans' work ethic and accomplishments have instilled within them a beautiful sense of pride and self-esteem that money cannot buy or replace. In Guatemala, I gladly gave of my time and resources and received a greater perspective of true wealth. I gained a stronger desire to pursue and appreciate the things that really add value to life. Today, count your blessings and say thanks for all the ways you are already wealthy.

August 28   You Already Have What It Takes

*Trust yourself. Create the kind of self that
you will be happy to live with all your life. Make
the most of yourself by fanning the tiny, inner
sparks of possibility into flames of achievement.*
~ Golda Meir ~

Congratulations to me! I just realized I have six pack abs. You do too! We all have those gorgeous stomach muscles (way down deep) that everyone wants, but some of us choose to become disciplined and focused on developing those muscles to the point they are pronounced and visible externally. Some of us say, "I'd like to, but I could never look like that," and buy their own excuses. We are created equally and our bodies are much more alike than they are different. The only reason I personally don't have a visible six-pack stomach is because I have not chosen to be consistently disciplined to do what it would take to reveal one. And if your desire to have a flat tummy is long gone, just play along. Here comes the point, and it's not about abs!

Many of us look at people and wish we had their talent, their skills, their friends, their assets, or their life. We tell ourselves they're different, special somehow. We lie to ourselves or we buy someone else's lie that we weren't meant to be great or to have a great life. A *lie* is all that is! We can have what we set our minds to have. We can be anything with the right effort, priority, intention and consistent action. The real question is, "Are you ready?" "Do you really want (fill in the blank)?" Are you willing to become uncomfortable to get it, because change is not always easy or familiar to manifest. Have you ever said, "I would give anything to have (fill in the blank) or be like so and so?" Really? Great! Start today. Who has what you want spiritually, emotionally, physically, relationally, or financially? They are no different than you. Stop making excuses and buying lies, and start creating your great life today. You *already* have what it takes!

August 29   Know When to Let Go

Okay I know up front this isn't the most poetic or elegant of lessons from nature. It's not about blue skies, blooming flowers, or summer thunderstorms. It's about … ticks. I can't think of one good thing about a tick except for maybe a lesson in letting go. My cat, Lucky goes outside and occasionally I have to remove a tick that he's picked up. Usually I can pull them off easily, but he has one now that just will not let go. In fact, I used tweezers to remove it and thought I got him, but upon a closer look, I only removed the tick's external shell with legs attached! The tick has completely lost its own identity and is firmly embedded in my cat! It's just a very small, flesh colored being, slightly visible on my cat's belly.

How many of us sacrifice everything we are—everything unique about ourselves so that we can stay in a relationship, or a job, or in a family we care about? Even to the detriment of ourselves and others? If most of your soul is buried and beyond recognition in any of your present day circumstances, it's time to back out! Let go! Trust that something or someone else will come along, bringing an interaction that will be mutually beneficial. Sucking the life out of someone or clinging to a situation doesn't allow room for breathing, much less growth. Take a deep breath. Get support. Trust and let go.

August 30   Becoming a Human (Who Is) Being

To love oneself is the beginning of a lifelong romance.
~ Oscar Wilde ~

One of my biggest challenges is staying too busy being a super "human doing," instead of a human (who is) being. My to-do list is frequently on multiple Post-it notes. I try to wake up early with the intention to write, pray, journal or meditate—something centering before starting the rest of my day. Too often I make the mistake of checking e-mail first. Then I spontaneously decide to change the HVAC air filter (because if I don't do it right this second I might forget for another month). Then I will "really quickly" unload the dishwasher, sort laundry, and then, and then ... and then the morning quiet time never happens.

Recently in the midst of this all-too-typical frenzy, I finally answered the call of my soul to have five minutes of quiet time outside, amidst the soothing sounds of nature. But my attitude was, *Okay, I'm here—let's do this! Let the amazing, spiritual connection begin! And could you hurry up please? I have a LOT to do!* Obviously, I wasn't feeling much connection with that attitude, but then I had an "a-ha" moment. Loving myself and being able to feel connected spiritually isn't something I snap my fingers to get. Rebuilding self-esteem doesn't happen overnight just because the awareness has come that I need to love myself more. Like any true love affair, the love relationship with myself happens over time. It gets richer over time. If I want to develop self-intimacy, I must be committed to the process of making myself available for genuine connection with myself, consistently. Will you commit to give yourself some quality time today? If you're not used to doing it, start with five minutes, but take yourself seriously—no cell phones allowed! With practice, we will discover who our best friend has been all along.

August 31   **A Human "Being:" Part Two**

Wonder how we would feel if a lover said, "Ok, let's go! I'll give you five minutes. Give me all you got, your VERY BEST in five minutes—*because I have a lot to do*!" That wouldn't feel good and wouldn't invite true connection. Why then, concerning self-intimacy, would I even begin to bare my soul for a five minute, hit and run encounter? I'm worth much more than that! No, my authentic self will stay hidden until the circumstances are more welcoming (when it's safe for the real me to come out for a meaningful connection). I can't expect a true spiritual connection while the timer is running!

Since I wasn't going to be able to rush through my morning time and magically achieve serenity with a snap of my fingers, I relented and gave myself twenty minutes to journal. With the morning sun warming my skin and the gentle breeze tousling my hair, I had a genuine, loving encounter with my inner self. The real Angela dared to come out when she sensed my full commitment to receive her and be present with her in a relaxed space. Twenty minutes wasn't much longer than five, in the big scheme of things, although, intention matters much more than minutes. (Five minutes with a familiar lover goes a lot further than five minutes with an occasional lover.) I believe I will get to a point when I can grab a brief moment of quality intimacy with myself when that's all I really have time for, because a foundation of familiarity and safety will have already been established consistently over time. I'm still building toward that right now.

Once I committed to taking the time to be still with *me*, all other to-do's vanished from my mind and I truly became present. Now once again, I am connected to me, grounded to my heart, and in love with my spirit. I am a human (who is) being again and can carry that with me into all I choose to do today.

September

The past is but the beginning of a beginning.
~ H.G. Wells

... human beings, by changing the inner attitudes of their
minds, can change the outer aspects of their lives.
~ William James ~

I am experiencing a calm, overcast morning on my deck. Notice I didn't say "enjoying" because my mind is focused on other things that don't produce feelings of joy. The cows are mooing like always, the birds are singing, and the palm branches are blowing in the wind, making a nice rustling sound. I'm aware and observant of all the soothing sounds around me, but I still haven't been willing to set aside the negative thoughts weighing me down. What are the benefits of holding on to hurt and sadness? It does allow me to feel sorry for myself and to possibly gain sympathy from others. It gets me off the hook from engaging in life and joy and happiness for as long as I choose to keep sulking and licking my wounds. Self-pity relieves me of the responsibility to step up to the plate of life and take some good swings. (Right now, I've laid my bat down and am sitting on the bench deciding if I want to play today or not.)

On the other hand, what's the benefit of saying a quick prayer, asking for guidance and relief, and then letting my pain and troubles go—surrendering them? For starters, I'm free to seek the gifts of the day. I'm free to be useful to myself and others. I am open to receive blessings and inspiration. I can look at the day before me—the same day *either way* I choose to see it—and start focusing on all the goodness around me! I can be expectant of a great day rather than deciding to trudge my way through it.

Given my choices I think I will pick myself up, ask for help with what's troubling me, and put life back in proper proportion. Forecast now says 95% chance of a good day, and I will take those odds! If you haven't already, I hope you will decide to have a great day, too!

September 2   **Weathering Storms Together**

What a beautiful, rainy morning from my covered deck. I love the sound of water, whether it's the ocean, a fountain, rain or even the lingering drips of rain running through gutters and drains spouts. I can see a pasture across the road that separates our backyard from a farm. Cows are often visible and audible, mooing for whatever reasons cows moo. What I see today begs the question, "Why do cows, horses and other such animals stand in groups during a rain shower?" I could understand them gathering together to share shelter, but when there is no shelter, many of them still cluster together during a storm. As I study the cows now, most are huddled together, while just a few are separate from the whole.

I've decided they are no different than us. When the storms of life are coming down, we will not only seek shelter whenever possible, but we benefit from standing amongst a group. There are some things we will walk through more closely with just one or two friends, but when our support network is full, I believe we feel more comforted and secure.

One of the most life-changing ideas I've ever heard is that my suffering is ordinary. I am not terminally unique! No matter what troubles any of us encounter, someone somewhere has already been through what I'm facing, or worse. Someone somewhere is probably dealing with it now and it's likely that someone somewhere will deal with this or something like it in the future. If I choose to believe my troubles are bigger and worse than anyone else's, I choose to separate myself from the group. When I see myself as one among many (no better and no worse), as opposed to "special" or "different," then I can benefit from the strength and support of others. Weathering a storm together doesn't change my circumstances, but it does help to know I have people who care. If you are struggling today, let someone in. A problem shared is a problem halved. You are not alone.

September 3 The Best That Can Happen

I came outside just like most mornings, dressed as I have for the past five months in shorts or summer PJs. It's overcast after a long rainy night, but it didn't "look" any colder than yesterday. It's not freezing by any means, but there is definitely a chill in the air that I wouldn't have known by just glancing outside. I wonder how often I judge things by appearances when there is absolutely no way I could honestly know the truth just by looking.

I can't look at a person from across the room and know if they're friendly or not. I can't look at a party invitation and know I wouldn't have fun. And I can't hear a brief description of a new idea or concept and without learning more, just decide it isn't for me. Are we closing doors before we ever allow them to fully open? Are we living in a very small box and for "safety" reasons, keeping it that way? Let's embrace two questions before we make judgments:

❦ What's the worst that can happen?
❦ What's the best that can happen?

I think we are all familiar with question number one. We make up that if we do X, we will feel uncomfortable, awkward, waste time, etc. Let's explore the alternative more often! The best thing that could happen if I do X is—I make a new friend, a priceless networking connection, I meet my soul mate, I learn something new and the biggest one of all … DRUMROLL PLEASE … I will have fun! I will live a little! I will feel good about myself because I took a risk and it paid off. I expanded my box!

Challenge for the day: follow your inner nudging to do something outside your comfort zone. Remember, what's the BEST thing that can happen? Often, it's even better than we'll ever imagine from the sidelines.

September 4   Gratitude Is the Secret Sauce

When we can be grateful for the life we have, we will be free to have any life we want. I have heard that advice so many times! Gratitude is a magical tool. It's free. Easy to use. It can be practiced anywhere and anytime. If our brains are functioning, we can consciously practice gratitude. I know firsthand that on some days, being grateful feels like quite the stretch. It might have to start with, "I'm grateful I have fingers." Or, "I am grateful I can walk." If that is your starting point and the best you can do on that day, great! It's something!

This morning I journaled out some frustrations, and I wasn't feeling particularly grateful for much. As I started affirming my release of the situations and people bothering me, I felt a shift. My eyes opened up, literally. Somehow, in surrendering my troubles and really believing that they would work themselves out, I could get back to the present moment. I'm filled with awe at the beautiful greenness of everything I see. It rained heavily last night and the earth is still wet. The stillness is breathtaking. To me, there is nothing quite like a morning after a storm. Lingering clouds hold the promise of sunny days to come. Quiet acceptance fills the air and hope for the new day unfolds.

As my gratitude overflows toward all the beauty surrounding me, I'm now able to mentally praise and edify the people and situations that were on my mind before. I experience a complete shift in perspective—I feel love and empathy where there was anger and frustration. Gratitude, compassion and loving energy are the secret sauce to any turnaround in attitude. Surrender and acceptance are the whipped cream and cherry on top! Where can you practice this in your life today? Who or what do you need to let go of? Who or what can you feel grateful for at this very moment? Start with fingers and toes if you must, then see where that takes you!

September 5   Thirty Minutes Goes a Long Way

Thirty minutes makes all the difference. I woke up early today and as soon as I sat down outside, that thought immediately popped into my head. During a sunrise or sunset, a lot can change in thirty minutes. On a commute to or from work, leaving thirty minutes later can mean an extra hour on the road. When I have passed a terrible, multiple-car pileup on the highway, I count my blessings and am so thankful I didn't pass through a half hour earlier. Serendipity or good coincidences can happen when I'm off my normal routine. I may run into someone I haven't seen in years I got gas thirty minutes later than usual. In other situations, a half hour may not make much difference but for me, to kick off the day right, waking up early can make a huge difference.

Quiet time alone nurturing your spirit by writing, reading, praying, meditating or just being still can have a positive impact that lasts the whole day. The benefits of having some time every morning—or some time throughout the day—start to have a compound effect over several days. Before you know it, a habit is created and if continued, your whole life will be impacted by regular time devoted to stillness and introspection.

If you don't already have a daily habit of "me" time, set the alarm earlier tomorrow and experiment. I find losing that half hour of sleep does not make a huge difference in my energy level, but it does make a tremendous difference in my daily outlook and overall quality of life. That in itself is more energizing to me than an equal amount of sleep. Thirty minutes a day makes all the difference!

Gods gifts put man's best dreams to shame.
~ Elizabeth Barrett Browning ~

Today I woke up not thirty minutes early, but a full hour earlier than usual! I guess "someone" wanted to show me, "Hey, you think a half hour makes all the difference? Try an hour!" I must say it is very mystical! I'm not sure if the sun has officially breached the horizon? It's dark, not dark as night but too dark to write outside. A thick blanket of fog conceals everything beyond 100 feet. I feel like a kid on Christmas morning! Hey, I just realized I have been given a birthday gift from my creator! Yes, it is my birthday, and moments like these are my favorites of all time. I am up at dawn before anyone else. The house is quiet. Creativity is alive. And waking up to fog is a treasure I can't get enough of. As a photographer, I have been known to jump in the car on a foggy morning and just drive until the beauty stops me in my tracks and I have to start shooting.

The sky is growing lighter now. Only ten minutes have passed and it's already light enough to write outside. While still a gorgeous foggy morning, I feel so grateful to have seen it just a few minutes ago in the near darkness. We need wonder! Variety! Something on occasion that stops time and makes us feel small enough to marvel at the mystery of creation. A new day unfolding. The magic of twilight. The majesty of the mountains. The infinity of the ocean. The vivid colors and smells of spring. The reverence of snow. The glory of fall's descent into winter. We live in a magical place and on any given day, if we look for it, we will find the magic. I cannot see a miracle moment of nature and not feel, and know, that everything truly is right with the world. I have danced with my creator this morning and as my birthday unfolds, everything else will be icing on the cake! Thank you! I am so humbled and grateful.

September 7   **Hope to Light Your Day**

How can a little light from a small lamp be so significant in darkness and be so insignificant in daylight? To me, that means in times of darkness or troubled spirit, a little bit of light and hope can make a huge difference. It really doesn't take much light in the grand scheme of things to impact a dark corner of my life, or maybe just a dark moment. The small lamp, in that moment, is a bridge to daylight. Once daylight returns, the lamp—or bridge—is no longer necessary or even visible. The troubled thought or season has passed and light fills my world again. Daylight may outshine my little lamp to where I can no longer see its impact, but it was just enough in my time of darkness.

Where are you in your life right now? Is it a season of daylight or one of darkness? You can find hope and enough light to guide you until daylight is restored. A book, a friend, a movie, a mentor... Find something today to provide a glimmer of light and hope if you are walking through a dark patch. Just a little bit of light is all you need to see the path ahead. Keep walking. Morning's coming!

September 8   **Hibernate or Incubate**

Hello crisp September morning! The promise of fall is evident today after a temperature drop yesterday—the first hint of a new season coming. It still *looks* like a gorgeous summer morning. Flowers are blooming, and the grass is green and lush. But it's an absolute fact that in about six or eight weeks, our landscape will change. Leaves will be transformed into their spectacular finale, the ground will go into hibernation, and growth will cease. We will walk through fall and winter, and then spring will emerge once again, barring any complete freak of nature never seen before.

Every season in nature and in life offers immense gifts unique unto itself. Sometimes it's tempting to fast-forward through the fall and winter periods to avoid the barren, cold, dark, colorless times. As in nature, these are just as important in our personal lives to prepare us for the next season of growth. We have some choices. We can hibernate—just hunker down and tough it out till something gives. We can resist and stay in denial to minimize loss and pain. OR we can incubate. We can use those dark periods to go "inside" to assess what happened and grow through it. We can ask ourselves how do we feel, what did we learn, and most importantly where do we want to go from here? In fall and winter, we design our own "spring!"

Did you ever sit down and look at a seed catalog? The choices are endless! Numerous varieties of flowers, vegetables and herbs are available. We get to choose what we plant in our lives! When we figure that out, life can get really good! It won't be perfect and it won't be permanent, because we're always promised change. But we do have the power to design our own life, and make the choice of what to plant, water and fertilize. Use the gift of change as an opportunity to reassess and decide, "What do I really want in my garden of life?"

September 9   Losing Sleep Over Bunnies

Returning home from a walk yesterday with my dog, Goldie, I noticed my cat, Lucky was acting peculiar in a patch of my neighbor's bushes. Out of nowhere, a little bunny darted to another set of bushes. Strangely, my cat didn't follow. I got a little excited thinking the bunny got away and Lucky hadn't realized it. I silently cheered for the bunny! I walked over to check things out, where Goldie caught the scent and got excited. She sniffed her way right up to the bushes and pounced! To my horror, Goldie had a bunny in her mouth! I wished I could've done something, but it was too late. Suddenly, another rabbit sprinted from the thick of those bushes and Lucky went after him! I managed to get my dog in the house, feeling terrible that another bunny was dead because I unknowingly brought Goldie right up to the hunt. At midnight last night, Lucky meowed outside our door and had another bunny with him! This one was still alive and I brought Lucky inside so the bunny could live—for now.

What's odd about all this? It wasn't the cat's or the dog's behavior. They were following their natural instincts to hunt. As much as I don't like it, it is the circle of life. What's crazy to me now as I look back at all of this in written form, is me running around trying to control the uncontrollable! I can't change anyone or anything but me. I can make my life pretty nuts attempting to make people and things go like I want them to, or trying to prevent undesirable outcomes that aren't mine to prevent.

I lost sleep last night chasing a bunny and a cat! How much time and sleep have you lost hoping to manage people and circumstances to manipulate life as you know it? How many of us don't do it once, but again and again? The definition of insanity is doing the same thing over and over expecting different results. Relax! Take a break! Your shift is over! Let someone else be crazy today while we work on cultivating serenity by practicing surrender and acceptance. We can't control the world, but we can control our reactions and perspective. Today I choose peace!

September 10   More Bunnies to Save

Not ten minutes after I wrote the last entry, I jumped right back into trying to control the uncontrollable! With Lucky watching intently, Goldie was sniffing extra hard around a plant cart we have in the corner of our deck, which usually means we have (or had) a visitor.

Cautiously, I pulled the plant cart away from the wall just enough to get a glimpse of brown fur, so I quickly pushed it back. Goldie went crazy and Lucky tried to get closer. I didn't know if "it" was alive, but I yelled for my husband to help. We managed to put both Goldie and Lucky inside, but Goldie's instincts were so strong, she went berserk barking and scratching to get back out. I had to put her out in the front yard, so she wouldn't tear up the window, door and blinds.

When we pulled the plant cart away from the wall, we found two baby bunnies all curled up together, eyes closed. We weren't even sure if they were alive. As my husband scooped them up, they were still breathing, although it seemed one of them may have had a hurt leg. The other seemed fine. They were small enough to both fit in the palm of my husband's hands. My cat must have brought them up to play some more before turning them into lunch, but they found a hiding spot he couldn't get to.

We carried them to a field and set them deep into a pocket of thick grass. They may not survive without their mama, and my cat or some other animal may get to them later today. These things I cannot control. I *could* control my animals eating them right in front of me, but once again I cannot change the circle of life. I laughed when I realized the irony of having just written about being willing to give up attempts to manipulate external circumstances and choose peace today. That lasted less than ten minutes! Before I knew it, I was engaged in chaos, once again trying to keep cats and dogs and bunnies apart! There are some lessons we will get slowly. There are some behaviors we will have to completely exhaust ourselves with before we learn to surrender. (I will probably always try to rescue the bunnies ... just sayin'!) It just takes what it takes. When we have had enough chaos, when we try for the last time unsuccessfully to change someone or something to our liking, when we have lost enough sleep and are finally, completely ready, we will let go and surrender and choose lasting peace.

September 11   Trusting Ourselves

Today I am thinking more about my pets' natural instincts. They were born to hunt, eat, sleep, smell and hear. They were born with curiosity. My animals have a need to belong, and to express and receive love. I've heard that a pet with an animal companion will live longer simply due to the benefits of that friendship. My dog was not born with self-doubt, self-criticism, or an uncertainty about what his gifts and purposes are. My cats trust their instincts and their senses unquestionably. They will leap up to our second story deck railing and effortlessly land on a four-inch board, fully confident in their skills. While they're focused on getting up on the railing to explore and live a little, I'm worried about them losing their balance and getting hurt! They know what they are capable of and they live as big as they can, occasionally pushing themselves to jump even higher than before.

Today, why don't we trust our instincts and honor our intuition? We were born with these abilities and if we've picked up the habit of doubt and second-guessing ourselves, let's recognize that is man-made. Awareness is always the first step to change. Next time you are facing a decision, ask yourself what you need to do or what you really want. Then listen! And trust the answer. We were born knowing what we need. Believe! Be bold! Be you.

It is time for parents to teach young people early on that in diversity there is beauty and there is strength.
~ Maya Angelou ~

I have two lush potted palms on my deck. They are nearly identical in growth and fullness and they sit in matching pots. For some strange reason, I can give them the exact same amount of water and one will drain so much the saucer will overflow and not so much as a drop will collect in the other. My analytical mind works to make all the puzzle pieces of life fit together, but this doesn't fit! Two identical palms having two very different experiences. One doesn't need much water at all and one can't get enough. But both are under a covered deck sitting side by side! I guess even with palm trees there are no two alike. I cannot continue to compare them to each other—they are different! Their needs are different. Continuing to not accept this fact means constantly having to get a towel to soak up the overflow of the one who doesn't need as much water. I just did it again today, thinking, *All the other times may have been a fluke and I bet today will be different!* Hello? Another example of the definition of insanity! Doing the same thing over and over expecting different results!

Accept people, places, things and circumstances as they are and stop trying to conform everything into neatly packaged boxes. Some of us are round, some square, some thirsty, some not. Diversity is a beautiful thing and keeps the world we live in interesting. Today I will appreciate the uniqueness I find even when I don't understand it all and I feel the urge to force all the puzzle pieces to fit. Today I can celebrate mystery and wonder, and be grateful I don't have all the answers!

*The truth is, what you do matters. What you do today
matters. What you do every day matters. Successful
people just do the things that seem to make no difference
in the act of doing them and they do them over and over
and over until the compound effect kicks in.*
~ Jeff Olson ~

I've been finding a lot of dead gnats near the two
lamps we keep on at night, and wondering how they were
getting in. This cool September morning, like the last
several mornings this week, I thought it safe to leave the
back door open to let the kitties go in and out as they
pleased. It seemed like the season of flying pests had
passed, but to my surprise, I saw a swarm of gnats
hovering outside and immediately closed the door! I
shuddered to think I've been letting them in every
morning where they could spread out and remain
undetected individually. I'm reminded about the power of
small changes of habits and subtle choices, and how one
by one, they seem inconsequential.

It's easy to think, *This one time won't matter.* We may
choose to skip the gym for a few days, or indulge in a
meal or two we know isn't the best fuel for our bodies.
We might decide to skip our morning rituals or other
important self-care and spiritual nourishment. Or, despite
knowing our budget is tight, we may decide to go ahead
and splurge "this one time" to buy "it," whatever "it" is
that we feel we cannot live without one minute longer.
Each of these instances on their own, if they only
happened once or twice, may not be a huge concern. The
impact is less noticeable as isolated incidents, but when
we step back and take a look at the cumulative effects of
several less-than-ideal choices, especially if those are
happening in multiple areas of our life over a period of
time, the compounded effect *is* a very big deal!

Without much thought, we may have muddied up our lives, our relationships, our finances, our bodies, our health, and our spirits. We didn't mean to do it. Had we been able to see the collective damage in advance, the large group of "pests" hovering outside BEFORE we let all of that into our lives, we would have quickly shut the door and made all the right choices. Where are you feeling the effects of detours that led you down a path you didn't want to go? Every small decision matters and that's exactly how you can turn it back around—by making one small move today that's aligned with your goals. It may feel insignificant at first, but every step in the right direction WILL ADD UP and put you back on the path to the body, the finances, the relationships and the spiritual life you meant to have. Start RIGHT now.

September 14   **Ready for the Blessing**

Exercising is good for me but not all exercise serves the same purpose. A really high-energy cardio workout at the gym holds a great emotional benefit for me, in the form of release and de-stressing. It's like pushing a reset button. Going for a walk is a way of moving my body, which also serves to recharge my spirit. A walk in nature helps me reconnect with myself and my creator. Walking clears my head and allows new ideas to surface. Today I got ready for the gym but I realized what I needed most was a walk. I put Goldie on a leash and off we went!

The smells of the crisp fall morning immediately began to soothe my soul. Deep breaths of fresh air filled my lungs and I exhaled the clutter in my mind. I was listening to personally recorded affirmations on my phone to fill my mind with healthy thoughts to dwell on. One statement regarding a large philanthropic goal of mine (I want to be able to give away one million dollars in one year to charity), stopped me in my tracks. I wrote it nine months ago and have read and listened to it many,

many times. But today, as I paused to imagine what it would feel like for this affirmation to be true in my life, I realized it can't come true until I'm ready and capable of experiencing greater abundance. I suddenly realized the saying, "God never gives you more than you can handle" applies not only to troubles, but to blessings as well. When I can be comfortable with abundance and greater fruit in my life, blessings—bigger crops so to speak—I believe my readiness, my expectancy will indeed manifest those things, but not a moment before I'm ready.

Imagine your life just got 1000 times more financially secure, you've realized your life's purpose and are doing what you were put on this earth to do. Your life is better now than you could have ever hoped for. Time and money are no object and you're having a huge impact on other people's lives. Are you ready for that? Could you embrace it or would you be waiting for the other shoe to drop—the good life to end? Is chaos more comfortable and familiar than calm? Are you more comfortable striving for something, than actually achieving/receiving it? Do you really believe you deserve abundance, purpose, influence—these blessings you seek? Do worry and fear feel more natural to you than peace and prosperity? If we want the good stuff, but that seems unfamiliar or daunting, we better find a way to get comfortable with it! If insecurity feels more secure to us than genuine financial, emotional and spiritual security, we have some work to do. Today I am grateful for the realization that my soul/soil has to be tilled, rich and ready in order to reap the bountiful harvest I pray for. I must be fully capable to receive, and comfortable enough to accept the dreams of my heart before they can become my reality. Before my circumstances can change, I have to change. I believe I've got some more walking to do to make that happen and to get me ready!

September 15   What Real Friendship Looks Like

In the sweetness of friendship let there be laughter, and sharing of pleasures. For in the dew of little things the heart finds its morning and is refreshed.
~ Khalil Gibran ~

Today I am grateful for a very close friend. Life has been extra busy and transformative for both of us lately, and we haven't connected much at all for the last three months. We got to spend time together last night, and I stand in awe at the power of *real* relationship. You know you have it when it doesn't matter how much time goes by, you can pick up right where you left off. The relationship feeds both people with spiritual encouragement and inspiration. Each person is able to help the other see how amazing they truly are, when doubt and perfectionism have produced "self-blinders."

Our shared passions and interests not only provide common ground, but the idea swap is like pouring gasoline on fire. The energy produced could power an airplane! Each person accepts the other—warts and all, without trying to change them. Relating is done with ease, *adding* life as opposed to draining energy. And occasionally, more of each self is revealed, just like the peeling of an onion. You get a glimpse of something even more precious about your friend to admire, love and hold sacred.

All relationships are unique and serve different purposes. Today I'm thankful for the friendships that have survived the test of time and change. They are worth preserving. A little time, attention and nurturing go a long way! Call a friend today or write them a note and tell them how much they mean to you. Focus more on *being* a good friend and you'll have all the friends you need.

Denial doesn't make it so! Today is supposed to be a record low of forty-three degrees. It's 7:15 a.m. and it's already dropped to fifty degrees. Close enough! Brrr! I'm outside anyway because soon enough the cold temperatures will drive me inside for good. We have a very dense fog. I can see the tree line separating my backyard from by neighbor's, but nothing beyond that. I could pretend that I live on a very magical secluded mountaintop for all I can see right now. Deep down I know the truth, but don't we do this in our lives at times? We drift off into a fantasy world and start ignoring things we would rather not see or acknowledge.

Fear of knowing the truth doesn't alter the truth. It's still real whether we look at it or not! Maybe we aren't doing something we set out to do? Without making any changes, we still hope somehow we will hit our goal anyway. Do you have financial goals where your actions aren't lining up with your intentions? Do you have health goals, but you're not doing what you said you would do? Have you set boundaries at work or at home that you know aren't being honored?

We all have things we've let slide. I've had a feeling I needed to evaluate my progress on finishing this book— add up everything I've written so far—because I haven't written as often as planned to meet my desired completion date. I've been kidding myself that I could somehow still finish on time. I knew the truth deep down, but I wasn't ready to look at it until yesterday. Rather than being about three months away from achieving my goal, I was actually at least six months away. I have made progress, but all those days I chose not to work on it added up.

Reality is not always kind, but I would rather live in the truth, than keep living in a fantasyland, with a rude awakening waiting for me on the horizon. Now that the fog has lifted, I can't ignore it any longer. So today I know exactly where I am on this journey and how far I still have to go. What truths are you avoiding today? What are you afraid or hesitant to look at? Go ahead, lift the veil. It's already real so we may as well acknowledge it, accept it and decide what, if anything, we want to do about it. Thank the part of you who knows the truth and let the rest of you catch up. Then give yourself some grace, set a new intention, and take a step in the right direction. The truth may not always appear to be our friend but I have an inner calm today from choosing to let go of illusions and live my life exactly as it is today. Come join me when you're ready! The truth WILL set you free!

September 17   Fruit Theory

Have you ever wondered why some fruit comes ready-to-eat, while others have a jacket or a protective coating that must first be removed? Apples, nectarines, peaches, grapes and berries are washed and then eaten. Bananas, cantaloupe, pineapples, watermelon and oranges must be peeled or cut to get to the good stuff. Is this just a random act of our Creator? Couldn't a pineapple just as easily have been given an edible skin? Its texture isn't any more fragile than a strawberry or a peach?

Personally I have no theories. We're all uniquely special, just like each and every variety of fruit. Our needs are not identical and they don't have to make sense to us or anyone else. We are who we are, and what makes us tick, what ticks us off, what excites us, inspires us, moves us to action, moves us to love and care is a very individual thing. I don't have to fit into anyone else's ideas or box. Mine is just fine thank you! Let go of expectations for you or anyone you relate with to be anything they're not. If someone in your life is "should-ing" all over you, it might be time to have a conversation, and if that doesn't work, maybe it's time to remove yourself from that "should-y" environment. A variety of fruit makes the best fruit basket because there's something for everyone. For today, be yourself and bear the fruits of your individuality proudly! It's okay to be a little nutty too, but that's another story.

September 18   It's Rarely the End of the World

After the big escapade a week ago of finding two baby bunnies on our deck and saving them from the jaws of my cat and dog, my dog, Goldie just hasn't been able to accept the fact that the bunnies are gone. On the morning it happened, she kept sniffing all around the deck in a panicked frenzy as soon as we let her back out (after we relocated the bunnies). Round and round she ran sniffing the deck furniture, always returning to the plant cart under which they had been hiding. I pulled the plant cart completely away from the wall so she could see without a doubt that they were gone. She was unsettled all morning. Goldie would come inside and then want to go right back outside to look for them one more time.

I felt bad for her. Acceptance can be painful, and we will stay in denial and resistance long after a situation has ended just to hold onto something or someone we cared about. We will hang on to a job we loved long after we've stopped loving it, kidding ourselves it will get better. Or maybe we'll stay in circumstances that we feel define us or give us a sense of self-worth, when deep down we know it's not working anymore. Often everyone around us can see it's over, "they" are gone, but we can't see it. Let them go. Let it go. Let her or him go. They're already gone anyway and holding on doesn't bring them back. Our denial doesn't change reality, it just means we're stuck in "Why?" and, "If only..." and, "Please, God, no!" Own your part. Forgive. Grieve. Whatever the situation calls for, do it. And know, you will survive this.

I have a friend who keeps a journal and puts special bookmarks on the days she thought surely it was the end of the world and she wouldn't live through it—whatever "it" was. Now, when she is encountering another really tough, "end-of-the-world" day or circumstance, she goes back to those special bookmarks to remind her that she got through that time and she will probably get through today as well. It has been a week now and Goldie is napping by the plant cart, probably dreaming of the bunnies that got away. She still gives it a good daily sniff to remember. I don't mean to make light of bigger problems we face but to Goldie, having bunnies on the deck was a big deal. Whatever you're going through, even if others don't get it, if it feels like a big deal to you, it is. Honor your losses, and your disappointments. When you can accept it, the hurt will start to diminish. The disappointment will fade. You will become open to living and loving again. Memories can offer comfort but it's also important to let the past be the past so today can be the best present ever.

September 19   **Feeling My Feelings**

Feelings are as real as the grass is green and the sky is blue. That doesn't mean they are always accurate. Something may make me feel like a bad mom, wife, daughter or sister but that doesn't mean it's true. I may feel like I love my job or my life one day, and hate it tomorrow. Nothing changed but my feelings. Feelings don't have to make sense or be justified to anyone, not even myself.

Today is a beautiful crisp sunny morning, yet I feel sad. I'm not sure why, but the only thing it might be related to are the tragic deaths of a couple we knew casually. I have told myself it couldn't be that, because we weren't close friends or family. However the grief started creeping in yesterday, the day after their deaths. I have wrestled with allowing myself to feel sadness about losing a couple we were not extremely close to. We did share a love of travel and these two were quite adventurous! Thank goodness they didn't wait till retirement to start living! Known for their generosity, they touched many lives. I will always remember them as a couple who really *lived*.

My sadness is real. Perhaps their untimely death has put me in touch with the reality of death. We are not promised another day, week or decade. We can be grateful for the breaths we're taking at this moment. Maybe they weren't close to me in the big scheme of things, but their kindness and passion for life touched mine, and today, I feel like I lost someone close to me. I give myself permission today to feel all my feelings, not just the ones that make sense. I don't always need to act on my feelings, but I do choose to honor them, and as I do, I honor all the parts of me that ever wanted to be known, seen and heard.

When I can fully embrace a feeling, it can then pass. When I run from them through busyness and other avoidant behaviors, my feelings pileup, waiting for my attention. They can pile up for years, making it a challenge to sort out how I feel and why. For today, I will allow my grief to register and I will be gentle with myself and my expectations of the day. It makes sense to me that a day saturated with grief may not be as productive as a day full of joy. At this stage of my personal journey, I would rather give up some productivity to feel my feelings as they come up than let them accumulate with residual effects on my life, my spirit my health, my relationships, and my business.

How are you feeling today? ARE you feeling today? Please join me in the full human experience and allow yourself to feel. Even if you don't understand it or can't explain it, your feelings are real and waiting for your acknowledgment. Feeling feelings is not a selective process either! Joy, sadness, anger, loneliness, love, gratitude, grief and fear are all natural expressions of life. Allowing yourself to experience the full spectrum of human emotion guarantees a full life.

September 20   See the Trees AND the Forest

It is not so much for its beauty that the forest makes a claim upon men's hearts, as for that subtle something, that quality of air that emanation from old trees, that so wonderfully changes and renews a weary spirit.
~ Robert Louis Stevenson ~

We've had so many foggy, rainy and overcast mornings that my view from today's sunny landscape is extra gorgeous. I'm up a little later too, so my first look was full sun and not sunrise. Everything is a gorgeous green. Beautiful rolling hills—the scene is magnificent! Every single tree I see is a complete unit, a whole tree and yet together, a group of trees really makes a visual statement. If all I saw was one tree here in my backyard, or especially in a forest, it wouldn't have the same impact. Together, many trees add splendor and composition—they create a scene. A group of trees are part of something greater than themselves, but it takes each single one to contribute to the full picture.

We are all unique individuals, each bringing gifts for the greater good. We are whole unto ourselves, but if we walked this earth alone, our journeys would be lonely. We need each other to complete our scenes, to add value, to complement one another's lives. Today I am thankful for family, friends, strangers and everyone in between. Somehow, someway you all enrich my life in a way I could never accomplish alone.

September 21   Solid Foundation

Depending on what time I wake up, and if it's sunny outside or cloudy, the color of the walls in my bedroom varies. They can be darker and more of a cool gray, or they can be brighter and warmer. It just depends on the natural light coming in. I delight in knowing that the name of the paint color we chose for our walls is "Happy Trails," a soothing, warm, ivory beige. Of course no one is altering the shade of paint on my walls in the middle of the night. Perspective, time and circumstances can only make it appear as if the wall color is different. Such is true in our lives.

Reality does not change every other day, however my thinking and my perceptions about myself and my life can change on a dime. If I let it, one phone call has the power to bring me up or bring me down, make me love life or make me hate it. My goal is to be so grounded in who I am, whose I am, what I want, where I'm going and why I'm here, that my perceptions and my reality remain one and the same. External circumstances and other opinions will not be able to challenge what I know to be true. Life will not always be "Happy Trails" without disappointments or unexpected detours. However, when I remain confident in myself, grateful for what I have and where I've been, and trusting that all things work for my good, my peace and serenity will not change on a dime. I will not sell myself short and buy anyone else's forecast of me or my life. Is your self-esteem built on rock or sand? Every investment you make in yourself, every solid person you surround yourself with, every inspiring book you read and audio you listen to are adding bricks to your foundation. Keep building!

September 22   Moving On

Yesterday I listened to an old recording of a sermon my mom had particularly enjoyed. The essence of the sermon served to introduce a few soul-searching questions. Stop asking yourself, "Why did I have to go through that?" And start asking instead, "Why did I survive that?"

I woke up as usual to birds singing this morning. They sounded cheerful as ever and it occurred to me I have never heard a depressed bird. I know that sounds absurd, but it made me think about the message I listened to yesterday. Many of us have justification to sing sad songs about our past. I know for a fact (unfortunately) that some of these birds have lost entire nests of babies because my cat discovered them. But their tunes never changed. Yes, my example is a stretch and of course grief is appropriate for any loss. What I'm referring to is our inner dialogue that sometimes goes on for years about the tragic events and losses we've endured in our lives. We choose to remain angry, sad or resentful, and a part of us gets stuck and is unable to move on. We can't change our past circumstances, but our future hinges on how we talk to ourselves about what happened. Gratitude for getting through it is a great place to start. Forgiveness sets us free! Today is a new day. I can ask myself what's bad about it or I can ask myself what's good about. Either way, I will get an answer and I will be right. The right *question* can change everything! Which mindset are you going to choose today?

September 23   Welcoming a New Season

Delicious autumn! My very soul is wedded to it,
and if I were a bird I would fly about the
earth seeking the successive autumns.
~ George Eliot ~

It's that magical time of year when we open the windows to bring in the crisp autumn air and let the old air out. The air-conditioning is off and so is the heat, marking the end of summer and the beginning of fall. When I'm tuned in and mindful, I can literally feel the shift in energy—that change is "in the air." It smells different too.

For me, a change of season heightens my readiness for a change of pace. I feel a transition is coming, not just in the weather but also in me. I'm usually much more aware of how an impending spring feels, with the promise of new growth. But right now, I'm really sensing how the upcoming fall season feels like going into an incubator. It's as if we're about to step into a place of rebirth and a time of renewal. It's time to surrender everything we've got and allow it to be repurposed for even greater good in the months and new year to come.

I also feel a sense of mystery and some uncertainty hovering in the air as fall approaches. Too often I want to direct and control the changes in my life. Of course this is no more possible than me trying to control when the leaves change color, but it doesn't stop me from trying! I have learned that attempting to manipulate the world around me is a quick way to lose my peace, serenity, and acceptance and puts me in a position of missing the gifts that are trying to unfold naturally.

All I can remember of previous fall seasons is not wanting summer to end, not wanting to go into the shorter days, the gray days. This year I'm not scared or resistant, but more trusting and surrendered. I don't know what's coming, but I know it's good! *And* I'm not going to just count the days till spring. I'm going to be present each day till then. All I have is today, so while it's great to anticipate and plan for the future, we also have to remember today is all we have. Be *here* and make the best of what's true today. Today I will get out of my own way and wait expectantly for the gifts of the season, trusting that everything—*everything*—happens for my good. The window of my soul is open to fresh air! Is yours? Give thanks for the present! Unwrap and enjoy!

On a walk early this morning, I saw a fascinating box on the curb (it's trash day). Partly because of curiosity and partly because I'm a salvager, I like to see what my neighbors are throwing away. The cardboard box had a picture on it of some kind of attachment that goes on an adult bike. It was more than the back half of a bike; actually it was everything but the front wheel. The bike attachment had a pretend handlebar and a long arm to connect it to the adult bike. Basically it would allow a child to feel like he was riding his bike, but actually Mom or Dad would be steering and doing most, or all of the work.

Immediately I saw a parallel between myself and what I believe about my relationship with God. I can choose what kind of spiritual bike ride I want to experience. I have my own handlebars and pedals, and the illusion of control. If the bike starts going a different way, I can tighten my grip on my handlebars and grit my teeth, trying to force the bike to go my own way. OR... I can accept the higher guidance and direction, relax and enjoy the ride. What if life really is as simple as enjoying the ride? Exploring new ground? Riding with complete trust in my driver, believing I'm going to see a lot of cool stuff and have a great experience along the way.

When we go bike riding, we start somewhere and finish somewhere we could easily drive to much faster. We don't though, because it's about the ride, not the arrival. Today, if life takes what seems to be a detour, I will relax and look for the gift. If we hit a rock and the bike turns over, I know God is there to pick me up and dust me off, and we'll get back on the bike and ride some more. Today, I will look for areas where I'm resisting and trying to control. I will let go and enjoy the ride.

Rest. We all need it. Some of us don't get enough. We push ourselves relentlessly to do more and more and more. Our bodies or our minds say, *I'm tired. Let's stop and rest*, but the drill sergeant inside us pushes onward. My cats and dog get crated at bedtime, so I know they're getting plenty of rest at night. I let Lucky outside first thing every morning as I go out to write. Some days, he will go right down the stairs to start his hunting and climbing adventures, and other days he will sleep some more first. Today he is on the deck floor curled up on his back, paws drawn up to his chest, cat napping. He is listening to his body saying, *Wait! A little more rest please!*

Learning to hear our inner voice is a skill that is easily forgotten. We can have so much noise in our lives that we are not tuned into our needs and desires. Every time we honor these requests, we strengthen the bond between our inner being and our outer doing. We say, *Your needs are important!* and our inner being feels heard and validated. That voice will get stronger and louder as we tune into it regularly, providing insightful intuition to our real needs, wants, hopes and desires. We can tap into all the guidance we could ever want or need! I once heard a pastor say, "God is calling but he's getting a busy signal and can't get through!" Ouch! Maybe it's time to clear the line? What inner nudging have you been ignoring? Do you need a break? Do you need more sleep? Need a trip to the beach? Time to quit the job you hate and go for your dream? Time to stop dating Ms. Alright so Ms. Wonderful can show up? If you will learn to listen, you will be guided to life, health and balance and the greatest love affair of all—the one with yourself (and your creator)!

It's almost October! I am looking forward to the leaves changing colors. It always seems as if that happens overnight, but on my last walk, I noticed a few leaves on one tree were already completely red and some have fallen. On the same tree, all the other leaves were still completely green. I've never noticed that before. What I thought was more an overnight sensation, is just like many other scenarios in life: someone's got to go first. When they do, they are such the minority that they are hardly noticed, but change has started. The Al-Anon Fellowship uses the phrase, "Let it begin with me." If I am inspired to take action that may seem absurd to some, let me do it anyway. If I recognize my relationships are unhealthy and no one else is willing to look at it or do anything about it, let it start with me. If I want to see more kindness in the world, let me start by being more kind.

A movement doesn't just happen. A starting point occurs when someone gets the courage to go against the norm, take a stand, chase a dream, and say no to optional misery. It isn't easy going first. The pushback can be tough. You may hear all sorts of reasons why what you're doing won't work. You may get laughed at, ridiculed even. Well-meaning people, sometimes those closest to you, will try to sabotage your efforts. Many of us live in safe little boxes and we don't want anyone else to leave the box, if we have to stay in it. Misery loves company? Yes, that's often true, even and maybe especially, if it's the people who love us. I love the saying, "Don't let the people who have given up on their dreams talk you out of yours!" They will say they only want what is best for you, but they are the ones who are afraid of being left behind. Do it anyway! Honor your inner prompts to go first. To be the change you want to see. To do something everyone says can't be done. The Wright brothers did it.

Henry Ford did it. Sam Walton did it. Mother Teresa. Nelson Mandela. Many courageous people went first. You can too! Remember, being "good" enough is the biggest obstacle to becoming "great." Mediocrity is comfortable. Average people need other average people around them to justify staying average. It doesn't have to be you!

September 27   Facing Forward

Lucky is my big, solid black cat. I look at him from a distance and often can't tell if he is facing me or facing away from me. All I can see is his silhouette—ears, head and body—and unless his eyes are open, it's hard to tell if he's coming or going.

We all wake up every day to a new day. One we have never seen before and one we will never see again. Time moves on without fail. People don't always go with it. Are you facing backward or forward? Do you linger in yesterdays and what-might-have-beens or are you enjoying the present and looking to the future? If it's hard to tell, that's probably your answer. Every day of life is a gift, but if we are looking in the wrong direction, or our eyes are closed, we will miss it. If you are reading this, congratulations! You're still breathing! You made it this far! Count all the reasons you have to be grateful right now! Go forward today knowing and expecting more good is coming your way as long as you are facing the present! Face forward. Today is a new day! Be expectant of guidance and favor!

September 28   Soul Sustenance

Routine maintenance. We do it for our cars, our homes, our teeth (hopefully!). We complete annual wellness exams and other periodic health checks like mammograms and colonoscopies. How frequent are our emotional and spiritual checkups? As we approach a day of fall outdoor cleaning to remove cobwebs, wash windows and clean out the garage, I am reminded that regular "soul" maintenance is crucial as well. Dirty windows of the soul could feel like lack of vision or apathy about the future. Cobwebs in the soul could be long forgotten hobbies or passions covered over. It is time to dust those off and revitalize the zest for life those once provided. Cleaning out the garage for the soul might look like getting rid of all the beliefs that don't serve you anymore. Fill in the blanks below with the first thing that comes to mind.

❋ I'm too _____

❋ I'm not good enough at _____

❋ I'll never _____

❋ I'll always _____

Drag those outdated beliefs to the curb and let the garbage truck haul them away! Write about how you want to feel and repeat these affirmations over and over until you have a new set of beliefs about yourself and your life. All of that may sound like a lot of work, but you're going to pay a price one way or the other. You can pay the price of hard work or the price of staying lost and misguided. You can develop some new habits or stay shackled to self-deceptions and misconceptions. You can start having fun or remain overworked and underplayed. It's a choice. If we let our home maintenance slide, it's only going to get worse and may even create bigger problems down the road.

Our spiritual well-being is no different. If you have gotten behind, just pick one change you are willing to make today. Maybe start with an assessment of where you are, where you have been and where you want to go. What does it look like? Feel like? Consider going for a walk and asking what you need more of to feel connected. Can you commit to regular walking, journaling or praying, even if you start with five minutes a day? May not sound like much, but if it's more than what you're doing, that's what we call progress!

What are you willing to do today that most people won't, so you can have tomorrow what most people don't? It's your soul and your life. Let's roll up our sleeves and do some work! There is nothing like getting everything clean and shiny after a hard days work, but when you do that internally, it feels even better!

September 29   Open Your Eyes

Denial. I can try to ignore the dust piling up, or the cobwebs accumulating. I can avoid looking at my kitchen windows up close, so I don't have to acknowledge how dirty they are. Not looking or *not* acknowledging doesn't make something *not* true. I can live in the dark with blinders on or I can choose to face my life.

We all know the Serenity Prayer: "God grant me the serenity to accept the things I cannot change, the courage to change the things I can, and the wisdom to know the difference." In order to change the things I can, I must first be willing to see things as they really are. I can't change everything at once, but one small action in the right direction can open up a channel of hope and lead to the next small step and the next one after that.

Today, have the courage to open your eyes and take a good look around. It's usually not as bad as we think or fear. With eyes open, you are also able to clearly see the abundance in your life. Knowledge is power. Awareness is key. No change is made until the need for it is recognized.

September 30   Three Steps to Peace and Progress

If I need to remove a big tree, I better bring an axe or it won't budge. If I want to catch a fish, I have to do more than will one into my boat! (Using a fishing pole and some bait are a good way to start.) Not long ago, I set an intention to take myself seriously and finish writing this book. I didn't realize until just recently that I've been fully expecting that to happen, even though I haven't been consistent with my daily actions to bring it about. No wonder I'm not seeing the desired outcome yet! I'm trying to catch a fish and I'm not even by the water!

For me, writing out goals, reciting affirmations, and practicing visualization are all additional forms of prayer. I identify my innermost hopes and dreams and make them known, while maintaining ongoing dialogue with God for guidance about my ideal path, and His will for my life. However, I can't just make a wish, a declaration, or a prayer, and sit on the couch waiting for it to happen! Taking action demonstrates my faith in what I'm praying for, and that's what can initiate the shift. No, I don't get everything I want—thank goodness! To me a closed door is a form of protection and/or re-direction, because I know all things work together for my good.

These are my three steps to peace and progress. My first task is to seek and define the "what," and start taking actions to move in the right direction. My second task is to also believe the "what" is possible, and that I'm worthy of good things happening to me. (Doubt or lack of faith can often keep me stuck receiving more life lessons to overcome my limiting beliefs.) My third task is to surrender the outcome (the "how") and be open to all possibilities that lead me to my ultimate goal, even though they may not be how I planned to get there. That's it! I'm *not* responsible for bringing the "how" into alignment—that's God's job! It's not always in the way I envisioned, but always in the way that serves my ultimate good. What intentions are you putting out today? Are you backing that up with action? Believe, act, then surrender and trust the delivery method.

October

Remind me each day that the race is not always to the swift; that there is more to life than increasing its speed. Let me look upward into the towering oak and know that it grew great and strong because it grew slowly and well.

~ **Orin L. Crain**

People may argue whether or not it really makes a difference to talk to their plants. I don't know about that, but I think everyone can agree on one thing—plants won't talk back! Imagine how crazy it would be to constantly talk to your plants and expect a reply? If they don't answer the first time, they're probably not going to answer the hundredth time either!

How often do we talk to certain people over and over with the hope of finally getting the response we've been seeking? We share our hearts and opinions, thinking each time if we say it just right, they'll finally listen and validate our position. Parents, kids, siblings, friends, and bosses—some people just can't hear us and will never be able to connect with us on certain issues. In recovery we often hear, "Stop going to the hardware store for bread. You won't find it there." Agreed? A hardware store is where you'll find nuts, screws and deadbolts!

Quite often, we all have people in our lives who can't provide "bread" and to compound matters, they may also feel the need to keep getting a response out of us that we are incapable of giving them. They may use our attempt to be heard by them as yet another opportunity to tell us why they *can't* tell us what we want to hear (all the stories keeping them from real relationship with us). The exchange serves no good to either party and the divide remains the same, if not wider.

I am learning that my peace is more important than my need to be heard by certain people. Insanity is doing the same thing over and over, expecting different results. Let's do something different to get those desired results! Today I will get my "bread" from the bakery—the people in my life who are good listeners and able to hear me (even though they don't always agree with me). Today, it feels good to know where to shop to get my needs met!

October 2   Bargaining for Change

The only way to make sense out of change is to plunge into it, move with it, and join the dance.
~ Alan Watts ~

It's all in perspective. Fifty degrees is really cold when you're used to seventy. Seventy degrees feels cold when you are used to ninety. Fifty degrees will feel like a warm front when I'm used to mornings below freezing. My spring and summer habit of writing outside every morning is something I cling to now with fall approaching. I know at some point I will not even attempt it, not even with blankets like today, and I will resign myself to writing in my cozy little chair inside. I have two palms on our deck that add the finishing touches to this great space. I know they will end up inside the house for the winter, but I will put that off as long as possible too.

Change is going to happen no matter how much we try to fight, fuss and resist. The bargaining process is an important one though. It helps us get ready. We will know we have tried everything we could think of to hold onto that which is familiar or cherished, and at last, we will surrender and accept the inevitable evolutions that come our way. Are you bargaining? What are you almost ready to accept? Good for you—you are right where you're supposed to be. You'll know when it's time to do something different. Savor it while it lasts!

October 3   Happy Dance Gone Wild

When was the last time you screamed *Woo Hoo!* When was the last time you made any loud sound from your mouth? We were given a voice and we can adjust our volume from a whisper to a battle cry. Do you use your upper volume range at all? It's liberating! I'm sitting by Old Hickory Lake and several flocks of geese have passed overhead. They aren't silent. They're honking as

275

loud as they can and inviting all who care to join! It sounds like they are rallying the troops and shouting *Woo Hoo!* on the way to their next adventure. Try it right now. Yell, *Woo Hoooooooooo!!!!!!* Really? That's the best you can do? You barely opened your mouth. Come on ... louder! *Woo Hoooooooooo!!!!!!* Okay, that's better. Do you feel that energy rising inside you? Our subconscious believes whatever we tell it, and when we purposely start whooping for joy, our spirit eagerly responds with excitement. It doesn't know why and it doesn't care. It *feels good* to feel good! Now try it again and this time, get up and do the Happy Dance as you yell! (Re-read April 1 if you need a refresher.) If someone thinks you're crazy? Congrats! You're doing it right! Practice this often enough and you will gradually believe it's crazy *not* to use your voice and move your body now and then. The best things in life really are free ... make all the noise you want!

October 4   Fog Part One: Releasing Self-Doubt

Don't be afraid to chase your dreams! I woke up to a mystical fog again and the photographer in me started begging to go shoot it. The doubter in me started in. *Where would we go? What if we don't get a perfect spot, or a perfect shot? The sun will come out any minute and you'll miss it. This will knock you off routine.* Have you had enough, reading that garbage of excuses? I got tired of hearing it too. I threw on some clothes, jumped in the car and headed for a nearby water hole I've always wanted to shoot. I got great images of the misty fog over the water and studied a beautiful white egret fishing for breakfast for over an hour. I got to see the sun burn the fog off the lake, which was also an awesome transformation to witness.

Every time I overcome my discouraging thoughts, I am rewarded for "doing it anyway." While it's useful to listen to my intuition, with practice I am able to discern caution from playing it small and staying inside my comfortable, safe routine. Forget the doubters in your head and in your life. Follow your instincts. They will lead you to treasure!

October 5   Fog Part Two: Stop Being So Civilized

Today, I woke up and answered the call of my inner photographer to go out and shoot some thick fog. It's quite a rush driving when you can only see about fifteen feet in front of you. Going thirty-five miles per hour with short-range visibility is a bit unnerving, but in an exciting way—at least today. I couldn't see where I was going, but I trusted it was going to be great. I felt like a kid on Christmas morning! Or a high school graduate leaving to go discover the world—rushing straight into the unknown with wild abandon and high hopes.

Why do we let this innate adventurous spirit become silenced so often by the "grownups" who emerge within us? We civilize our spirits and sequester our passions. We choose safety and security because someone said that makes more sense. Who are the real "crazy ones?" This morning I got to see an egret fly, bathe and fish—I can't see that sitting on my couch! No, that wasn't on my "agenda" today, but how do you pencil that in? The call of a world waiting to be discovered is in you. Unplanned wonder awaits you. Take a detour today and let the explorer in you come back to life!

October 6   Courage to Be Fully Alive

Today is a special day for a very special man in my life. (HAPPY BIRTHDAY!) We are going to make a *big deal* out of it! Did you ever hear someone tell you, "Stop making such a big deal about that!" Or, "Settle down now, and stop acting like a child." We've even said that to our children, when acting like a child is the most age-appropriate thing to do. (I'm not discounting the need for discipline, this is just an observation of our language).

All too often our spirits are conformed to fit into society, into school, into church, even into our own families. Our behavior is regulated so much that we may think it's not okay to jump for joy and act crazy. To cry when we feel sad. Or to laugh out loud when something's funny. We are encouraged to wear our quiet little masks and politely die a slow, numbing death. We are hardly living, as opposed to celebrating the full spectrum of the human existence. It's called a spectrum, which indicates that life is meant to be lived in a range of experiences, not as a safe, uniform spot somewhere in the midst of conformity and oppression. We need all of it to feel alive! Highs and lows. Loud and quiet. Fast and Slow. Celebration and grief.

A pastor once gave a sermon on how we've all but stripped the masculinity out of our sons and made them … nice. So we have compliant men who are afraid to take risks, make decisions and boldly be who they were created to be. And then we criticize them for it, and wonder what happened to the real men in the world? My husband is a huge fan of *Wild at Heart* by John Eldredge, who says, "Deep in his heart, every man longs for a battle to fight, an adventure to live, and a beauty to rescue." Referring to himself, Eldredge says, "I wasn't mean; I wasn't evil. I was nice. And let me tell you, a hesitant man is the last thing in the world a woman needs. She needs a lover and a warrior, not a Really Nice Guy."

Just for today, stop being so "nice" and politically correct, and demanding the same from everyone else. Let's be unashamedly ALIVE, whatever that looks like today. For us, that means a big celebration. We are going to sing really loud and probably do a few Happy Dances. We are all alive, aren't we? That alone is reason to celebrate. Let's make today something worth remembering.

October 7   **Rising Above the Storm**

Recently I heard the most fascinating nature fact. Eagles will fly straight into a storm to push through it and rise above it, while all the other birds will wait it out among the safety of the trees. So while it's storming down below, the eagles are above the clouds, flying around in the sunshine! I know this is possible because I have been in an airplane that did the same thing. We climbed past the turbulence and storm, and came out where it was nothing but blue skies and sunshine!

Turbulence is not pleasant, in the sky or in our lives. It can be really uncomfortable or even terrifying: the loss of altitude and suddenly feeling jolted, the feeling that we're no longer in control and the storm is strong enough to knock us off balance. None of this feels secure, but the only way through is … through. And the fastest way to sunshine is going into the storm and rising above it. Are you ready for a higher perspective? Do you feel like flying today? Are you an eagle, or are you everybody else? I thought so—race you to the top!

October 8   **Perfectionism Keeps Us Stuck**

Our front sidewalk is lined with monkey grass. It's very thick and lush, but it's starting to spread and take over our other shrubs. I have heard it is good to cut them way back every year, but I've been afraid they would look awful until spring, so I've never done it. Perfection and fear are two very powerful factors in determining many choices I make (or don't make). I have learned to recognize their presence in a decision and am beginning to overcome the power they have held over me. Fear of making a mistake. Fear of looking bad. Fear of not doing it right. Julia Cameron in *The Artist's Way* says, "…in order to do something well, we must first be willing to do it badly." I have always put pressure on myself to do everything perfectly, even if it was my first attempt. The usual result—no action at all! If something was "good enough," that kept me from attempting to make it great for fear of failure. I am learning to ask, "How important is it?" and, "What's the worst thing that can happen?"

I got out the electric trimmers this morning without further hesitation and started cutting the monkey grass back. It looked awful but it felt great to conquer fear. With a trusting spirit, I kept cutting and cutting without a clue of how to do it "right." When I thought I was done, I got a rake to clear away all the loose trimmings and debris and saw it actually looked pretty good! Very neat and tidy. Not perfect, but I did it! It looks good now and it will look great next spring. How many times have we left something alone and unchanged, despite the urge to try something new? How often do we stay stuck in relationships or jobs because we've settled for "okay," afraid to go after "great?" Staying comfortable can keep us from pursuing our dreams. When I have pushed beyond discomfort, fear and perfection, I have always emerged with a renewed sense of confidence and self-satisfaction. It feels good to push through and dare to be everything I am destined to be. Are you holding yourself back? Is there something you want to attempt? To try? To change? GO FOR IT! You'll be so happy you did!

October 9   Follow Your Own Course

I'm sitting by the lake this morning on a gorgeous sunny day. A flock of geese announced themselves from a distance, so I watched them approach. As they got closer I saw something very unusual. They continued to fly overhead, but two geese broke out of the V and headed to the right by themselves. They did a ninety degree turn, and headed off in the opposite direction. I've never seen geese in flight leave their flock and am thankful for the reminder that's it's okay (and actually *fabulous*) to be different from everybody else.

Under any circumstances, if you find yourself heading in the wrong direction or at least the wrong direction for you, break formation and change course the moment you realize it! Go solo or bring a like-minded buddy along for the adventure, but do it and forget about what everyone else thinks and expects of you. You are the only one who can hear the desires of your heart. Be true to you and the rest will work itself out.

October 10   Fall's Gifts

Fall is here! Fall is here! Yesterday I made the annual trip to get mums and pine straw. I pulled out the dying begonias in my pots and replaced them with brilliant, budding mums. My front door now has a gorgeous array of fall foliage in bright reds, oranges and yellow. Today we will be filling our landscaped beds with pine needles, providing the rich aroma of autumn. Traditions and rituals are a wonderful way to recognize changes of the season and special days. They provide a sense of belonging, purpose and order. We celebrate the big stuff but let's remember to celebrate the little stuff too, and incorporate other traditions to look forward to on a more regular basis.

We can commemorate a really good day with a candlelit dinner. I remember my dad once taking us out to the restaurant of our choice for good grades, so maybe that's an idea for your family. Maybe every time you hit a savings milestone, you take a trip to the dollar store and splurge a whopping five dollars on something? This past summer I purchased popsicles for a visit from my nieces and I started rewarding myself with the ones that were leftover each time I finished yard work. I really began to look forward to that refreshing treat after sweating through some manual labor, and so did my inner kid!

How about picking out a fancy cupcake or some pretty flowers just to celebrate another day in paradise? Our spirits love to rejoice. Let's party more often!

October 11   Gratitude Is a Choice

If the only prayer you said in your whole
life was 'thank you,' that would suffice.
~ Meister Eckhart ~

Know when to say when! It's cloudy and forty-five degrees this morning so rather than writing outside today, I'm inside with the fireplace going ... what a treat! In everything there is something to be grateful for. I may have to look a little harder in some situations, but I can always find some reason to be thankful, or at least some way to appreciate that the situation could have been worse.

Being thankful is a choice, a state of being, because I can also always find a reason to complain. Which feels better? Being miserable and complaining? Or finding the gift and being grateful? Exactly! I'm not perfect, so if I catch myself looking at the glass half empty, I know it's time to shift my focus and count my blessings. Today I will start by being thankful for the three inside-only cats curled up with me on my blanket by the fire. I would have missed this cozy morning if it were warm enough for me to be outside on the deck.

October 12   First Day of the Rest of Your Life

One of the most tragic things I know about
human nature is that all of us tend to put off living.
We are all dreaming of some magical rose
garden over the horizon instead of enjoying the roses that
are blooming outside our windows today.
~ Dale Carnegie ~

We learned today that a former classmate of mine passed away over the weekend. He was barely into his forties and I feel sure he planned to live longer ... a lot longer. We are not guaranteed any set amount of time, but I started counting up how many days I might have left using the best case scenario. With very rough math, I arrived at about 15,000 days remaining on earth. The number didn't matter. Just seeing any number—any finite number—was enough to make me embrace the idea that like everyone else, my days are numbered, and each one matters.

It is so easy to live day after day like we will live forever. Or to put off doing "X" until next month, next year or maybe when we retire. I am reading a fascinating book that encourages people to imagine there is no "retirement" to look forward to. Don't spend forty years of your life doing anything less than what you love, in hopes of some pay off at the end. Do it now! (Whatever IT is for you.) There is never a good time to make a change, start a business, or tour the world. Today is as good as any.

What if I fail? Well, what if you succeed? If you had to choose what you want to do for the rest of your life, what would really excite you? While it may not be feasible to change your entire life tomorrow, put a plan down on paper. State what you want. What action steps can you take to navigate to the life you could only dream about? Is there someone who is already living your dream who you can talk to or read about? Start asking some questions and doing some research. Today really is the first day of the rest of your life. Wake up and make it count!

October 13   **Stop "Taking" Offense**

Today I was walking and noticed a buzzard circling overhead. I am mesmerized by the ability to fly and love to watch anything in flight. At one point I was staring up at him with a goofy grin and he flew right over me—

straight over me, about a hundred feet up. It occurred to me that he could "relieve himself" right at that moment and ruin my fascination with him should it hit me in the face, or even worse, land in my open smile. Now that would be totally random, a complete coincidence and yet, how often when something or someone comes along and out of nowhere, suddenly "poops" on us—we take it personally? That's no crazier than if my buzzard friend this morning dropped a "gift" on me unexpectedly. It wouldn't have been because he was trying to do it "to me." We need to stop taking everything so personally! Going through life easily offended seems to bring me a constant supply of reasons to be upset! Things just happen. People have bad days and say things they don't mean. If the clerk was rude in the grocery store, say a silent prayer that her day gets better. If someone forgets your birthday, let it go! Unless you're telepathic, you have no way of knowing what that person is thinking or why they did or didn't do something. Chances are good it had nothing to do with you, and they were just lost in their own world. Living in a state where you assume everyone is doing things "to you" is a miserable way to live.

Recently I went out of my way trying to help someone out, but somehow it backfired, and this person became highly offended. Not only were they angry, they missed my good intent completely. I had spent an hour trying to do something nice for them but "thanks" never crossed that person's mind. It was a great lesson for me! I've probably done that too and missed the "gifts" people were trying to hand me.

If reality is ninety percent perception, let's start assuming the best instead of the worst. Give people some grace. Imagine for a second it's NOT about you. And if you accidentally step in the mud as you're running to your car in a sudden downpour only to find someone has parked too close and you have to climb in through the passenger side, take a deep breath, shake off the rain and let it go. It's just life. No one's out to get you. In fact, we can choose to be grateful for what *is* going right, and maybe even learn to laugh at life, while we grow in patience and compassion. Give it a try … it beats the alternative!

October 14   Small Steps Land Big Rewards

*"The journey of a thousand miles
begins with a single step."*
~ Lao-tse ~

My husband and I were out walking this morning and stumbled upon a garage sale. I love to find treasures but he didn't have time to stop. I did, so I told him to keep going and I would soon catch up. After browsing for five minutes—no treasures to be found—I started running to catch him, about a block ahead. I don't run very often anymore because of my knees, but I thought that would be the only way to catch up. Then it occurred to me that as long as I jogged or walked faster than his pace, I would eventually reach him. I didn't have to kill myself to get back to where I would have been.

Hopefully we all set goals—specifically written goals, because goals that find their way to paper are proven to have a greater chance of showing up in the real world. Dr. Gail Matthews, a professor at the Dominican University of California, recently demonstrated this fact in a study, and also proved that your chances of reaching your goals increase if you share them with someone else. Your success will be even higher if you check in weekly with that person, or a coach, about your progress. However, even in the best of circumstances, life happens and we get off-track or behind schedule and it can seem too daunting to get back on track. We may tell ourselves we will never be able to make up the lost time and because we aren't up for sprinting, we throw in the towel.

Consider the alternative. One or two consistent actions, slightly more than what you are already doing, compounded by time, will make a huge difference. No great sacrifices needed! Exhaustion, insomnia, injury, or a decline in health also not required.

What area in your life, business, relationships or finances had you hoped to see more progress by now? Identify one thing you can start doing today or this week to get you going again. You don't have to move a mountain today or chop the whole tree down this week. Calculate where you will be in three months from now if you take that consistent small action daily or weekly. Consider where you will be if you don't change anything. Which scenario will make you feel better? I agree! Let's get started!

October 15   Silver Linings

The sky is cloudy this morning, but the hint of sunshine is *literally* creating a silver lining. So that's where that saying comes from! And it does bring hope to an otherwise dark morning. Even on days where there's not enough break in the clouds to see it, the sun is always there. I was raised to believe in a silver lining in every circumstance. No matter what, I have a deep knowledge that everything is working for my good, and I trust that things will always work out.

I'm such a fan of metaphors, which demonstrate in real life what might be true in other situations. It's easier for me to trust the "sun" is always present in my life too, even on days when I can't feel it or see it. If I want, I can choose to believe it will be dark and cloudy forever, but that doesn't feel good at all! And it is a lie. I don't know of anyone who has lived a life completely void of "sunshine" and blessings. Today, if you find yourself stuck in darkness, *choose* to believe the "sun" will shine on you again. Chances are, the sooner you expect it, and the more you expect it, the sooner it will happen. Choose how you will feel today. Go on, give it a try!

October 16 Avoidance Doesn't Change Things

Have you ever ignored something—a feeling, a situation—and just hoped it would go away? Every now and then that might work, but it usually doesn't. I have a pulled muscle so I'm exercising less. When I think it's better, I exercise again only to discover it's still there. Much like a bear that goes into hibernation for the winter, it isn't really gone, just hiding. I have been told some "silly" exercises I can do to make it feel better, but I'm resistant to those. I just want it gone!

Avoiding grief, pain and confrontation doesn't change anything. If we really want to heal, we must work through whatever is going on or face the person or situation we're avoiding. The only way through is through. Everything else is just a temporary fix or postponement. Is there a "bear" in your life? Something you hope will resolve all by itself? Try journaling about the fear that is blocking you from looking at it. Awareness is always a good start!

October 17 Avoidance Strikes Again

Pet hair, dust bunnies, crumbs from breakfast—whatever the culprit(s) may be in your own home—lay scattered around my kitchen floor much more often than I like. Until someone invents a magical solution, floors get dirty and need to be cleaned. Ideally, I will sweep it all into a pile, guide it into a dustpan and dump it in the trash. It would be crazy to get my broom out and sweep everything into corners and under rugs, just trying to get the mess out of sight, right? But how often do we do that with our feelings and the messy circumstances in our lives, trying to avoid the pain and discomfort of coming to terms with issues that plague us? Avoidance strikes again! Why not take the effort we spend trying to keep everything hidden and under the surface, and instead, journal about it, talk it over with a supportive friend and face it head on? Once we do that, we will feel so much better! If it's time to "clean house," pick up your broom (pen, phone) and just get started. You don't have to do it all in one day, just pick one place to start and begin. Your de-cluttered soul awaits!

October 18   Find Your Pulse

"To live is the rarest thing in the world.
Most people exist, that is all."
~ Oscar Wilde ~

It's prime Haunted House season. My son paid good money to stand in line so he could walk through a haunted house and have people try to scare, shock and spook him. (You can probably hear the sarcasm!) I've never been a fan of haunted houses or scary movies, but it's definitely big business. Lots of people like to be scared! Is it because they already know it's going to be okay when it's over? I imagine it's a huge endorphin rush, too, that edge-of-your-seat, what's-going-to-happen-next feeling. While haunted houses aren't my thing, I do endorse at least occasionally seeking the thrill of adventure.

Excitement plus uncertainty plus fear—sounds crazy, but many of us will pay for that! Maybe because it's so intense that it forces us to be present? And yet, it's definitely an escape from the hum drum of life. Maybe the biggest outcome is simply feeling alive? Too many of us walk around with barely a pulse, day after day after day, caught up in a routine existence. If you are really daring and courageous, but haunted houses aren't your thing, maybe a tandem skydive is the way to go? (Pun intended. I finally did that and it was awesome!) If extreme living isn't for you, choose an activity in the next few days that is exciting—something that will make you feel alive and re-introduce you to your pulse. Take a spontaneous road trip with no particular destination, and no reservations. (Pun intended again!) Or try a salsa class. Even a brisk cold walk in chilly air can do the trick. Beware of a life lacking in adventure and excitement. Pay attention when you're saying *No* if somewhere deep inside you a voice is saying, *Yes! Please!* Avoid being haunted by missed opportunities to really live. Say *Yes* to a full living experience!

October 19   Life Is Precious

All life is precious, even the smallest baby field mouse. I am not exactly sure how he got to our yard, but a one week old field mouse survived my curious cat and dog, and was lying asleep in the grass beside our driveway. I thought he was dead, as we find remnants of our cat's excursions all the time. When I came home, my husband was attempting to dropper-feed this tiny little creature who was alive after all. We made him a bed in a Pop Tart box with tissue and wood shavings. We have four cats and a dog and we are trying to nurse a baby field mouse! As crazy as it seems, it's hard to turn our backs on this little life. He's not going to make it. He is not eating and even if he lived, he has no future within a mile radius of my hunting cats. But we feel better for trying.

Just to hold this tiny creature and marvel at such a small miracle of life has been a gift. We all have purpose and no matter how insignificant we might feel on any given day, we are no small miracle! We have life inside us! LIFE! We are not machine or battery operated. We are powered by the most supreme Creator and the most sophisticated collaboration of systems. We are only alive for a designated number of days, so make them count. Embrace your individuality! Celebrate your life today and the life in everything and everyone around you. Enjoy the gift of life for as long as you can and realize how very special you already are, just because you are here.

October 20   **Broaden Your Horizons**

I heard an amazing statistic cited from the 2010 Framingham Heart Study. Men who go on a real vacation once a year will cut their risk of heart attack by approximately thirty percent. Women who vacation at least annually will lower their risk of a heart incident by fifty percent! When was the last time you went on a real vacation? We live in a world where there is something for everyone—beaches, mountains, and cold or warm climates. We can choose relaxing getaways or activity-based vacations like skiing, hiking, scuba diving, sailing, or cycling across Europe. Mark Twain said, "The world is a book and those who do not travel read only one page." We have an incredible world to explore!

Five years ago, we found a travel club who is pioneering ways to save money and create a greater experience for like-minded individuals wanting more out of life (without breaking the bank). We met great people and became friends with a couple who had never traveled much before. Now they've been out of the country, not once but three or four times. Where there's a will, there's a way but you have to be open to finding it.

Travel helps create a life that is memorable and rich. Right now, start thinking about and researching a place you've never been before. Arranging your first adventure as a day trip to the next town over can be a great warm-up to planning your dream vacation. Decide how much you would need to save per month to make it happen. Stop paying for cable if you have to, or have a yard sale. Give up that which is not bringing you life … to get more life! If you don't travel, it's time to stop watching "life" happen for other people and make plans to experience it firsthand. Release any belief that travel and exploration is only for wealthy people, because there are a lot of free adventures everywhere, within a brief car ride. Allow your desires to surface, get creative financially if necessary, and JUST DO IT! Please contact me with your stories of how you stretched to explore something new, and how that felt! findingthegift.com

October 21   **Travel NOW**

Talking about travel has me really fired up, because so many people wish and postpone, but seldom act. If you need inspiration—travel! If you need clarity—travel! If you need to restore your soul—travel! I can take a walk in my neighborhood and be inspired, so I can just imagine my insights if my next walk is on a beach in Costa Rica! Or if my next bike ride is through Italy! Or anything else outside my usual path. Heightened moments and experiences can often bring heightened awareness. What's going *right* in our lives? What needs changing? Are we living our lives on purpose? Immersing myself in nature helps me provide those answers, but … immersing myself in nature and culture through travel and adventure can be like getting those answers on steroids!

It's time to break out of our comfort zones and really live! No more excuses. No more putting it off. This is your life and the clock is ticking. The sand is filling the hourglass. This isn't a dress rehearsal. Do not wait in hopes of seeing the world when you are "retired." Look at the word retired. Take off the RE and what do you have—tired! What if life throws an unexpected curve and retirement looks different than what you hoped? You have no guarantee you will live that long, so travel now. Enjoy adventure now, at the height of your physical abilities! While your knees, back, shoulders etc. are still healthy and functioning. Live a life full of mini-retirements now! Adopt a no-regrets mindset. If I have to choose between travel and a Starbucks every day, more designer purses to fill my closet, or that newest phone or video game—it's a no-brainer for me. Come join me!

October 22   Accept and Move On

Today is a gorgeous fall morning, cool but sunny. If I wanted it to rain, well, that would be too bad. I am not powerful enough to change the weather. Why, then, do I think I can change people? Lately, I'm struggling with having imaginary conversations with someone whose mind I would like to change. I have stated my request with supporting information. She has stated her unwillingness to do it my way, based on her past experiences. Even though I have discovered new supporting information that further reinforces my position, she isn't going for it and it's time to let this issue drop. I need a job done and this person is so perfect … all except for her unwillingness to do it the way I need it done. That's called a deal breaker. It's time to move on and find the person I'm looking for. Note to self: quit trying to fit pickles into a toothpick jar! Accept people as they are with grace, tolerance and love. If they can't meet my needs, let them go and find someone who can. We don't have to settle for less. I don't have to tell myself, "This might be as good as it gets." That is a lie of mediocrity and fear! On this one issue, I have allowed myself to waffle back and forth all week. I finally asked myself today, what is the right answer, for me? I have known it all along, and today, I am ready to admit she isn't the right person for my job. Know what you know. Quit doubting your truth! Make a decision and use that energy toward action instead of indecision and mind-wrestling. I can't enjoy this beautiful day or much of anything else when I am engaged in imaginary conversations! Hello world, I'm back! Clarity has won again!

October 23   Standing Up Without Standing On

This is really odd. Yesterday I wrote about needing a job done and finding the perfect candidate only to have her tell me she can't do what I wanted, based on her seven years of experience. My twenty years of experience say otherwise, as do the colleagues I double checked with. I have moved on, it's a done deal and I have felt much release in making that decision. Ironic as it may be, as yesterday unfolded, I had to train a new business partner for another project. (I am an entrepreneur at heart and always have several projects in motion!) This person is brand-new, and knows nothing about this type of work, but seems eager to learn. We got everything set up, and created a good solid plan of action for the next several days. Later that same day, he sent word that he wouldn't be able to follow the plan we created, and expressed hope we could still work together if I would consider doing things his way. I am all for new ideas and challenging old ones, and for some reason, that's often a role in life I've been assigned to play. This, however, felt like an acorn lecturing the oak tree, telling the oak tree he's going to take a different approach. Thankfully, I've learned I can grow from everyone who crosses my path!

Between today and yesterday's experiences, I can only conclude I'm being given a lesson in open-mindedness, or a lesson in standing up for what I believe to be true, and in either case, holding out for what I want and need, without settling for anything less. I think it's the latter. Once again, I have a choice. I can choose to reverse roles and let the new guy with zero experience call the shots, or I can reaffirm what my leadership role is, and gracefully inform him that I can only work with people who are coachable. I do admire his enthusiasm, but unfortunately, it's pointed in the wrong direction for what I need.

We teach people how to treat us by what we say or don't say, do or don't do, tolerate or don't tolerate. If I don't like how I'm being talked to or treated, I have choices. I can leave the conversation to gather my thoughts. I can make a request for what I would need to continue from this point forward. And at any time, I am free to leave the relationship. I don't have to change "me" to deal with every person that comes along. Someone who doesn't value my worth is not worth my time and energy. Today I seek interactions and cooperative efforts with people who value me—my heart, my intentions, my loyalty, my knowledge, and yes, my experience.

October 24   God Box

In recovery circles, I often heard people talk about something called a "God box," so finally, several years ago, I created one of my own. When someone or some situation is persistently troubling me and stealing my peace, I can write down my concerns on a piece of paper and place it in my God box. The God box is an act of surrendering, and a bridge to acceptance. It's kind of like planting a seed in the ground. I bury the seed and for a while, it's out of sight. If the seed comes into my thoughts, I can easily let it go again with full trust that the seed is exactly where it needs to be. I know when the time is right, I will see evidence of growth and the fruits of my actions. How crazy would it be for me to dig up a planted seed multiple times throughout the day to check on it? It's just as crazy to keep mulling things over in my mind that disturb me, especially if I've done all I can do about it.

Now when a troubled thought returns, it's much easier to let it go because I know I have "planted it" in my God box, and He is taking care of the situation for me.

Growth, resolution, change—whatever needs to happen is cultivating, and in time I will see the result of letting go and trusting that the solution is in process. A God box can be anything: an empty tissue box, a decorated shoebox, or a trinket box. It can be as plain or as fancy as you please. The magic is on the inside! Good things happen by writing my troubles down and placing them in the box— and leaving them there! I repeat, *leave them there*! Today, give this a try. Write one concern down and tuck it away. When it comes back to mind, and it will, see it tucked away safely and remind yourself someone else has it for now. You are on break! Let it be, and enjoy the serenity a simple act of surrender can bring.

October 25   Extraordinary Perspective

To me, photography is an art of observation. It's about finding something interesting in an ordinary place... I've found it has little to do with the things you see and everything to do with the way you see them.
~ Elliott Erwitt ~

We have a standing joke where I live: "if you don't like the weather in Tennessee, wait till next week!" We have sudden weather changes at times that are quite dramatic. One winter, my dad came to visit. The Saturday before he arrived we had an unseasonably warm December day in the seventies. During his visit just seven days later, the temperature was below zero! Today we are enjoying sunshine and higher temperatures than usual. This is late October and right now it's in the eighties! The weatherman says storms are coming this weekend, bringing in a cold front. Next week they say we will be lucky to see fifty degrees. Knowing the storms and cold weather are coming soon, other people are here at the park with me soaking up the sun and the warmth, jogging, walking dogs, and feeding the ducks.

In life, we often don't get a forecast telling us to really enjoy the next few days, weeks or months because it's all about to change. To be honest, I'm not sure I would want advance notice of significant change. I do try to live with heightened gratitude for my life exactly the way it is, knowing it won't be this way forever, while solidly trusting whatever comes my way will be good, too.

I often say, "Ordinary life is extraordinary when viewed from a higher perspective." Today is a perfect example of an ordinary moment that suddenly shows me a glimpse of the bigger picture. I am grateful for today's awareness to take a moment to look around and soak up all that I see—cherishing smells, sounds, sights, touch, people, places and things. Of all the truly spectacular things I have been blessed to see and do, these ordinary moments are the most precious to me. Take a look around you today and really get present. Can you see the gifts?

October 26   We Control Actions Not Outcomes

"Your proper concern is alone the action of duty, not the fruits of the action. Cast then away all desire and fear for the fruits and perform the duty."
~ The Bhagavad Gita ~

When I am frustrated, could it be that I'm trying to make things happen according my plan and other people or circumstances are not cooperating? Life isn't Burger King and I don't always get to "have it my way!" Often the harder I try, the more resistance I meet! I got up in time to see the sunrise today. It never ceases to amaze me how fast it can move from behind the tree line on up into the sky. Guess what? I had nothing to do with it. I'm just sitting in my chair watching. The grass is covered with a thick dew this morning. That wasn't me either. And, no, I don't tell the birds to sing. Sometimes when I start falsely believing I'm the center of the universe, I can step back and take a look at all the wondrous things that happen outside of my control. When I'm pushing too hard, I might be trying to do more than my part.

I am responsible for the footwork, the action steps and that's it. I can lose my peace in a heartbeat if I also choose to believe I am responsible for every outcome. I don't know what you believe spiritually, but what I know for certain is that I'm not running the show! The sun is continuing to rise and no one is asking me how high it should go. When I can trust there is a power greater than me taking care of things and watching out for me, I can relax. What a relief to let go and know I'm only in charge of my decisions and my actions. I can look for the gifts and how all the rest of it plays out. If you are wrestling with someone or something today, go back and read October 24. Write the issue down on a piece of paper, put it in your God box and forget about it for now. Accept that it is not your job to resolve, however the one who raises the sun every morning might be able to work on it, if you will let Him.

October 27   Created to Create

Originality is the essence of true scholarship.
Creativity is the soul of the true scholar.
~ Nnamdi Azikiwe ~

We took a road trip to Dallas yesterday. Twelve hours in a car is hard on the body! Even two to three hours without a break is enough to stiffen our joints and make it hard to hop right out of the car and walk normally. The human body is designed to walk and yet just a few hours in one position leads to "dysfunction"—difficulty with an otherwise normal human function. I believe another of our innate abilities is to create. If we have no creative outlet for two to three months, we may have irritability pop up as a consequence of restricting our natural capabilities. If we go two to three years without engaging in any creativity, we may see even more evidence of "dysfunction," and we will probably experience a lack of fulfillment (though we may not realize why). If we wait twenty to thirty years without being creative and true to the way we were designed, we may have full-blown dysfunction in the way of depression, unhealthy relationships, bad habits, apathy, loss of physical health—complete bankruptcy of the soul.

In our culture, it's so easy to fall into a confined lifestyle, where we're practically robotic without a lot of variety. We do everything the same, over and over. We may not use much of our creativity or imagination, so those innate functions get rusty and stiff from lack of use. It can happen before we realize and then perpetuate over time. Creation is life. Creativity invites life energy to live in you. You don't have to be a traditional artist, but we all need to create, to give life, to dream, to bear ideas, to play, to follow passions, to experiment and to explore new paths. What creative activity—creat-ivity—can you do today to put some *life* back into your life? Can you experiment in the kitchen? Try something new on the menu at your favorite restaurant, or maybe even explore a new restaurant? Can you make a small wardrobe change to create a new combination that you've never worn before, using the clothes you already have? Can you invite creativity into your job and relationships? Can you find an alternate route to work, paying attention to the different landmarks you see? Reignite the spark that makes you ... YOU!

October 28   Rooted Together

*"We cannot climb up a rope that is attached
only to our own belt."*
~ **William Ernest Hocking** ~

My husband and I went for a walk this morning in Dallas near our hotel. I have never seen so many varieties of trees in just a couple blocks! I saw several I had never seen before in my life. One group of trees was very unique. Instead of one big trunk and lots of branches, these seem to grow their branches straight out of the ground—they had no trunk. I took a picture of them. I thought about everything I've written using trees as metaphors and how important it is to have a strong trunk or strong foundation. I suppose these trees have everything they need underground to hold them up—a very strong and sophisticated root system.

These trees together represent communities to me, or individuals grouped together on a project, vision or common goal. Individually they may not be able to stand alone, but together they are strong and function as one. I don't have to know all the answers or be able to do everything by myself. As long as I am partnered with like-minded people, together we can accomplish what neither of us could do alone. It's okay to put down my superhero cape and lean on my friends. Together our strengths unite and complement and we're all the better for it! Comradery feels pretty good too! Find out where you belong and plug in. Take a risk and link up with some like-minded friends with similar interests. It might be like dating. You may have to try several groups of friends before you find the right fit.

October 29   THE Secret of Success ... Shhh!

My husband and I attended a leadership pow-wow yesterday for one of our businesses. We were among thirty leaders gathered together casually in someone's home, using the premise: iron sharpens iron. Everyone was hungry for the latest tips and success strategies from the top performers of the year. A few people were having extraordinary results and we were sure they had discovered the formula to shortcut our road to skill mastery and high achievement. But we didn't really hear anything original or different. Finally, the last speaker shared the best tip of all: there is no magic pixie dust! We all know what to do. Just go do it more often, better and faster than anyone else!

When someone is having more success than us in business, relationships, or finances, it's easy to feel like they must know some secret or that maybe they're just lucky. Usually winning in business or life comes down to the following three things. The first one is application of knowledge. We all have access to unlimited knowledge, but application of knowledge is the real magic. The second part of the winning formula for success is a firm decision. Whether it's to succeed, to improve, to have loving relationships, to stop a bad habit, or whatever—a firm decision must accompany the effort. The third component of the secret code is motivation. Tapping into a personal incentive that is bigger than any of our excuses is possibly the most important "pixie dust" of all. The reason for doing something, the *why*, must be stronger than any obstacle likely to stand in your way, or it's too easy to give up. These three elements are the Miracle Gro of life. You can't go buy them in the store, but they are free to those who seek them. If our plants and flowers deserve Miracle Gro, why not our lives?

Josiah G. Holland declared, "The mind grows by what it feeds on." Read, listen, study, pray, meditate, journal. Commit to spending ten to twenty minutes or more every day feeding your mind and soul. Get up early if you have to. And for today, spend at least ten minutes getting clear on what you really want and why. Write down a goal and then jot down your "why" but don't accept your first answer. Whatever your response is, ask "why" again. And again. Drill down until you get to the very bottom of the truth and you will find resolve you never knew you had.

October 30   A Healthy Need to Achieve

It is only in adventure that some people succeed in knowing themselves—in finding themselves.
~ André Gide ~

A few days ago, our dog bolted down the deck steps and ran as far as her electric fence would allow her to go. I really thought she would decide these "visitors" were worth bursting through the fence, even if it meant getting a little zinger, but she stopped just short of the boundary. There were several deer back behind our tree line, and I happened to see them just a few seconds before Goldie did. They took off when she went nuts. What beautiful creatures they were, racing through the fields! Goldie was thrilled just to briefly engage in the chase, even though she probably knew all along she would never catch them. That wasn't the point.

We were born to run, to race, to pursue and then to rest. Remember playing hide-and-seek, tag, duck-duck-goose, musical chairs, and kick the can? As adults, we have marathons, hunts (I am not a fan), fishing, Black Friday early-bird limited specials for the serious shopper, and auctions (silent or otherwise). Even costume contests provide an adventurous quest for many of us. The point is to engage in life! Go after something! Use a little healthy competition to spur you on to greater creativity! Even if it's just a challenge to yourself to be a better you. Set little goals. Big goals. Go after it and remember—the prize isn't only in catching it. We may not always cross the ultimate finish lines we pursue, but have fun on the journey. Find and share encouragement with friends you meet along the way. The journey is often the real prize.

October 31   Everything Is a Treat

Trick-or-treat! Growing up, one of the best memories I have is sitting in a rocking chair with my mom and younger brother at bedtime. My mom would occasionally read us a story at night. The only book I can remember was a children's storybook from the Bible. I will never forget at age nine hearing a story from the book of Romans that said, "If God is for us, who can be against us?"

From that story, I developed the belief that everything is working for my ultimate good. Sometimes in my life, I get a "trick," and sometimes I get a "treat." It doesn't really matter because in the long run, I see everything as treats. Some of the worst things I have ever experienced have led me to the best things I have ever experienced. I absolutely love this quote, often attributed to John Lennon, but my research shows it was originally created by Brazilian writer, Fernando Sabino. He said, "In the end, everything will be okay. If it's not okay, it's not the end." I trust that today, whatever I am walking through is leading me on a path of favor and blessing, even if the rainbow is just out of sight.

November

If one advances confidently in the direction of his dreams, and endeavors to live the life which he has imagined, he will meet with a success unexpected in common hours.
~ Henry David Thoreau

November 1   Observation Leads to Appreciation

It's so beautiful this morning with bright sunshine and cheerful birdsong. Just another day in paradise! I'm studying Goldie and Lucky. They don't appear to be driven by mindless chatter. They are looking around, but relaxed and seemingly content, fully accepting of this moment and their role in life. Observant. I can't fully appreciate anything without taking some time to stop and notice my life, and the people and things in it. In this moment of mindfulness and gratitude, I can breathe deeper. I let peace wash over me in timed, increments of breath. Peace in, chatter out. Peace in, stress out. Nothing but here and now. Get present. Observe. This is my life. I see it. I feel it. I am thankful and centered. The chatter has stopped. My cat is off to explore the fields. I'm refreshed and ready to explore my day now too! How about you?

November 2   No Strings Attached

After six days on the road, it's good to get home to our son, our furry children, and our own bed. I wanted to just hug the living daylights out of my son and animals! While hugging, Lucky, our biggest cat, I wrapped my arms around him so tight that he actually whined to let me know it was too tight. I missed him so much, I just couldn't help myself from squeezing so hard. There's a difference between loving and hugging, and outright restraining. We all want to participate in relationships voluntarily. It never feels good to be forced beyond our own comfort levels, or restrained against our will. Relationships can be kind of like fishing (hopefully without the sharp hook part): catch and release. Catch and release. Allow people, friends, and loved ones to come and go at their own pace, at their own frequency. I don't mean break vows or other serious infractions of committed relationships and marriages. But let each party participate with choice, rather than force.

We don't need to control someone or latch on so tight that they can't breathe and be themselves. If we do that and they *don't* leave, what remains is not what or whom we admired in the first place. All we really have at that point is a prisoner, or a puppet. Cut the strings and let them dance their own dance, while you dance yours. Chances are good if you allow and appreciate your friends' and loved ones' individuality and respect their boundaries, you won't need strings, control or manipulation to keep them in your life. They will stick around voluntarily to soak up the acceptance and unconditional love you have to offer. Speaking of acceptance and unconditional love, I have discovered I have to give it to myself before I have any to give to others. Begin today by loving what is ... starting with YOU.

November 3   Get in the Driver's Seat

Everywhere I look this time of year I see orange. Orange leaves, orange pumpkins, harvest decorations on mailboxes and doors. And being from Tennessee, we see a lot of orange football this time of year—Go UT! Go Big Orange! Today on a walk, I noticed the fattest, furriest, bright orange caterpillar about two feet off the curb, headed toward the middle of the road! What was he thinking? He was about to become orange squash! I picked him up and put him back in the field he must have crawled from. I think we often get tunnel vision. We have our sights set on something and we pursue it with blinders on. Before we know it, we've gotten so far off track and we don't even realize it. Thank goodness for friends who love us and support us, and aren't afraid to say, "Hey! What's up? Did you mean to end up here?" or "Do you realize what could happen if you keep going in this same direction?" Or maybe we have been heading down a path for so long, we can't even remember why we went that way in the first place? We just keep trudging along because it's what we've always done and what everyone else has been doing, and we never even question if that's still where we want to go. Autopilot is on and no one is behind the wheel.

Pretend I just picked you up and set you back down in a safe, neutral place. East, West, North, South—you can go anywhere you want to. You can go in the opposite direction if that's what you want. You are in the driver's seat! Even if all your friends are going left, but you feel led to go right—do it! Trust your gut! If you don't do it now, when will you? This is your chance. What do you really, REALLY want? You already know the answer. Have courage to listen and take action—even if it's just a baby step. Even if it's just doing a little research. Do one thing today to live your life on purpose, starting with just getting honest. Ask yourself, *Am I really in the driver's seat of my life and paying attention, or am I living on cruise control?* Whatever the answer, give yourself grace and celebrate new clarity. An awakened soul is better than one who doesn't even know they're asleep.

November 4   Strong Foundation

Nature is a powerful demonstration of being balanced and grounded. She's never in a hurry and you don't usually see chaos or indecision in nature. Everything always looks true to what is—nature wears no masks. If it looks calm and sunny, it is. If it's storming wildly, it is, and yet, it will pass. Sometimes nature can create human chaos, but nature always restores itself to balance, to a relaxed state of ease. The goal is always finding balance amidst opposing forces. A cold front, a warm front. Drought, flooding. Challenges and variables arise, and nature endures the circumstances the best it can, but not everything survives the extreme weather. However as a whole, nature always restores itself back to balance, to a state of acceptance and original being.

This is a powerful lesson that reminds me to be firmly grounded in who I am at all times, yet be flexible when variables come my way. I accept there will be change, abundance and loss. My goal is to remain as steady as possible in my spirit, and when I'm stretched, to preserve my soul, my life, as best I can. If I veer off course, I choose to move back toward balance as soon as possible, so that once again, I am relaxed and grounded, back to doing what I came here for—to be me. Check in with yourself. How balanced and grounded do you feel today? My wish for you is to take several deep breaths to connect with your spirit and then proceed with your day as you—the real, balanced you.

November 5   Different Strokes for Different Folks

I really believe there is someone for everyone and that beauty is in the eye of the beholder. Someone's junk is another man's treasure. Many things in life boil down, not to right or wrong decisions and choices, but to personal preferences. We see a particular tree when we walk through our neighborhood. In my opinion, this is quite possibly the ugliest tree I've ever seen. It's some sort of blue spruce variety, but it's the most crooked, scraggliest tree ever. It's in the front yard of a corner house, meaning this tree is center stage! If it were my house, I'm pretty sure that scrawny eyesore would be cut down tomorrow. I'm exaggerating … a little. It reminds me of a Christmas tree from the cartoon movie, *When the Grinch Stole Christmas*. The owner must like that tree (or at least, not dislike it enough to remove it). It is unique and it does have character. It definitely must be a conversation starter. Or maybe no one else sees it like my husband and I do?

When I'm so sure of something, when I've formed a solid opinion and decided I'm "right," I have to remember there's probably someone else who is just as convinced of the exact opposite. We are both right. It's our opinion. Our perception. Our perspective. Our feelings. Our beliefs. Allow people the dignity to believe as they do. There's a big difference between having a healthy debate and close-mindedly badgering someone to finally see your point of view. As the old saying goes, "A man convinced against his will is of the same opinion still." Many times we need to agree to disagree and appreciate individuality. What a boring, monotonous world it would be if we all thought alike. We would dress the same, drive the same car, plant identical flowers in our yards. Look for and offer your blessing for the diversity you see today and dare to be uniquely you as well!

November 6   **Change What You Can**

"You must take personal responsibility. You cannot change the circumstances, the seasons, or the wind, but you can change yourself."
~ Jim Rohn ~

It's an election year and after months of campaign ads, internet posts and e-mail persuasions, we all got the opportunity to vote today. Each candidate had some plans that didn't sound so great and others that seemed pretty good. I trusted my instincts and cast my ballot, knowing that regardless of what happened at the end of the day, it was going to work out—it always does. We are here for such a short time. Can we all just get along, be kind to one another, do the best we are capable of at any given moment, be our authentic selves and respect differences in opinions? A lot of people were happy with the outcome, and quite a few people weren't (I guess that's true in most elections). Social media has given us a platform to publically complain and rally the troops into our own corners. I'm perplexed at how opinionated people can be, when they feel they have the support of their peers to criticize political candidates and bash the government. They seem so angry and I wonder if these people are just unfulfilled? Many people will join any fight but their own. They stay in jobs they hate, where they trade the bulk of their time away from family for a paycheck with benefits, all to have an *illusion* of security, allowing every last dream inside them to die. It's too convenient to blame everyone else, instead of taking responsibility for their own lives and making necessary changes.

Jim Rohn has a fabulous audio recording I just love and can't recommend enough. In *The Art of Exceptional Living*, Mr. Rohn shares how he was deep in debt, "had pennies in [his] pockets," and blamed the government, the economy and taxes for his financial predicament. Ultimately he had to change his philosophies because this was the same government, economy and tax structure in which other people were doing quite well. Like everything on this earth, we were all born with specific dreams and purpose. Have you settled for a life of mediocrity and "security?" I know I did for a long time. External circumstances beyond my control redirected my path. While at the time, life got really different and challenging, today I am so thankful for the wake-up call that put me back on my authentic path. *It's never too late!*

We are fortunate to live in a world of free enterprise. Take advantage of all your giftings, passions and freedoms and make a decision that the rest of your life will begin anew today! Yes it might involve risk, but you already know what you've got if you do nothing new. You really can have the life you dream of, if you are willing to dream and then take action. Choose your battles. Do what you can to make your country a great place to live, but fight even harder to make your life a great life to live. If we all took the time spent venting on social media and applied it to our own personal development—that's where real change can happen.

November 7   Re-Find Yourself

A tree is a tree. It may stay a tree or it may become a house, a bench or a book. The tree may be burned to warm someone, or it may become a boat to carry someone off to a distant shore. A friend of mine has a business making jewelry out of odd items that have served other purposes—watch parts and bottle caps for example. They are being re-purposed, given new lives when the one they knew ran its course. We are no different! We hopefully will continue to evolve as the years go by. Just because you started out on one path doesn't mean you have to stay there! Often we learn, we grow, and we alter our course. Then we learn, and grow, and alter our course again. You are the captain of your ship, the master of your soul! You get to decide what's next. True, sometimes you have more or less choice about a change in direction, but you get to decide what you do with the changes that come your way. Live a grand life. Then live another grand life. Mix, stir and repeat until your very last breath. Whatever you do, make it a story worth telling. Create the best obituary you can think of. Live your life. Refine yourself. Re-find yourself.

November 8   Wake Up And Chase Life

I woke up today just like any other day, but when I looked outside, I stopped in my tracks. Through the windows that overlook our backyard, I saw a breathtaking layer of fog. This morning, however, the thick blanket of white started *behind* the first tree line. The bright green trees were set off by the muted trees behind them, creating a startling contrast. How can I be so in love with fog and all the ways it changes the landscape? I can't get enough of it! I quickly grabbed my camera and captured it to the best of my ability, shooting from my deck. Even as a professional photographer, however, there is no substitute for what I see with my own eyes. My neighbors are leaving for work. Do they see it? Do they slow down too, and appreciate this majestic moment? It's going to be gone in less than an hour. It's already changing and the fog has now covered everything.

Soak in the breathtaking beauty that surrounds us constantly. It's only thirty-six degrees this morning, but I've got my coat on over my pajamas and I'm not going to miss a minute of this. The sun just got brighter and changed the landscape again! Open your eyes and ears. Your soul feeds on beauty and there is always a feast waiting if you'll take the time to look for it. Now the fog is so thick that the cars have completely disappeared, and so has everything behind the first row of trees. I may have to jump in the car with my camera and chase the fog this morning.

One hour later: I threw out all of the reasons not to break my morning routine. I brushed my teeth, dressed quickly and started driving, stopping whenever and wherever I could, to capture the magical landscape. Often I parked the car a little precariously, or I found myself having to walk in the road to get the shot I wanted. I think that's part of the thrill—taking a calculated risk. Stopping the car on a foggy, two-lane back road to jump out and grab a shot before the next car comes. The whole time I was racing the clock, because fog doesn't last forever. Hmmm … *Chasing what I cherish, to get all I can before it's gone.* That sounds like a great approach to life. A little risk is always better than a lot of regret. Go after something today!

Today is Sunday. I don't usually mention that because on any given calendar year this entry is read, it most often won't fall on a Sunday. However today's inspiration has to do with the particular days of the week. When I think of Monday through Friday, I have an imprint of work. It's all about production and often specifically, income production. As a mom and a wife, those days also mean juggling. I have to be personally productive while maintaining the laundry, stocking the fridge, and preparing meals. Additionally, I have to navigate doctors, dentists and vet visits, as well as piano recitals and football games. Saturdays are usually full of home or family projects that can't or didn't get done during the week, mixed in with a little, "We should do something fun as a family." (Even my fun is driven by should's!)

Sunday holds the least amount of should's. I woke up today thinking at first it was Monday and the "should factory" in my head started to crank up. Then I realized it was Sunday and the weight of the world dropped off my shoulders. It's just 7 a.m. I have "permission" to write and read and daydream. I don't feel I "have" to do too much of anything today. I want to learn to live with less should's Monday through Saturday. Many times, I force myself to do something, just to feel productive, even when I'm caught up. I've done this for so much of my life that it feels difficult to give myself permission to relax when the critical things are completed. It's hard to stop finding busywork for myself and to realize down time, creativity and fun are also necessary ingredients to a satisfying life.

Maybe it's time to fire that internal Monday through Saturday boss? To start working with my authentic self instead—the one who knows what balance looks and feels like. It's time to release the inner "should" boss. If I can do it on Sunday, there is hope for Monday through

Saturday. Today I will remember what Bertrand Russell boldly declared, "The time you enjoy wasting is not wasted time." I hope you will too!

November 10   Quality Over Quantity

Do you have a "should" voice in your life? Where did it come from? I look around at my animals, the trees, the grass and sun and I feel pretty certain they don't operate with an inner "should" boss. Does your "should" voice also tell you that you're only as good as the things you produce—your tangible evidence of success? Is or was there someone in your life who first voiced those beliefs, which you then automatically adopted as the truth? Even a highly productive assembly line has quality control checkpoints built in. Quantity doesn't matter if the quality suffers. Is it time to do an inventory of your life? Has your life become robotic as you focused more on quantity versus quality?

Evaluate the belief templates you operate by on a daily basis. Be willing to let go of the ones that just aren't true. Establish your own quality of life checkpoints. What are the minimal criteria that you require in your life to maintain a quality standard that is nonnegotiable? In other words, how much of the following do you need to maintain a satisfactory quality of life: fun, recreation, creativity, vacation, social interaction, physical activity, mental stimulation, opportunities for inspiration, meditation, culinary delight, variety, risk, excitement, stability, and spiritual nourishment? Design the life you want, and measure it on a regular basis, because if *you* don't do it, who will? It's easy to get off track but with regular and honest evaluation, it's also easy to get back on track. Aim for the highest levels of quality to please your number one customer—YOU.

November 11   **Gently Intentional**

"Let us spend one day as deliberately as Nature, and not be thrown off the track by every nutshell and mosquito's wing that falls on the rails."
~ Henry David Thoreau ~

I stumbled across this quote and it resonated deeply within me. It also provided a strange comfort that being easily distracted was just as true a century ago as it is today. "As deliberately as Nature" at first sounded like an oxymoron to me, no different than "as fast as slow." "Deliberate" sounds so harsh and strong and "nature" seems so soft and easy going. Maybe that is the deeper point? Maybe we are to be deliberate and intentional, while maintaining a gentle disposition? Deliberate doesn't mean we bully our way through life, fixed intensely on getting what we want, but that we are clear about our path and we take the necessary steps in that direction. Our pace is easy *and* our resolve is strong. Today, when I find myself chasing my own tail and every other thing that moves and distracts me, I will recognize that I've gotten off track and temporarily lost my sense of relaxed focus. I will come back to a calm, centered place and reset my course to match my intentions for the day. I will be deliberate about my choices and gentle in my renewed approach. Feeling stressed and stretched is always our clue to step back, breathe and start gliding again.

November 12   **Mapping Our Dreams**

You are never too old to set another goal or to dream a new dream.
~ C. S. Lewis ~

Intentions. Goals. I find I have a much greater chance of staying the course when I have clearly defined my intentions and goals on paper. There is power in the written word. Our thoughts come out of our racing, jumbled mind, down through ink and onto paper. Suddenly, they exist outside of me. I see tangible evidence of the intangible inspirations, hopes and dreams I have been carrying around in my head. The "map" is visible now and no longer merely abstract wishful thinking. Without maps or GPS and a designated destination, how will we get where we want to go? I can't get to California if I'm walking toward New York! Take a few moments to chart your course for today, making sure today's map is aligned with the bigger picture of what's important to you and where you see yourself going and growing. Be sure to include some fun and R&R along the way!

November 13   Sunny Days, Rain or Shine

Wherever you go, no matter what the
weather, always bring your own sunshine.
~ Anthony J. D'Angelo ~

Yesterday we woke up to a drastic temperature change with rain, and a dark, gloomy sky. All too often, I'm influenced by bad weather setting the tone for my day. For me, a rainy day just doesn't give me the same internal reaction as waking up to sunshine. I went about my day with a little less bounce in my step. I carried an umbrella into a noon meeting, which took place in a room with no windows. An hour and a half later, I walked outside and didn't notice that anything was different at first. Something felt odd, but I couldn't quite put my finger on it. As I drove to my next appointment, it hit me like a lightning bolt! The rain was gone, replaced by bright sunshine, blue skies and fluffy clouds! It was eerie, and I doubted remembering correctly that the day had started off so dark and rainy. I felt myself sit up straighter and come alive, as if to say, "it's sunny now—better act like it!" The reminder for me is that I have the power to feel and act "sunny" any time, by simply making a decision to do so. I don't have to be a victim of the weather or other life storms to send me off riding a roller coaster of ups and downs. Is there sunshine in your heart today, right now? Good, it can be a great day if you choose it to be.

November 14   Spreading the Love

As I greeted my cat, Fancy, this morning with her breakfast, she didn't move toward it as she usually does. I realized she needed a hug more than food today. I picked her up and stroked her till she purred and then set her back down to eat. Food, water and shelter (and clothing for those of us who don't walk around on all fours!) are not enough. We all need love. We need to feel cared for, to know that we matter. And we need to give love just as much as we need to receive it. Ironically, the end result is the same!

Let your family and friends know that you care, with an extra dose of sincerity today. We hug and say I love you so habitually to our families, so next time, stop and do it deliberately. Sometimes as I give my husband a hug and tell him I love him, I hold his shoulders extra long, stare at him till I've caught his attention and then suddenly we're both out of autopilot mode. I joke as our eyes are locked and say, "Eye contact isn't eye contact if you don't look into the eyes!" Show a stranger they matter by looking them in the eye for a moment and giving them a smile. You'll both feel good! Opportunities to give and receive love are all around, and most of them are free! As a pet parent to five animals, I guess I'd better start spreading the love!

November 15   Do Your Dance

Do all birds fly south for the winter? I think not. We still have plenty around here. I witnessed an incredible display of beauty and creativity in the sky a few days ago with my friend, Todd. A multitude of birds were flying together. Hundreds, maybe thousands of black dots were moving along in a straight line with each other. The majority stayed together, but occasionally, I saw a small group moving like synchronized swimmers. Every so often, a few birds broke formation to create shapes and designs in unison, while the masses continue to fly straight. It was beautiful, graceful.

Had every bird been participating, it would have seemed more like chaos. However, against the backdrop of the masses, these artistic formations were easy to spot and appreciate.

We need the masses and we need the artists—the souls that have their own dance. We each have an artist inside us who needs to break formation from time to time and let the world see our individual expressions and interpretations of beauty and creativity. When the time is right, do your dance! The world will benefit from it and celebrate with you as you break formation to be uniquely and wonderfully you.

November 16   Gratitude Is Always in Season

Thanksgiving is coming up soon and serves as a great reminder to take inventory of all that we have to be grateful for. I'm grateful I was born with a hunger for insight and personal growth. By picking up this book, you apparently share that pursuit with me as well. I'm grateful for revelations in times of stillness, confirming the journey is worthwhile and full of rewards along the way. I am grateful for the mirrors in others which I encounter daily, because they help me see myself in truth. I am grateful for the courage to take action, when what I see in those mirrors falls short of who I know I was created to be. I am thankful for the comrades I've met and continue to meet along the way. I am grateful for the heartaches and the ability to know now that my past is my passage to the new and improved me. I am grateful I am willing to release old beliefs and adopt new ones, including the belief that I am worthy of receiving all the gifts noted above. What are you grateful for today?

November 17   Press Play and Pause More Often

Retail merchandising for the holiday season seems to happen earlier every year. It used to be that the stores took one holiday at a time and when that one passed, within twenty-four hours they would clear the aisles and set up for the next holiday. I saw Christmas decorations available for purchase in early October this year! That's two holidays too soon! Halloween and Thanksgiving hadn't even happened yet. It's still not Thanksgiving yet and a week ago, I overheard two people bragging they had already put their Christmas trees up. It seems they wanted to hurry up and get it out of the way. How many of us are living our lives with the fast-forward button pressed? We're rushing to get ahead only to have something new constantly added to the list so we are always behind. Living chaotically is a habit and a learned behavior. We can unlearn it with intention and a daily devotion to staying present and enjoying the moment. Today let go of fast-forward or rewind, if that's where you're stuck, and hit *play*. And yes, it's okay to press pause occasionally to really soak up the moment. This is your life. Enjoy the show!

November 18   Imaginary Leash

The only person you are destined to
become is the person you decide to be.
~ Ralph Waldo Emerson ~

Goldie and I went on a walk this gorgeous autumn afternoon. The brilliant neon orange trees were glowing in the late afternoon sunlight and the sky was bright blue, with white, fluffy clouds. All the cares of the day just disappeared from my mind and I was free again. We have

318

a street in our neighborhood that still has only a few houses, although recently they completed two more. Usually on this street, I let Goldie off the leash so she can run wild through the undeveloped land alongside the road. We all need to run free now and then. I haven't been doing it as much lately though, because one of the new neighbors has a dog they let roam free. Today we circled the cul-de-sac, and once we passed the last house, I let Goldie off the leash. She trotted along as if nothing happened. She had no idea she was free and just kept her pace beside me on the street. I had to run away from her into the grass to show her she was off the leash.

How many of us voluntarily buy into the boxes and chains we trap ourselves with? We are the only ones keeping us stuck. We buy into the should's, the what if's, ought to's, and have to's so much that we forget what free feels like. Worse than that, some of us don't even realize anything is wrong—that we are not actually free. We move along doing what we're supposed to do, never challenging the beliefs we have tied ourselves down with.

Are you living the life of your dreams? Do you dream of living a different life? Do your dreams even surface anymore? Today can be a new beginning because awareness is the first step. Maybe you just need a little more life in your life, rather than a drastic change? Join a bowling league. Buy an arts and craft kit. Volunteer at a homeless shelter. Pack an overnight bag and drive until it looks like an interesting place to stop. Just do *something* different. Maybe it's time to really assess the path you're on, or examine the detour you accidentally took so long ago. What can you do about that? When you think about what you really want, instead of saying, *I can't*, ask yourself, *How can I?* Look around. The leash has been imaginary all along. You are free!

Today has me thinking more about yesterday's walk—and the subject of freedom. There are people living their dream life and people who can imagine what that might look like, but don't see how it's possible to make the transition. And there are those who don't even know what their dream life would be. Some of us know exactly what our ideal life looks like, and we know how to make it happen, yet we still stay where we are. Why? Brendan Francis sums it up, "Every man, through fear, mugs his aspirations a dozen times a day."

Fear makes us afraid to trade today's comfort for tomorrow's uncertainty. We have fear of the unknown. Fear of failure. Fear of success. We don't just worry about trying and failing; we worry, *What if it goes right?* Even then we would be uncomfortable outside the box called security! We would be vulnerable to disappointment striking unexpectedly. Our illusion of control may be shattered forever. Hmmm... Maybe we should just stay where we are, always knowing we could go for it if we really wanted to? *I don't think so!*

Imagine your life twenty years from now with the same degree of fulfillment you're experiencing today. How does that look and feel? Remember, it's not just, "What if you do?" There's also, "What if you don't?" To me, the certainty of regret for choosing to remain stagnant and safe outweighs all other fears combined. Following up his earlier statement, Brendan Francis offers hope if we're struggling with fear, "Many of our fears are tissue-paper-thin, and a single courageous step would carry us clear through them." List on paper all the pros and cons of moving forward. Journal about your fears. Then make a small goal and achieve it. Then another. Then another. Before long, you will break out of the box and never look back.

November 20   **Resolve to Take Action**

Some days I just don't know what I'm going to write about. Then I'll do something random and the inspiration hits me. The thing is, if I want to write a book, I have to sit down and pick up the pen and paper and be prepared to receive thoughts, words and ideas. If I waited for the whole book to come to me, I might be waiting a long time. In other words, I "act as if" I'm expectant of getting what I need to write about when I sit down to write. Sometimes I don't get it until I'm into the first few sentences. Make a decision. Commit to action. Suit up and show up. Take a step in the right direction and see if the next step becomes clear. New York writer Peter DeVries quipped, "I write when I'm inspired, and I see to it that I'm inspired at nine o'clock every morning." I couldn't agree more! Moving forward is a choice. We can often reach our goals with small, consistent daily disciplines—little measurable chunks that add up. Today is as good a day as any to get started on one of your own goals. Guess what? You don't have to wait till January first to make that New Year's resolution. Make one today and get a big head start!

November 21   **New Horizons Just Inches Away**

Today I was wondering what to write about and was determined to find something. I journaled first to get my pen flowing, then something caught my eye. We have a cat bed that sits on a bench by a window. The cats jump up there all the time to nap and daydream, while looking out into the world. I guess it's never crossed our dog's mind to jump up there. She's a Terrier, so she's low to the ground. She isn't tall enough to see through our windows, so she has very few opportunities to watch the outside world from inside the house. We have a few French doors, but she has to look through the blinds. Our

321

front door is glass, but it's frosted for privacy, so it's not the same as looking through a clear windowpane.

Something inspired me to coax Goldie to jump up on the bench so she could enjoy the wide panoramic views of our backyard. It was a stretch physically and mentally for her to make the jump. Goldie was hesitant but with my continued encouragement, she checked out a few different angles and made the leap of faith to get out of her comfort zone. In the window seat for the very first time, Goldie just sat there and stared, looking all around. Such a simple thing, and yet she was seeing that view for the first time ever. Ever! All this time, this new vista has been just mere inches out of her usual reach. If I put a small step stool by the bench, Goldie could hop up there and see outside as often as she wanted to.

How close are we to something magnificent? What few inches are keeping you from a whole new perspective? Look around your world and think outside the box. Better yet, look for ways that God and the people and circumstances in your life are coaxing you to stretch those extra inches to expand your world. Check it out, explore the angles and make your approach. When the next opportunity comes along, try that too. Maybe you started out to achieve a goal and didn't think you'd ever reach it. But now you're in the last phase and you may just be inches from your goal so ... *stretch!* You can do it! Wherever you are, you may be closer than you think to attaining completion, reaching a new level, or gaining a whole new perspective. A whole new view! Life-changing expansion! Stretch! Just ask Goldie—she's happy she made the leap.

November 22   **Releasing Expectations**

Today I am thankful I can give myself some grace. I don't have to be perfect. With the holidays upon us, it can become a season of pressure and expectations. Too easily, I can get caught up in trying to make each experience the best it can possibly be, and worry if I'm pleasing everyone. Or I can decide my sincere efforts on any given day will be enough. I don't imagine God stresses out every day trying to figure out what to serve up when it comes to weather. He doesn't agonize over deciding if he should provide a sunny day, a foggy day, a warm or cold, rainy day. I'm sure He doesn't deliberate over what people will think of him if he offers up three stormy days in a row or doesn't make it snow on Christmas. Who knows how the weather is determined, but it's certainly not always perfectly pleasing, is it?

People are free to have their expectations of me, but that's their business, not mine. I am free to do what I'm capable of and what I choose to do, and let the rest be. I have a yardstick for peace in these situations. If I can take action in generosity, joy and love, and remain absent of resentment, I can feel pretty good about my choices. If something doesn't measure up to those guidelines, I may have to ask myself if I'm people-pleasing and being codependent. Or am I bringing my own expectations into a situation, trying to control the outcome or get something in return? In twelve-step recovery, we like to say, "Expectations are premeditated resentments." That's dangerous territory for me, to be avoided whenever possible. Today, I'll do my best and that will be enough. I hope you can also let whatever you do, be just right too.

November 23   **Year End Self-Care**

The holidays can be a memorable time with family and friends. Traditions and rituals are sacred this time of year. However, all the festivities and gatherings, with all the preparation that goes into them, can really take us off our own personal rhythm:

❧ Our daily habits of nurturing our bodies, minds and spirits are often interrupted.

- We get less sleep; we eat more and at odd times.
- We may have time off from work and other regular activities, which removes some of our daily structure and changes our usual flow.
- In juggling everything and everyone, we may spend less time reading, writing, praying, walking and exercising—or whatever else you do to stay centered.

It's important to be flexible for special occasions, holidays, company and other memorable events that take us out of our routine, but it's equally important to find the balance along the way so we can fully enjoy those special times, feeling our best. Be sure to monitor your level of self-care and never let it get too low.

Besides family and social gatherings, we literally deal with heavier traffic and an overall, year-end crunch which can generate even more stress as we juggle the additional demands on our time and the extra "traffic" in our minds. Pay attention when you sense your internal pressure is rising, and have a plan for letting off steam. A phone call to a listening ear is a great way to defuse rising tension. Writing, meditation, taking a walk, or making a trip to the gym are also great ways to slow down the chaos long enough to feel grounded again. Listening to calming or inspiring music can quickly restore a sense of balance and peace. Know what works for you and use these tools as often as needed at anytime you're feeling too low or too high and need to come back to center. I love the holidays and I also love going back into my own personal rhythms when they pass. The normalcy returns, providing the stability we all crave. But for now, tune into yourself and take good care!

November 24   Best Holiday Gift

In Asian languages, the word for 'mind' and the word for 'heart' are same. So if you're not hearing mindfulness in some deep way as heartfulness, you're not really understanding it. Compassion and kindness towards oneself are intrinsically woven into it. You could think of mindfulness as wise and affectionate attention.

~ Jon Kabat-Zinn ~

We had a visitor show up last night! Our dog, Goldie had wandered off and while we searched for her, another dog found us! That dog followed my car all over the neighborhood while I drove around slowly, calling for Goldie. We eventually found her, and had *two* dogs when we got back home! We're at max capacity with our four-legged family members, and since several of them are feline, we couldn't invite our visitor inside. We left food, water and a blanket outside, only to find our new friend snuggled up on the outdoor couch this morning, like he owns the place. Apparently he has decided he's home!

Isn't that what we all want? A place to feel loved and cared for? A place we belong? If you have that, give thanks and offer what you can to those two-legged and four-legged souls who do not. Generosity and compassion are two of the greatest gifts to give this holiday season. The more you give away, the richer your life will be! Need a quick fix for the holiday blues? Help someone who needs clothing, shelter and food. And love. Give love away every chance you can and you'll have more than you could ever spend!

November 25   Let Joy Light the World

We decorated for the holidays this past weekend. In the midst of getting everything out of storage, I asked my family what started such a tradition anyway? Why do millions of people put a tree inside their homes and adorn it with ornaments? Everyone thought about it for a moment and then my son said, "Because it's pretty." I'm sure there's a long, historical answer, but enough said! We don't always have to explain and justify everything we do. Our actions don't always have to be logical. Even if we are the only one in a million who does what we do, so what? If we like it, if it feels good, if it brings us joy, if no one gets hurt and it's not illegal, unethical or immoral, then just do it! And enjoy the smile it puts on your face. If we all committed to doing one thing each day that made us feel happy, we could light up the whole world with joy.

November 26   A Daily Gratitude Practice

"The more you praise and celebrate your life, the more there is in life to celebrate."
~ Oprah Winfrey ~

November is the perfect time of year to focus on being thankful: good health, relationships, friends and family, our jobs, our homes, and our freedom. Many of us can count some or all of these as blessings in our lives. What else? What else are you truly grateful for? Look around. Listen. Feel. Take stock of everything you have appreciation for. Holding gratitude in your heart generates a high vibrational frequency that attracts even more good to come your way. Count your blessings often. For extra benefit, make a daily gratitude journal, listing at least five new things every morning or night.

In addition to what's noted above, I am deeply grateful for nature, music, role models, reverse role models (who teach me what NOT to do), nature seasons, thick fuzzy blankets and socks, fast cars, adventure, adversity (without adversity, personal growth is much slower), my furry loved ones, sidewalks, hot baths, dark chocolate, apple cider, boots, things that sparkle, laughter and piano music filling my home, and much, much more! For a real challenge, make a list of all the people, places and things you are grateful for. Do this alone or with a group. When you run out of things to write, go through the letters of the alphabet to jog your memory some more. Keep this list and your daily gratitude journal handy for rereading frequently. Turkey hunters practice making turkey calls to attract birds to come their way. Practice using gratitude to attract more goodness to come your way. Cheers!

November 27   Grace and Choosing to Forgive

No one's perfect! Our relationships are bound to disappoint us from time to time. A sure way to stay dissatisfied and unhappy is to continually focus on what you don't like about this person. It may be your spouse, another family member, your boss, a coworker, a friend or a neighbor. If you're tired of being frustrated and ready to take action to feel better (and that is important because sometimes we want to stay miserable for a while), write down a list of all the positive aspects of this person. These are all the things you like about them, what they do well, and what you would miss about them if they were gone. Whatever you're focused on will expand. If you want to keep feeling bad, keep focusing on the negative. If you're ready to feel good, focus on what you can be grateful for in that relationship.

With sincere effort, I find this practice changes my perspective 98% of the time. If it doesn't, I'm not really ready to let go of my bad feelings yet, and am choosing to stew a little longer in the pain. Two incredible truths I lean on a lot: acceptance is the answer to all my problems, and forgiveness is giving up the *right* to be angry. We always have a choice about how we want to feel. Do you want to feel good today? Me too!

November 28　　Disappointments and Indecision

Disappointment offers clarity and I am always grateful for insight. A while back, I was invited to participate in a collaboration effort of authors. After going through the proof copy, it became apparent there was either a misunderstanding, or I was uninvited somewhere along the way! If I'm honest, I didn't have a lot of energy invested in this opportunity, but now that it's gone, I realize I did care about it. The old saying, "You don't know what you've got until it's gone" rings true. The great thing about disappointment is that it shows me how I really feel. When something doesn't work out and I feel relief, I get the confirmation it wasn't right for me anyway. It's good to gain the insight and not put any further effort into something that isn't a priority. But if something doesn't go my way and I feel disappointed, I realize how important it really is to me, and I can either try to resolve the situation, or look for a similar opportunity, and this time, be more dedicated.

I deal with indecision this way too. I will tell someone my dilemma, and then ask their opinion. What would they do? They respond and I will either agree with them and feel peace about my choice, or I will know their solution is absolutely not what I want, and now I can confidently and with new clarity, go do the opposite. It's like a fitting room for decisions. Try a few on. Even if you've yet to find one you love, you will rule out several less than ideal options, and that is always forward progress. We really can't make a mistake. We get to experience lessons and continually learn more about ourselves and what we value. Learning is living and living is learning.　Knowledge is power and self-knowledge may be the greatest gift of all.

November 29 False Evidence Appearing Real

"Fear is a darkroom where negatives develop."
~ Usman B. Asif ~

The wind is really howling outside—loudly. You could even say it's raging fiercely, although intellectually I don't believe the wind has any feelings at all—it just is. Because I choose to make that interpretation, I feel scared and unsafe, and I just want it to stop. I'm struck by how quickly I can notice the way something *appears* to be, pass judgment that it's *true*, and then act in accordance of the *truth* I just made up!

How much more do I make up about people and circumstances in my life? Someone hasn't called me back so I decide they must be mad at me. She didn't say she liked my haircut, so I conclude it must not look good. He was extra quiet tonight, and I wonder what I did wrong?

Why do I give my peace and power away so easily? I get to decide how I feel about every aspect of my life. I don't have to torture myself with assumptions about people and circumstances. I can choose to feel bad or good, by being more intentional with my thoughts. How do I want to feel, is the real question. So the wind is really intense right now but until I hear differently, this is just wind. I can stay stuck in fear, but what if instead, I said, "WOW! The wind is really up! I bet people with sailboats and kites could have some fun today!" That may be a stretch, but I can reassure myself with the truth that right now I'm cozy inside and my home is solid. Perception is powerful, and within my power to choose. If anything appears to be screaming trouble at you today, take a step back and ask yourself what is true. Go with that and assume the best until you hear otherwise. Most of the time we worry for nothing!

We lost a very special friend yesterday. Our beloved cat, Lucky, was hit by a car right in front of our house. We weren't home, but our neighbors were kind enough to call us and move him out of the road. Death, grief or any sort of trauma affects each of us in different ways. When you are faced with a tough circumstance, give yourself permission to feel what you feel and take care of yourself however you need to. I had to tell my husband, "Please don't judge how I deal with death and I won't judge you either." Lucky was a beautiful, large, sleek black cat. He moved like a miniature panther. Lucky lived a full life, indoors and outdoors. He loved to hunt, climb trees, sleep in the sun and he never met a stranger.

Everyone loved Lucky. He loved people and life. I can only hope my obituary reads as well! Have you ever thought about how your obituary will read? What will people say? What lasting influences did you create? It's never too late to think with the end in mind, literally. I want it to be said that I lived BIG, loved BIGGER and served BEST! Live today like you want to be remembered! Lucky inspired several other entries and mentions in this book and I will greatly miss his gentle, adventurous spirit. He taught me a lot. Cherish what and whom you love. Tell them, show them. Think about the seeds you're planting and what will harvest when you're gone. We truly are not promised tomorrow. Good night Lucky. Thank you for helping me find the gift! Each of my animals has their own song and this was his:

Lucky, Lucky little star. You're the very best by far.
Like a diamond in the sky. Lucky, Lucky, you're my guy.
Lucky Lucky little star, you're the very best by far.

December

In the midst of winter, I finally learned that there was in me an invincible summer.
~ ***Albert Camus***

December 1   Patience Learned From a Feather

Patience is a virtue, and never more needed than when chasing a feather! Yesterday while cleaning, I noticed a random, red feather had somehow landed on my finger. Without thinking, the kid in me threw it up in the air to watch it float around. When I immediately realized I would have to pick it up again anyway, I lunged for it and missed. Every time I grabbed for it, the feather escaped me by the sheer force of the air and energy I directed toward it, in my effort to catch it. The more rushed my attempt was, the *more air* the feather floated away on. I nearly stepped on one of my cats in my focused pursuit! I finally realized, if I wanted to catch it, I would have to gently follow the feather's natural direction, and be ready to receive it with open hands, when it was ready to land.

I thought of how hard I chase things at times, trying to force something in my life. I was reminded to follow the guidance I receive when I am patient and trusting. As long as I'm willing to move in sync with my guidance, I will be led to the prize. In fact, it may even land in my hand when I've done my footwork and let go of trying to *make* it happen. I won't have to force anything! What a relief! And a great reminder to trust in the process, do my part, and patiently surrender the outcome.

December 2   Choosing Sunshine

"That the birds of worry and fear fly above your head, this you cannot change. But that they build nests in your hair, this you can prevent."
~ Chinese proverb ~

I am sitting on my deck in my PJs in the sun, even though it's barely above freezing. A cold day can feel warm if it's sunny outside. What about our troubles? They're like a cold day. We can stay in the shade and feel miserable, cold and helpless. Or we can seek out the sunny spots—sunny people, sunny music, sunny places, sunny books. They're all around us, year-round, regardless of the "weather" in our lives. Plug into sunshine! It feels better! We will always have "cold days," but "sunshine" makes it a little easier. Make a decision to intentionally seek out some sunshine today, whatever that looks like for you. Let it pour in and warm your bones. Allow it to fill you with hope and offer a different perspective of the same cold day. Some things are beyond our control—but some things are not!

December 3   Ok to Change My Mind

I started my morning quiet time out on the deck again today. It's bitter cold, but sunny. Though it's only ten degrees less than yesterday, that ten degrees makes a lot of difference. At first, I felt torn. The birds were singing so loudly, inviting me to come out and listen. News flash! I don't have to miss out on the whole experience of being outside in the morning, just because it's windy and cold. I'm so used to all or nothing thinking! I can enjoy the brisk morning air, sunshine on my face, and the sounds of chirping birds. When I get too cold, I can change my mind and go back inside any time I want. I can listen to myself. *Yes! I want to go outside.* Then, *Wow. It's cold. I'm ready to go back in.* I don't have to make myself stick it out to spend my mornings outside, or any other choice I've made for that matter. It's okay to try something and then decide it's not for me. Listen, and your spirit will tell you exactly what you need and want.

I guess I get to implement that philosophy right now! Everything was going great until the sun went behind the clouds and the wind kicked in stronger. I grew up believing you had to be tough, and my old beliefs like to remind me with messages like, *Stick it out! Act like you're not cold!* Today, thankfully, I know when to say enough is enough, and I can remove myself from a situation, a relationship, or a cold porch that is no longer good for me.

If something doesn't feel good, I don't have to do it! If it started out good and then went downhill, I can change my mind! I don't have to let the quicksand climb up to my neck before I decide to get out. Today if anything becomes uncomfortable, I can decide if it's something I can learn and grow through. I don't want to give up on everything the minute it becomes hard, because many times, the tough situations are our best teachers. But if my intuition is screaming for me to do something different, I can trust and listen to her. And make a change, even if just for today.

December 4   Mind-Reading Isn't Very Reliable

Today it's very windy outside and the ground is damp from overnight rains. Even though it's early December, in Tennessee, the temperature can vary in extremes. I'm looking outside at the wind beating the trees around and trying to figure out—from inside—if it's freezing or warm. How often do I sit back and try to guess about a situation or how loved one is feeling? Or worse, assume I know the answer and act on that without ever confirming it first? It would be silly to decide to go on a walk today, bundle up for freezing temperatures, only to get out there and find that it's unusually mild.

When I'm unsure about something or someone, I can ask! Check it out, before I act it out. If I stay "inside" my head, it's pretty hard to mind-read accurately. Go "outside" and see what's really true! Today, make your next step based on fact, not assumption. Truth is always better than fiction, even if it's not the answer we wanted. At least we know it's real and can take the next step based in reality.

December 5   Someone Watching Over Me

Recently we were driving along the highway, and I was drawn to all the newly leaf-less trees lining the road. In the top branches were birds' nests and squirrels' nests! I've never seen so many! I'm sure they've been there all along, but with the leaves all gone now, today I noticed them. For me, I felt hope and reassurance in this. Many times we doubt what we can't see. And yet it's already there or it's just around the corner, or it's coming our way in the next day, week or month.

Faith is believing in things we can't see. Trusting we are being cared for and provided for on a higher level—beyond the scope of our own hands. As I look up into the barren trees, the multitude of nests remind me of all the work that goes on "above," just out of our realm of sight. Though we can't see it, it doesn't mean it's not happening, or it's not there. I'm grateful for all the preparation and care that's continually in motion on my behalf, whether I see evidence of it today or not. Someone is watching over you too, caring and preparing for you as well.

December 6   Prescription for Living: RIP Lucky

Sadly, our cat, Lucky was suddenly removed from our lives recently. His body may be gone, but his spirit and memories live on. He was a great inspiration to me of living a life full of adventure, pursuit, love and stillness. When he was hunting in the fields behind our house, it was *game on*. Nothing could distract him and he proudly presented us with his trophies—or part of them. He took his cat-napping seriously too, as many as possible, outside under trees or curled up on something soft. He taught me to cherish favorite objects and places. He loved hiding under our low Japanese Maple on a bed of freshly-laid pine needles. Often Lucky just enjoyed stillness, taking it all in, enjoying every breeze and every breath with a look and air of quiet serenity.

When he spent time inside, Lucky got his fill of love and sense of belonging from us and his furry indoor siblings. He loved everyone and was quick to purr to show his appreciation. Lucky didn't judge others by their outsides, or because they were different from him. He was nurturing to a new kitten we adopted and was best friends with our dog, Goldie. Lucky had a heart big enough to love everyone. Sometimes he was content to just be near us, and other times he wanted to snuggle in our laps. Still other times, Lucky wanted to nap in solitude, in a quiet part of the house, away from everything. He inspired me to know what I want and need, and to seek it without apology. Lucky really lived, and day by day I am learning to do the same. Adventure, pursuit, love, belonging, and stillness. If you have all of that, I don't know what else you could need or want.

December 7   Our Optimal Environment

We have a small Friendship plant that we bring inside for the winter. My cat, Herschel, likes to snack on this plant, so I put it on a top storage shelf in the laundry room by the window to keep it safe until spring. I don't get to enjoy looking at it as much in the winter, but at least it's safe from the cat, it's getting light, and I see it enough to remember to water it. The crazy thing is the plant absolutely thrives in there, way more than outside!

We can all thrive in our optimal environment. Where that is may not be the most obvious answer. We may find we are happiest or most productive in an unlikely job, a different circle of friends or living, visiting, or exploring a place we've never thought about going before. Observe how your life feels to you. Do you love your environment and relationships? If there's a question mark in any area, it doesn't necessarily mean it's time to make a change, but stay aware of how you feel. Watch for clues. Look for "coincidences." If your intuition tells you something over and over, trust yourself. Go and be where the best YOU can thrive!

December 8   Want to Feels Better than Have to

Have you ever asked yourself, *What do I need to get done today?* In other words, what do I need to have finished today? Past tense. Fast tense. I do, and often. I just realized that reflects how I feel a lot of the time. What do I *have* to do and how *fast* can I get it over with? For what? To get to the next list of have to's, ought to's and should's? Too often I am racing to some mysterious finish line. If I'm not careful, I can get in a rut and view everyday life as one big chore I must check off my list so I can get to the good stuff. How crazy is that? Everyday life is the good stuff! A life is the sum total of many single days.

It occurred to me to ask a different question today: *What do I WANT to do today?* This reflects me running my life, not letting my life run me. This question nurtures empowerment, rather than fostering a victim or martyr outlook. I do have a few appointments and other obligations today, but I created those. I'm the one who made a choice to say "Yes" to those. We each design our lives, voluntarily or involuntarily. Life feels a lot better when we take ownership for ourselves and our circumstances. We may not get to choose every circumstance we will ever encounter, but one hundred percent of the time we do get to choose how we feel about it. How we talk to ourselves and others about it. How we think about it. And what we're going to do about it. What actions will we take?

Today, I'm going to own my day. It's all mine. I get twenty-four hours. If I've created obligations and commitments I don't like, it's my choice to honor them or not, and to agree to them again, or not. If I have agreed and given an employer a portion of my day, it's my choice. Regardless of how I earn income, I can go to work and earn money, or I can stay home and embrace the consequences of that decision. We are only "stuck" if we decide it's easier to be a victim than to take responsibility for ourselves and live our lives on purpose. I am in charge of me and help is available as often as I seek it. As the Serenity Prayer suggests: "God, grant me the serenity to accept the things I cannot change, the courage to change the things I can, and the wisdom to know the difference." Amen and amen. Enjoy your day. Enjoy your life.

December 9   Lend a Hand When You Can

Our task must be to free ourselves by widening our circle of compassion to embrace all living creatures and the whole of nature and its beauty.
~ Albert Einstein ~

A few days ago, my well-laid plans for the day completely unraveled. I was headed downtown for an appointment when I encountered heavy traffic from an earlier wreck. I decided to reschedule and explore Plan B, to take care of an unplanned errand nearby. I exited the interstate, which put me in a completely different area from where I had originally intended on being that day. In the course of taking a detour, I found a gutsy, stray cat walking around a side street looking lonely and hungry. It was cold and drizzly and barely above freezing. Since I had enough time before my next appointment, I went to a nearby grocery store and got this scrawny, wet cat some food. I guess he was more hungry than frightened, and proceeded to eat the entire can. I stayed to offer protection while he ate, and I pondered if I should try to rescue him. It felt too soon to get another cat after just losing our beloved Lucky less than a week ago. After a long deliberation, I decided to take him to our vet for basic immunizations, and get him cleaned up while I figured out what to do with him. It's so easy to justify turning our backs on people and animals that need our help. Yes, it's true—offering help can mean complicating our own lives. I'm grateful for what I have and am willing to endure occasional inconvenience when I can help those less fortunate. *There, but for the Grace of God (go I)*. Who can you help today?

December 10   Compassion for the Furry Ones

Yesterday when I came upon a stray cat and had to decide whether or not to rescue him, I opted to let the cat choose. Not knowing how feral he could be, I got a towel out of my trunk. When I went to pick him up, he let me swaddle him in the towel, nice and snug so I could safely drive with him in my lap. He fell asleep and purred the whole way. I really didn't know the right thing to do, as far as me and my family (and other pets) were concerned, but I knew it couldn't be wrong to try to help this little creature of God. There is a beautiful Scripture about sparrows, "Not even a sparrow, worth only half a penny, can fall to the ground without your Father knowing it" (Matthew 10:29 New Living Translation). While it's true I can't save them all, I can offer help to the ones that cross my path, especially when the situations involve coincidence or synchronicity, such as this cat showing up in my last-minute change of plans. I never would have seen this cat had it not been for the wreck on the interstate that rerouted my whole day. I believe in going with the flow and trusting in the unexpected detours we encounter along the way. If we act upon good intentions, generosity and love, how can we go wrong? Keep your eyes open for random coincidences—they could be a blessing in disguise for you, or an opportunity to give back just a little of all you've been blessed with.

December 11   Lessons from a Stray Cat

I am a sucker for a stray cat. *But it was cold and rainy! He was so tiny!* I justified to myself. I promised I would get a shelter to take him, so I had the vet take a quick look at him—which turned out to be a her—and brought her home, *temporarily*. Her sweet demeanor changed abruptly when she smelled our other animals. Actually that's a huge understatement—she went crazy! I guess she has been fighting it out on the street since she was born, a year and half, according to the vet. She was so little, I thought I'd found a six-month old tom cat, and that if worse comes to worse, I could keep "him" outside. Maybe because of her small size and being female, she's had to be extra aggressive to stay alive, amidst other street cats and dogs? We sequestered her in our bathroom, where she is extremely content, playful and loving. I see so many lessons:

- ❦ A safe environment can make all the difference in the world. Find your place!
- ❦ Even when I'm really and truly safe, I may not know that yet. I may have to "act as if" and trust I'm being taken care of until I start to feel more comfortable and can believe I'm really okay.
- ❦ It's hard to recognize what a healthy environment (job, relationship) feels like, if all I have ever known is chaos. Chaos may seem more familiar and therefore more comfortable, because it's predictable. However, an open mind can lead to greater things.
- ❦ The very things that saved her life (aggression, defensiveness) may become the blocks for really living life fully today. When the tools for survival

no longer help, but hinder, it's time to get new tools.

- There will always be tension when dynamics shift, or when the players change (in groups, at work, in families). Until a new leader emerges, there is a struggle for position. Some will always want to be followers and avoid confrontation at all costs (Harvey). Some don't want to lead, but they won't allow others to push them around without a fight (Fancy). Some just want to play (Goldie), and some are up to the challenge to lead (Herschel). Everyone has a place that is perfect for them.

Jasmine—yes, doggone it, we gave her a name!—is figuring all this out to see where she fits in her new home. Excuse me, her *temporary* home, ahem. Learn what you can, when you can, from whom you can. Lessons are all around!

One year later: Jazzy is still with us. She was way too aggressive to be taken in by a shelter, but she has come a long way in a year. She chases and swats at our dog, Goldie, who can't seem to remember she is the dog and Jazzy is the cat. Jasmine loves to launch surprise attacks on all the other cats, but she no longer lives in the bathroom by herself. I can only hope in another year, she will be even less aggressive with her furry siblings. No person, no situation, and no animal is hopeless. Love, compassion, willingness and determination can conquer most obstacles and facilitate rehabilitation and redemption.

Two years later: Jazzy is a permanent member of the family and has a new best friend in Herschel.

December 12 — As True as an Evergreen

There's something so true about evergreens. All year long they are constant and … true. As all the other trees' leaves come and go, evergreens are always green and full. As I look out over a cold, barren December landscape, the evergreens stand strong.

In a world that is constantly changing, I am grateful for the few things that have remained a steady presence and influence in my life. My roots and family of origin have made me the person I am today. They have given me a hunger to be better today than I was yesterday. I'm grateful to have known true love, in all the ways that has evolved over the last twenty-plus years. I am thankful for other dear friendships, which have stood the test of time. Most of all, I am grateful for the consistent effort I continue to make to know and grow myself. Everywhere I go, there I am. As strong and true as an evergreen. Just like ... you.

December 13   The Gift of Unplugging

Today is unseasonably warm and downright balmy for December! We had a gentle storm all night, but now the rain has ceased. Occasionally I hear distant thunder. The sky is overcast with an eerie yellow tint spilling onto the landscape. I have both French doors wide open to the back deck. It's breezy and it sounds like hundreds of birds are singing. My cats are on the deck taking it all in too. This is a moment I could sit and revel in for hours. The calm seeps down into the depths of my bones and the crevices of my soul. Automatically my breath slows and deepens and I haven't got a care in the world. I am tethered to the earth and one with all creation. Clarity is found in moments like these. Inspiration is born—away from cell phones, laptops and other distracting devices. Technology is wonderful, but I must find time to completely unplug for a little while each day, a couple of long weekends, and ideally, a few weeks each year. Find a place to unwind and reconnect with yourself and the magic of nothing. It is *everything*.

December 14   Get Uncomfortable to Grow

Behold the turtle. He makes progress
only when he sticks his neck out.
~ James Bryant Conant ~

Our resident scaredy-cat, Harvey hates the vacuum, but he taught me a few good lessons today. As I was vacuuming closer and closer to him, he stayed very alert on top of the sofa just in case he needed to jump and run. I could see the bigger picture and knew he was in no danger at all. Just before I finished the area near him, he jumped down to run away. He was almost in the clear, had he just stayed put!

Number one, this was progress for Harvey. He tolerated his discomfort longer than usual, when he normally would have bailed at the first sight of trouble. Number two, had he been willing to be uncomfortable just a little while longer, the trouble would have passed and not affected him in the least. Number three, by acting on his *unsubstantiated* fear, Harvey put himself at greater risk!

If we are not uncomfortable very often, chances are, we're not growing. Or if we get uncomfortable and bail too soon, we may miss out on a gift, helpful insight, or some other lesson. Practice discerning the difference between fear and intuition, especially if the fear is based on old, unsubstantiated beliefs like, *The vacuum will hurt me*. (Intuition should never be overlooked and honest fear serves an important purpose. Today, we're focusing on those worries and fears that may not indicate a real danger.)

When you're safe but uncomfortable, stretch a little more each time. If you stick around long enough, you may see there was nothing to fear at all and get to enjoy a boost of self-confidence and a sense of accomplishment. Often the trouble we get so worried about is just *noise* that if ignored, would go away on its own. Today, look for one place to practice courage or challenge an old fear. Don't quit right before the miracle happens!

December 15 Relationship Lessons from a Cat

I recently rescued a small, skinny cat off the street. I brought her home and named her Jasmine. Watching her initial defense mechanisms and interaction strategies with our other three cats and our dog has been insightful. I see all sorts of parallels in the human experience. We all come hardwired to some degree, based on our past relationships, circumstances and experiences. The strategies in relationships which we have developed, might have been necessary in the past, but may no longer be useful in the present. If we're not getting the results we seek in our significant relationships—our family, our work, our church, or our social circles—we may want to explore *our* behavior and make some modifications.

- If something in our spirit is growling, or worse, hissing, people around us pick that up and it isn't inviting at all. Some may find it entertaining and stick around just to see what we will do next, but their guard will stay up.

- Making a habit of launching surprise (verbal) attacks, catching people when they're totally off guard or vulnerable will not create the atmosphere of trust and safety necessary for authentic connections.

- People need to know where we stand. It's natural for most of us to explore other people's boundaries. How much will they take? How far will they let something go? Will they turn their head and act like nothing happened? Do they mean what they say or do they just have a loud bark? We learn what we can get away with, who will command our respect, and who will try to push us to our limits. A little bit of assertion goes a long way.

Examine the boundaries of your relationships. Is there enough give and take, or is it lopsided? We really do teach people how to treat us. They learn our limits by taking actions and observing our responses. If you don't like how a relationship feels, start changing *your* responses to their actions. At first, you may experience resistance. They may like things just the way they are and may not be happy when you change things up. Stay firm. State your needs, goals, desires and requests. Redefine your boundaries. Some people will respect you even more for your new clarity. For others, your awareness and growth may bring about a natural conclusion to the relationship as you have known it, and neither may choose to continue the connection. And of course, there will always be bullies who will prey on the weak. You don't have to be the bully or the weak one any longer. Relax, relate and re-learn when necessary. Be the spouse, friend, sibling, coworker, or neighbor that you want others to be for you. It's never too late to grow a little more.

December 16   Gratitude to Start Your Day

Waking up with gratitude is such an incredible way to start the day! I attended a sales convention recently and the speaker shared that he had spent most of his life angry and he didn't even know why. At one point, he was about to lose his job over his grumpy demeanor. At someone's suggestion, and very begrudgingly, he began to start each day with a gratitude list. At first he hated doing it and didn't see the point. He hated his life and felt he had nothing to be thankful for. He wrote down things like, *I'm grateful for being able to breathe. I'm glad I have eyes.* In time, thanks to this daily discipline to cultivate a sense of appreciation, he gradually learned to appreciate the tiny apartment that cost him \$1100/month. He decided that having a car with a broken door handle was better than no car at all. He began to proclaim, *I am grateful for all that I have, and all that is yet to be! For all that I am and all that I am yet to become!*

At that moment, nothing changed about his circumstances, but everything changed about his life. He had a new perspective. He carried himself differently. He viewed others with appreciation. Because he changed on the inside, his outside eventually changed too. This speaker's life is as different now as night and day, with more abundance, freedom and joy than he ever dreamed possible. Before I put my feet on the floor today, I focused on something I'm thankful for until I could feel it in my heart. The more grateful I can be about my life, the more life gives me reasons to be grateful.

How about you? What are you grateful for right at this moment? Take a second or two to send positive vibes and prayers of thanks to that person or situation. Hold it in your mind until your heart warms over and you're smiling on the inside. Now, that's how you start a day right!

December 17   **Time Is on Our Side**

Treat yourself to a sunrise every now and then. I get up pretty early anyway, but if I wake up extra early, I have two choices. Go back to sleep for half an hour, or get up and enjoy the stillness. If I'm lucky, that will include a sunrise. I have learned that the extra thirty minutes of dozing doesn't equal the reward of getting up. Today the fields are blanketed with a thick white frost and the sky started out slightly pink as the sun was just beginning to break through. That was gorgeous in itself and worth seeing. But to see the sunrise unfold, and to watch the entire sky transform in a matter of moments was magical and powerful.

We all have circumstances in our lives that we wish would shift a little faster. Whether it's a bad situation that can't end soon enough, or a dream or goal that seems to be taking forever to realize, we all have situations we deal with that feel slow to show change. However, change is happening all the time, we just don't see it. When dawn shifted to daylight and transformed the entire landscape in a matter of minutes, I felt blessed to witness this rapid transformation. For me, it's tangible proof that we are always in motion. The power of possibility becomes more real than ever. I feel uplifted and encouraged to trust that the intentions of my heart are manifesting all the time. We don't always get what we want, when we want it, but we do always get what we need, when we need it. Thank you, God, for the powerful element of time to transform each of our own horizons.

December 18   Law of the Magnet

I have used a particular philosophy much of my adult life, and my son got this lecture when he started dating. I'll call it the Law of the Magnet. Magnetic forces can either attract or repel. We all have this energy inside us doing the same thing. Think about how it feels when we're around people who are demanding and controlling, or needy and insecure. Their energy is trying to overpower us to get their needs met at our expense. Your energy naturally says, *Run!* Whether they are pushing at us or trying to pull us in, the force is out of balance and our healthy reaction is to step back. When we really want to be closer to someone or learn from someone, but they are aloof or just super busy, we may feel the urge to pursue them even more. It's like the old saying, "You want what you can't have." Your energy wants to chase after them, but they feel your elevated pursuit and consciously or unconsciously, they may want to keep running away from you.

If one person needs the exchange of energy more than the other, the relationship will be off-balance. I have found this to be true in every relationship: friendships, love interests, and family relations, as well as in business among internal company relations or between the company/client interface. Imagine you have a device that reads magnetic energy. Notice in each encounter you have today if you are being pushed or pulled, or if you are the one pushing or pulling. Observe, grow in awareness and make any necessary adjustments. If only it were that easy, right? Just focus today on what you learn about your interactions. Give yourself a pat on the back for any new awareness, because that's the first step to getting more balanced in your relationships.

December 19   Perspective is Everything

Perspective gives us the ability to accurately contrast
the large with the small, and the important
with the less important. Without it we are lost...

~ John Sununu ~

I realized something very important this morning. The chair you sit in can change your life! I was trying to journal and kept jumping up to deal with this or that and changed chairs each time I returned to the deck. I noticed how each chair offered a different view. Some were highly desirable—gazing out over our acre of land, trees and the neighboring farm. Some were just okay—looking across the deck at our patio furniture. And I could have even chosen a chair that faced a brick wall! Sometimes you need the brick walls. You need the timeout. You need the contrast so you can go inward and remove yourself from all distractions. If all you ever looked at was beauty, how could you continue to have the same level of appreciation for it? In every case the setting was the same. The chair I chose made all the difference in what I got to see and enjoy. Perspective is key. When I'm not feeling stimulated, inspired, hopeful, or serene, I will remember to change chairs—try a different angle, look at things from the opposite direction. Often, it's the way I'm looking at my life that makes all the difference.

December 20   **Looking Inside**

This morning I am reminded of a hit song by the country band, LoneStar that said, "The view I love the most is my front porch looking in." We turn our Christmas tree lights on in the mornings, when it's dark and cloudy like today. The soft glow adds comfort, coziness and beauty, offsetting the gloomy weather outside. The tree is beautiful at night when the darkness provides maximum contrast, but my husband and I agree—the soft glow of the tree in the morning while the outside is dimly lit is our favorite. Out of habit, I turned the tree lights on this morning and came to sit in the back of the room in chairs that face outside. But today, what I really want to look at and appreciate is the tree and the fireplace, not the outside like every other morning. Earlier in the book, I discussed my "furniture-moving" rules. Today I ignored them and moved my chair so it faces in, instead of out. I love this view! I've never enjoyed this view before because of the usual furniture arrangement. I am full of appreciation for the glowing tree decorated with care, the stockings dangling above the crackling fireplace, the cozy leather couch with a fuzzy blanket stretched over it, beckoning me to cuddle up.

Looking in your home and in your life, what do you see? What are you grateful for? Taking this a step further, let's practice turning our focus inside ourselves while letting all outside circumstances fade from our consciousness. What do you see in there? What are you feeling? What are you grateful for, about *you*? It's a busy time of year. It's easy to get caught up in everything and everyone else, neglecting self-care and attention. Today, give yourself the gift of some quiet time looking inward. Ask yourself what you need? What you want? Allow peace, love and gratitude to fill you up. Let your light shine bright for you and all the world to see. *You* are beautiful!

December 21   **Cycles of Growth**

Today was supposed to be the end of the world in 2012, according to the Mayan calendar. In my lifetime, I have experienced Y2K, which was also supposed to be world-ending, and a few other similar claims that, thankfully, never came to fruition. I have also had days where I personally thought *my* life was over. I thought, *I can't possibly live through this,* but I always did.

How about letting today be the beginning of a new and improved you? I am guessing that because you're reading this book, you are open to further growth regardless of how much you've already accomplished personally, spiritually and emotionally. Or maybe you're just starting your personal development journey? Either way, those of us who are actively seeking to better ourselves are continuously growing through a series of metamorphosis.

We were meant to fly, not crawl, but we can't do one without the other, and we will not do both at the same time. Embrace the cocoon when we're in it. We need that time of incubation to nurture our souls, ideas and dreams. Appreciate the time we spend grounded, while we allow our wings to fully develop. Soak up the lessons, the challenges and the disappointments that help form us, and clarify what we really want and how we will get there.

Savor the times of flight, Butterfly! Let's soar into our peak moments! Relish the occasions when we have truly arrived on the mountaintops of life, accepting that it, too, is temporary. Then welcome the renewal process, where we get to start on a new part of our journey. It may feel like the beginning all over again, except we always bring the growth from the previous cycles with us. So we are never really starting over.

Like a painting, the first coat of color offers no depth. As each layer of color is added, the painting gets richer, deeper with more contrast, giving it more life. Paul Gardener said, "A painting is never finished. It simply stops in interesting place." We are never finished either. For today, embrace wherever you are in your masterpiece of life. Keep adding brushstrokes, some for beauty and interest and some for contrast. Life happens along the way and no one else can paint your picture but you. Don't worry about how it will look in the end. Remember the backside of a tapestry is always a big mess, so give yourself some grace as the art of your life comes alive. Just keep moving forward and trust in the process!

December 22   Practice Being Where You Are

Mindfulness helps you go home to the present...
~ Thich Nhat Hanh ~

We've had fierce winds and rain for two days and today it's finally calm. The wind brought a cold front in and for now, his job is done. Wind is nowhere to be found. Jasmine, the cat we rescued a few weeks ago, came home yesterday after her spay surgery. She is our feistiest cat by far, but yesterday she crawled into my closet and slept the better part of twenty-four hours. Work when it's time to work. Play when it's time to play. Rest when it's time to rest. Whatever you're doing, do that.

How many of us have a hard time focusing on work, allowing distractions to turn a two-hour job into a four-hour or two-day job? How many of us have difficulty enjoying downtime and vacation because we can't stop thinking about work? Can you relate to not being able to relax and go to sleep because your mind is racing? Then the next day we're not only distracted while trying to work, we're sleepy. Stop the cycle! Be where you are when you're there, and let the rest go.

There is a phrase in the workforce called presenteeism, which is a cousin of absenteeism. It means you're there in physical form, but you're checked out. Check back into your life! De-clutter your mind. When we try to do or think about ten things at once, we don't do anything really well. Just for today, take ten minutes—set a timer!—to be where you are and nowhere else. If your mind wanders, stop and focus on your senses. What do you hear, see, smell, touch? For some of us, the question is, what are we saying? I'm guilty too often of having a conversation while multi-tasking, and having to ask for things to be repeated because my ears checked out. Simplify! End the confusion and mental noise. Bring yourself back to the moment and stay there until it's time to shift. Happy grounding!

December 23   Blessed Is the Giver

I woke up to the sound of the garbage truck entering our neighborhood and got the nudging again, for the third time now, to run out and give him a Christmas bonus. About eight years ago, I read a magazine article which had a tipping guide for service providers, suggesting we give them an extra bonus at the end of the year. One of the many people listed was the garbage man.

Since then, I've tried to be more aware of the people who provide a service to us and show them some appreciation. It doesn't have to be much. This year, I've struggled a bit with laziness and not wanting to run out in the rain but today, when I woke up and heard his loud brakes, I knew if I hurried, I would have just enough time to put some cash in an envelope and hand it to him personally at the curb.

He had already finished dumping our trash when he saw me running out to meet him. I gave him the envelope and thanked him for doing such a good job all year. He was so appreciative; I wished I'd given him more! I wished him a Merry Christmas. He thanked me and put out his hand, and I shook it. I went back in the house as he got inside his truck, opening his envelope. I know I got way more than he did! The gift of giving when done with a pure heart, in love, expecting nothing in return, is truly a blessing for the giver.

I was like a kid on Christmas morning, running back into the house. It felt good to be obedient to my spirit, and it felt even better to offer a small gesture of kindness to a stranger as deserving as anyone else. It was definitely worth getting out of my comfort zone (and bed). As I hear his brakes continuing to make stops in our neighborhood, I can't help but smile. In that small, but pure connection, I felt the spirit of Christmas. I'm not tooting my own horn. I was just a vehicle God used so both the trash man and myself could share a moment of humanity at its finest. Find someone to show some unexpected appreciation to today. Maybe an extra tip to a server or to your dry cleaner? Honor your inner nudgings and the world will be a better place. For sure, your heart will be blessed as you bless others.

December 24   Finding the Gift

*We start with gifts. Merit comes
from what we make of them.*
~ Jean Toomer ~

Today is a gift, and that's why it's called the present. Using traditional Christmas analogy, let's explore how to approach *Finding the Gift* on any day of the year!

I get to choose what to "open" or rather, how to perceive my day. If my attitude is less than ideal, I may get a day full of coal! When I'm feeling somewhat observant and spiritually open to receiving a blessing, maybe I'll find a cute "stocking stuffer," a little happy somewhere along my path? Maybe someone will pre-pay for my coffee at the drive-thru, or maybe I'll notice a lot of people are smiling at me today. If I'm really centered and spiritually connected, tapped into being thankful for my life today exactly as it is, perhaps my day will be *full* of presents? First parking space everywhere I go. Green lights all the way. A friend calls just to say hello and tell me they've been thinking about me and really appreciate me. Regardless of what really happens, I am walking in the flow and I can feel it. I don't have to muster up a Happy Dance, it comes naturally because my perspective is positive, and everything around me is feeding my attitude of gratitude even more.

But maybe I'm feeling a little low today? To climb out of it, I will need to make a decision—do I want to stay stuck, or am I willing to take some action and go looking for my gift? I will check the usual places—call a friend, walk the neighborhood—but it's a good idea to keep my eyes open for other "hiding places" where I might "Find the Gift," like maybe a hike at a new park where I'm suddenly delighted to cross paths with a doe and her fawns. Maybe instead of working from home, I make an effort to get around some other people. Maybe a conversation with a stranger at a coffee shop turns into a very coincidental and mutually beneficial meeting.

Sometimes the best gifts come in the most unexpected wrappings! It may not even have a bow on it! I will look for gifts in familiar places daily and be open to new surprises and blessings along the way as well. Whatever I look for, I find.

December 25   What You Really Believe Matters

For those who celebrate Christmas, *Merry Christmas!* I'm up with our animals enjoying the quiet solitude before everyone else wakes up. We have the ability to make every day a gift full of peace, joy and laughter. We don't need a special occasion. Life is the sum experience of the stories we are telling ourselves mentally. Many people revisit the Christmas story in the Bible every year to remember the meaning of Christmas. Maybe there are stories or beliefs you're telling yourself regularly that aren't so delightful, aren't worth rehashing and are definitely not creating feelings of peace and joy, or a life worth anticipation.

Our inherent beliefs have influenced the choices we've made, and the life we now have. If we want something different, we need to change our beliefs before we can ever hope to change our lives. One of the pioneers of modern personal success philosophy, Napoleon Hill said, "What the mind can conceive and believe, it can achieve." Today, write down three to five of the most predominant negative thoughts that run through your head. Now rewrite each statement in the positive form, and in the present tense.

- *I never have enough time,* becomes, *I have all the time I need to do what must be done today.*
- *I will never get out of debt,* becomes, *I am financially secure beyond my wildest dreams.*
- *I am worthless and I don't deserve anything good,* becomes *I deserve favor and blessing. I deserve financial success and happy relationships.*

Your specific negative chatter can be used to create exactly what you really want. If the chatter is poison, think of these affirmations as the anti-venom—the exact remedy to target those old beliefs. Read them daily. Speak them out loud. Add new ones as needed. Record yourself saying the affirmations and listen to them often. Our subconscious minds believe whatever we tell them. When said with conviction, you will feel an immediate energy shift. Good feelings attract good things! By giving yourself the gift of positive beliefs, you can create a life worth celebrating every day of the year! Happy Re-Creating! Ask (believe) and you shall receive.

December 26   The Gift of Silence

Everything has its wonders, even
darkness and silence, and I learn, whatever
state I may be in, therein to be content.
~ Helen Keller ~

Another Christmas season has come and gone. Outside, it looks the same as yesterday, but seems less magical somehow. More quiet. Still. Isn't that funny? Nothing is different between today and yesterday, except for myself and the excitement and expectations I carry into the day. I can choose to see every day as special and full of gifts. Whatever I think, I am right.

Today the stillness of the season is its own gift, a momentary break from all of the holiday hustle and bustle. Later, I will be out in the post-holiday traffic, but for now, I stare out my window and relish the stillness of the landscape and I'm thankful for the gift of being quiet and serene.

December 27   Love Yourself First

How important is the last word? Do I care more about the people I'm in relationships with or my need to be right? I got a memorable tip one time from a woman I greatly admire. Even if you get what you want from people (a sale, an apology, an agreement), how they feel when they walk away from the interaction is the real sign of victory. If I win the battle but lose the war, I haven't won anything at all.

Relationships are like leaves—they are strong, vibrant, colorful and they experience the change of seasons. They add fullness to our lives. A tree that is less healthy doesn't bear as many leaves. How I'm doing in relationships is a direct reflection of how I'm doing in relationship with myself.

Do I give myself what I need or do I have to take it from others? Do I approve of myself or do I depend on approval from others? Do I believe in myself? Do I recognize my goodness? Do I forgive myself for mistakes? What I see in myself is what I will see in others. We are mirrors for one another, to show us what we like and what we may want to examine and change.

To the degree I accept myself—strengths *and* weaknesses—I will accept others exactly as they are as well. Elisabeth Kubler-Ross said, "The ultimate lesson all of us have to learn is unconditional love, which includes not only others but ourselves as well." Grace, tolerance, patience, kindness, acceptance, love. Be generous with yourself first and you will naturally extend the same to the people in your life. Pick one attribute above and practice it on yourself today.

December 28   Sunshine Goes a Lot Further

I read a fable where the wind and the sun decided to have a contest to see who could make a pedestrian take his jacket off first. The wind blew fiercely, harder and harder from all directions, but all the pedestrian did was clutch his coat even tighter. The sun shone brightly and warmly, and the pedestrian took his coat off willingly.

This story encourages me to lay down my attempts to control people and circumstances. No one likes to feel forced into anything, and I usually don't enjoy the result as much, knowing someone has merely complied, but not very willingly. There is a better way to interact with people! Love, kindness, warmth, gentleness. Using these spiritual principles in everything we do not only makes those around us feel good, we can't help but feel good also.

Whether it's someone in business, your best friend, your child, your pet, or even possibly the clerk at the dry cleaners, someone may be having a rough day or rough moment and a little kindness can go a long way. Look for opportunities to be kind, loving, warm, and gentle today. Go spread some sunshine!

December 29   Life Lessons from the Dog

Today is a great day for a walk! I strapped Goldie in her harness and we set out for our morning adventure. I decided to put myself in Goldie's paws today, and I feel like I learned a few things. Goldie becomes really excited when you ask her if she wants to go for a walk. You would think I've asked her to go on vacation! She approaches every walk with the same level of intensity and enthusiasm. She is open and actively looking to make a huge discovery. She's constantly looking around, taking in everything. I doubt she's ever distracted by worry or fear! Sometimes I accidentally kick the gravel when I walk and a small rock runs up and bounces off her. If that happened to me, would I just say, *Hmmm*, like she seems to do? Then quickly dismiss it and go on to focus on all the wonderful things around me? Or would I say, *Hey! You did that to me on purpose! Why did you do that?* and carry a grudge?

This last one was the biggest lesson for me. Things happen sometimes and it's easy to take it personally. To get caught up in being offended—being a victim—and completely miss out on the joys and wonder all around me. It's easy to say, *God did this to punish me,* or *Well that's just my luck!* Sometimes "it" just is, without any rhyme or reason. Say *Hmmm* and let "it" go! Get back to what is good. It's all around you, just waiting to be discovered. Approach each day like a dog on a walk:

❦ Expect to find something exciting
❦ Don't be afraid to get messy

- Run when you can
- Rest in the shade
- Drink when the water appears
- Be in the moment
- Say hello to the people you meet
- Mind your own business and let everyone else mind theirs
- Be grateful

It's your walk, and your life. It's up to you how great it is!

December 30   Honest Self-Assessment

If we do not change our direction, we
are likely to end up where we are headed.
~ Ancient Chinese proverb ~

The year is coming to a close. It's time to pause, look back, and look ahead. Am I aligning my actions with my intentions? Is my life headed in a direction I want to go? If I want something different, do I have a plan of action to go with my desire? Today's a good day to reflect, always remembering, however, this is also just a day like any other. If I didn't accomplish a goal I set last week or last year, it's not the end of the world. This is just another twenty-four hours, not a reason to beat myself up. Re-evaluate missed goals. Are they still important? Were they ever truly important? It's okay—wherever I am, I got here in perfect timing.

My goals for today: accept myself, accept my life, embrace the lessons, and look for ways to turn the obstacles into opportunities. Know that it's okay to be where I am today, and remember, at anytime I can choose to make a decision to embrace a new direction.

December 31   Live Like You Were Dying

Answering a question about what surprised him most about humanity, the Dalai Lama replied, "Man sacrifices his health in order to make money. Then he sacrifices money to recuperate his health. And then he is so anxious about the future that he does not enjoy the present; the result being that he does not live in the present or the future; he lives as if he is never going to die, and then dies having never really lived."

It's quiet on my deck, and only a few birds are singing. The day will build with a seasonal excitement as we all anticipate bringing in the New Year tonight, whatever that looks like—huge party, big night on the town, quiet evening with a few friends, or a virtual celebration on TV. What if we approached each day of our lives as a chance for a new beginning and something to celebrate? We don't have to wait for a new calendar year to get excited about our lives, or to get the resolve to try something new or different. Whether it is January 1, May 13, September 22 ... this is your life! Start living now! Take music lessons! Start ballroom dancing! Go on that trip! Take one action toward being healthier! Tell that dysfunctional relationship goodbye! Chase after your dream before it's too late! Any day is a good day for a new beginning.

Do you know anyone who really lived their life, full out? We love the movie *Secondhand Lions* about two bachelor brothers recounting all their crazy, overseas adventures. Some stories were so far-fetched that people started to doubt these characters were real or these events really happened. At the end, someone came from far away to see for himself if these were men or myths. He asked, "So these men really lived?" He was told, "Yes, they *really lived*."

I have a strange habit of looking at obituaries every now and then, looking for those I admire. One of my favorites was about a man whose obituary read as a celebration of his life and all who knew him. It said he was a grill master and that he earned his nickname dancing on tables in the Florida Keys. He left this world right on the golf course, one of his many passions. I never knew him, but I wish I had. His obituary challenges me to live a story worth telling. It's never too late to create a better story. Like it or not, we are all going to die. If we truly accepted that, how much different would our approach to life be? Write your ideal obituary today, or at least the highlights. Now go live every minute of it, *Finding the Gift* every single day!

Finding the Gift

YOU ARE INVITED!

Stay connected with Angela and
other FTG Friends!

www.FindingTheGift.com
A **FREE GIFT** for *you*? Of course!

When you join FTG Friends, you will
immediately receive the FREE eBook:
*Top Ten Secrets to FINDING THE GIFT
in Your Own Life!*

Angela has created an online community
where you can share your own insights and
chat with the group by commenting together
on posts. You can also contact Angela with
suggested topic discussions for future blogs!
As a site member, you have an all-access
pass to articles and resources ... AND
You will be the first to see new content, new
posts, and announcements, PLUS receive
free and special offers.

Open eyes get more gifts to open.
Cheers to us all *Finding the Gift* today!
Invite your friends!

Twitter: @findingthegift
Periscope: @findingthegift
Facebook: Angela Howell, Author
Instagram: AngelaHowell4Life

i

About The Author

Angela Howell was born in Mason City, Iowa. She moved thirteen times and attended eight schools before she graduated high school in Tennessee a year early, with honors. She went on to earn a marketing degree at Middle Tennessee State University.

Angela has long been on the road to personal freedom and *Finding the Gift*. She survived a lengthy battle with anorexia and bulimia, and proceeded to earn multiple sales awards and top recognition with several Fortune 500 companies. During her twelve-year career, she gained valuable sales and motivational training, which she finds highly applicable to life. Despite business success and marrying the man of her dreams, Angela still felt life was lacking. Spiritually empty, she had sworn off God and religion years prior due to childhood extremes. Ironically the eating disorder that almost killed her, gradually brought Angela back to God and greater life fulfillment by way of the Twelve-step recovery approach.

Through books, seminars, recovery groups and creative circles, as well as ongoing spiritual development and healing, Angela is finally walking her own true path. She is passionate about sharing the journey with others and uses her coaching program to help clients create *A Life Worth Having.*

As a speaker, Angela shares her compelling story of triumph with a variety of audiences. Committed to advancing eating disorder awareness, she serves on the speaker's bureau for the Eating Disorders Coalition of Tennessee (www.edct.net), and is a facilitator for the Body Project (www.bodyprojectcollaborative.com). She has also owned her own photography studio for ten years.

Angela is married to her first husband, G. Patrick Howell, a former undercover agent. Patrick is also her third husband! Their marriage and love affair is quite a story all its own, and has been ongoing for over thirty years (including her crush on him at thirteen, when he was a youth worship leader). Together, they have a nineteen-year-old son and for the moment, four cats!

Please visit Angela at www.FindingtheGift.com. Your FREE gift awaits!

A LIFE
WORTH
HAVING

Are you ready to break out of your comfort zone to experience more joy and more peace—more lasting purpose and fulfillment than you ever thought posible?

Are you willing to embrace new beliefs about who you are, what you are capable of and what you really deserve?

If you are *truly* ready to transform your life, and would like personal guidance, support and accountability to help you do that, please contact Angela right now to inquire about reserving a place in one of her upcoming, online groups. You may also want to learn more about scheduling individual coaching sessions with Angela.

The BEST you is ready!

www.FindingTheGift.com/Contact

Recommended Reading

These are just some of the books in my personal library, in no particular order. Everything you'll ever need to know is already in a book somewhere—find it! I read a lot using an open mind and the motto, "Take what you like and leave the rest!" I challenge you to do the same. I won't shun an author simply for having different beliefs, if the content as a whole inspires me or makes me think.

I love to rummage through used bookstores and thrift stores looking for gold. There's nothing like highlighting the points that really speak to me so I can re-read the cliff notes another time.

God revealed the insights for *Finding the Gift*, but these authors provided the philosophies to interpret them. Of all my earthly treasures, I am most excited to leave behind my journals and books—the paper trail of how I came to be me.

The Bible (in many translations)
The Artist's Way by Julia Cameron
The Vein of Gold by Julia Cameron
Codependent No More by Melodie Beattie
Simple Abundance by Sarah Ban Breathnach
The Big Book of Alcoholics Anonymous
The Power of Intention by Wayne Dyer
The Dream Giver by Bruce Wilkinson
The Magic of Thinking Big by David J. Schwartz, Ph.D.
Think and Grow Rich by Napoleon Hill
Rich Dad Poor Dad by Robert Kiyosaki and Sharon L. Lechter
Cashflow Quadrant by Robert Kiyosaki and Sharon L. Lechter
Start with Why by Simon Sinek
Body for Life by Bill Phillips
The Four-Hour Workweek by Tim Ferriss
The Slight Edge by Jeff Olson
How to Win Friends and Influence People by Dale Carnegie

The Surrendered Wife by Laura Doyle
The Millionaire Messenger by Brendan Burchard
The Secret by Rhonda Byrne
The Reason for God by Timothy Keller
Abba's Child by Brennan Manning
The Art of Happiness by The Dalai Lama
The Seat of the Soul by Gary Zukav
Men Are From Mars Women Are From Venus by John Gray
Nonviolent Communication by Marshall Rosenberg
A Walk Across the Room by Bill Hybel
Flip Flop CEO by Finney, Muirhead, and Roberts
15 Invaluable Laws of Growth by John C. Maxwell
Loving What Is by Byron Katie
Your Best Life Now by Joel Osteen
How to Be an Adult by David Richo
A Million Miles in a Thousand Years by Donald Miller
Gifts from the Sea by Anne Morrow Lindbergh
Boundaries by Cloud/Townsend
Getting the Love You Want by Harville Hendrix
Secrets of the Millionaire Mind by T. Harv Eker
The Art of Exceptional Living by Jim Rohn
The Strangest Secret by Earl Nightingale
The Four Agreements by Don Miguel Ruiz

I also love to read memoirs and fiction featuring characters who are transformed by life's challenges.

The Traveler's Gift by Andy Andrews
The Noticer by Andy Andrews
Illusions by Richard Bach
At Seventy by May Sarton
A Gracious Plenty by Sheri Reynolds
The Rapture of Canaan by Sherri Reynolds
The Glass Castle by Jeannette Walls
An Invisible Thread by Laura Schroff and Alex Tresniowski
The Invisible Wall by Harry Bernstein
Skin and Bones by Sherry Shahan

Index

A

B

C

D

E

G

U

Made in the USA
Middletown, DE
18 April 2016